First World War
and Army of Occupation
War Diary
France, Belgium and Germany

3 DIVISION
Divisional Troops
Royal Army Service Corps
3 Divisional Train (15,21,22,29 Companies A.S.C.)
1 January 1916 - 31 December 1916

WO95/1410/2

The Naval & Military Press Ltd
www.nmarchive.com
Published in association with The National Archives

Published by

The Naval & Military Press Ltd

Unit 10 Ridgewood Industrial Park,
Uckfield, East Sussex,
TN22 5QE England
Tel: +44 (0) 1825 749494

www.naval-military-press.com
www.nmarchive.com

This diary has been reprinted in facsimile from the original. Any imperfections are inevitably reproduced and the quality may fall short of modern type and cartographic standards.

© **Crown Copyright**
Images reproduced by permission of The National Archives, London, England, 2015.

Contents

Document type	Place/Title	Date From	Date To
Heading	WO95/1410 3 Divisional Train Jan 1916-Dec 1916		
Heading	3rd Division War Diaries Divisional Train S.S.O January To 30th June 1916		
War Diary	Godwaersvelde	01/01/1916	31/01/1916
War Diary	Godewaersvelde	01/01/1916	31/01/1916
War Diary	Boeschepe	01/01/1916	31/01/1916
War Diary	Hooggraaf Westoutre	01/01/1916	31/01/1916
War Diary	Godwaers Velde	01/02/1916	08/02/1916
War Diary	Moulle	09/02/1916	29/02/1916
War Diary	Godewaers Velde	01/02/1916	05/02/1916
War Diary	Boschepe	06/02/1916	11/02/1916
War Diary	Wemaers-Cappel	12/02/1916	12/02/1916
War Diary	Larecousse	13/02/1916	27/02/1916
War Diary	J 36.C Sheet 27. B	28/02/1916	29/02/1916
War Diary	Boeschepe	01/02/1916	05/02/1916
War Diary	Eperlecques	06/02/1916	29/02/1916
War Diary	Boeschepe	01/02/1916	06/02/1916
War Diary	Wemaers Cappel	07/02/1916	07/02/1916
War Diary	Quembergue	08/02/1916	11/02/1916
War Diary	Quemberge	12/02/1916	16/02/1916
War Diary	Quembergue	17/02/1916	24/02/1916
War Diary	Quemberge	25/02/1916	29/02/1916
War Diary	Moulle	01/03/1916	06/03/1916
War Diary	Godwaers Velde	07/03/1916	31/03/1916
War Diary	J 36. C. Sheet 27.B La Reeousse	01/03/1916	13/03/1916
War Diary	Near Boschepe	14/03/1916	30/03/1916
War Diary	Eperlecques	01/03/1916	01/03/1916
War Diary	Ouderdom	02/03/1916	11/03/1916
War Diary	Boeschepe	12/03/1916	31/03/1916
War Diary	Quemberge	01/03/1916	05/03/1916
War Diary	Boeschepe	06/03/1916	31/03/1916
War Diary	Duderdom-Vlamertinghe H 14 Sheet 28	01/03/1916	10/03/1916
War Diary	Hoograaf G 32 A	11/03/1916	18/03/1916
War Diary	Hoograaf	18/03/1916	24/03/1916
War Diary	Hoograaf G 32 A 55	24/03/1916	31/03/1916
War Diary	Godwaers Velde	01/04/1916	05/04/1916
War Diary	Fletre	06/04/1916	25/04/1916
War Diary	Goin De Poperinghe	26/04/1916	30/04/1916
War Diary	Godwaresvelde	01/05/1916	12/05/1916
War Diary	Sletre	13/05/1916	30/05/1916
War Diary	Boeschepe	01/04/1916	05/04/1916
War Diary	Schaexken	06/04/1916	22/04/1916
War Diary	Croix De Poperinghe	23/04/1916	30/04/1916
War Diary	Boeschepe	01/04/1916	01/04/1916
War Diary	Meteren	02/04/1916	24/04/1916
War Diary	Bailleul	25/04/1916	29/04/1916
War Diary	Hoograaff	01/04/1916	05/04/1916
War Diary	Eecke	06/04/1916	30/04/1916
War Diary	Croix De Poperinghe	01/05/1916	26/05/1916
War Diary	Fletre	27/05/1916	31/05/1916

War Diary	Fletre		01/05/1916	01/05/1916
War Diary	Croix De Poperinghe		02/05/1916	29/05/1916
War Diary	Fletre		30/05/1916	30/05/1916
War Diary	In The Field		01/05/1916	31/05/1916
War Diary	Bailleul		30/04/1916	23/05/1916
War Diary	Meteren		24/05/1916	30/05/1916
War Diary	Sheet 28 M. 32. G.5.3		01/05/1916	27/05/1916
War Diary	Fletre W.5d 78 (Camp) W.5d 52 (R.P)		28/05/1916	30/05/1916
War Diary	Eecke Q27 G.2.9 (Reflling Point) Q21 D.5.2		31/05/1916	31/05/1916
War Diary	Fletre		01/06/1916	17/06/1916
War Diary	St Martin (St Omer)		18/06/1916	19/06/1916
War Diary	St Martin		20/06/1916	30/06/1916
War Diary	Fletre		01/06/1916	16/06/1916
War Diary	Staple		17/06/1916	17/06/1916
War Diary	Esquerdes		18/06/1916	30/06/1916
War Diary	In The Field		01/06/1916	30/06/1916
War Diary	Meteren		31/05/1916	04/06/1916
War Diary	Westoutre		05/06/1916	10/06/1916
War Diary	Shaexen		11/06/1916	17/06/1916
War Diary	Monnecove Nordausques.		18/06/1916	29/06/1916
War Diary	Eecke Q 27 G.2 9 Q.21 G 5.2		01/06/1916	06/06/1916
War Diary	Fontaine Houck X.4.C. (Gun Roads) Refelling Point X.4.C.2		07/06/1916	10/06/1916
War Diary	X 4 C 4.4. Fontaine Houck		11/06/1916	13/06/1916
War Diary	Houlle		14/06/1916	30/06/1916
Heading	3rd Division War Diaries Divisional Train S.S.O. July To 31st December 1916			
War Diary	Stomer		01/07/1916	01/07/1916
War Diary	Heuzecourt		02/07/1916	02/07/1916
War Diary	Bois Bergues		03/07/1916	03/07/1916
War Diary	Flessells		04/07/1916	04/07/1916
War Diary	Corbie		05/07/1916	09/07/1916
War Diary	Grove Town		10/07/1916	26/07/1916
War Diary	Treux		27/07/1916	31/07/1916
War Diary	Esquerdes		01/07/1916	02/07/1916
War Diary	Bois Bergues		03/07/1916	03/07/1916
War Diary	Flix Court		04/07/1916	04/07/1916
War Diary	Dours		05/07/1916	06/07/1916
War Diary	Bray		07/07/1916	30/07/1916
War Diary	Treux		31/07/1916	31/07/1916
War Diary	In The Field		01/07/1916	31/07/1916
War Diary	Monnecove (Nordausques)		30/06/1916	01/07/1916
War Diary	Domesmont (Doullens)		02/07/1916	02/07/1916
War Diary	Vignacourt		03/07/1916	04/07/1916
War Diary	Poulainville (Amiens)		05/07/1916	05/07/1916
War Diary	Grove Town Railhead Bray		06/07/1916	29/07/1916
War Diary	Ville Sous Corbie		30/07/1916	30/07/1916
War Diary	Houlle		01/07/1916	12/07/1916
War Diary	Grove Town (Bray)		13/07/1916	31/07/1916
War Diary	Treux		01/08/1916	12/08/1916
War Diary	Grovetown		13/08/1916	15/08/1916
War Diary	Forked True Grovetown		16/08/1916	21/08/1916
War Diary	Flessells		22/08/1916	22/08/1916
War Diary	Bernaville		23/08/1916	24/08/1916
War Diary	Frohen Le Grand		25/08/1916	25/08/1916
War Diary	Flers		26/08/1916	26/08/1916

War Diary	Mouchy Cayeux	27/08/1916	27/08/1916
War Diary	Vaudricourt	28/08/1916	31/08/1916
War Diary	Treux	01/08/1916	14/08/1916
War Diary	GroveTown	15/08/1916	31/08/1916
War Diary	In The Field	01/08/1916	31/08/1916
War Diary	Ville Sous Corbie	31/07/1916	10/08/1916
War Diary	Grove Town Bray	11/08/1916	21/08/1916
War Diary	Monton Villers	22/08/1916	22/08/1916
War Diary	Flen villers	23/08/1916	24/08/1916
War Diary	Mezerolles	25/08/1916	25/08/1916
War Diary	SeriCourt	26/08/1916	26/08/1916
War Diary	Eps.	27/08/1916	28/08/1916
War Diary	Vaudricourt	29/08/1916	30/08/1916
War Diary	Treux	01/08/1916	11/08/1916
War Diary	GroveTown	12/08/1916	31/08/1916
War Diary	Vaudricourt	01/09/1916	22/09/1916
War Diary	Bomy	23/09/1916	30/09/1916
War Diary	Grove Town	01/09/1916	07/09/1916
War Diary	Frechencourt	08/09/1916	08/09/1916
War Diary	Doullens	09/09/1916	09/09/1916
War Diary	Boubers	10/09/1916	10/09/1916
War Diary	Bergueneuse	11/09/1916	11/09/1916
War Diary	Mines Marles-Les	12/09/1916	12/09/1916
War Diary	Vaudricourt	13/09/1916	24/09/1916
War Diary	Mines Marles Les	25/09/1916	25/09/1916
War Diary	St Quintin	26/09/1916	30/09/1916
War Diary	In The Field	01/09/1916	30/09/1916
War Diary	Vaudricourt	31/08/1916	22/09/1916
War Diary	Burbure	23/09/1916	23/09/1916
War Diary	Boncourt	24/09/1916	30/09/1916
War Diary	Bomy	01/10/1916	04/10/1916
War Diary	Monchy Cayeaux	05/10/1916	06/10/1916
War Diary	Bertrancourt	07/10/1916	17/10/1916
War Diary	Bus les Artois	18/10/1916	19/10/1916
War Diary	Bus	20/10/1916	24/10/1916
War Diary	Bus Les Artois	25/10/1916	27/10/1916
War Diary	Bus les Artois	28/10/1916	31/10/1916
War Diary	St Quinton	01/10/1916	05/10/1916
War Diary	Anvin	06/10/1916	06/10/1916
War Diary	Etree-Wamin	07/10/1916	07/10/1916
War Diary	Raincheval	08/10/1916	16/10/1916
War Diary	Louvencourt	17/10/1916	31/10/1916
War Diary	In The Field	01/10/1916	31/10/1916
War Diary	Boncourt	30/09/1916	05/10/1916
War Diary	Bethonval	06/10/1916	06/10/1916
War Diary	Canettemont	07/10/1916	07/10/1916
War Diary	Arqueves	08/10/1916	15/10/1916
War Diary	Louvencourt	16/10/1916	31/10/1916
War Diary	Flechinelle	01/10/1916	05/10/1916
War Diary	Heuchin	06/10/1916	31/10/1916
War Diary	Bus les Artois	01/11/1916	30/11/1916
War Diary	Louvencourt	01/11/1916	30/11/1916
War Diary	In The Field	01/11/1916	30/11/1916
War Diary	Louvencourt	01/11/1916	30/11/1916
War Diary	Bus les Artois	01/12/1916	31/12/1916
War Diary	Louvencourt	01/12/1916	08/12/1916

War Diary	Bus	09/12/1916	31/12/1916
War Diary	Louvencourt	30/11/1916	07/12/1916
War Diary	Authie	08/12/1916	31/12/1916
War Diary	Louvencourt	01/12/1916	04/12/1916
War Diary	Authie	05/12/1916	31/12/1916
War Diary	Louvencourt	01/12/1916	08/12/1916
War Diary	Bois De Warnincourt	09/12/1916	31/12/1916

WO 95/1410

3 Divisional Train
Jan 1916 – Dec 1916

SSO
SO III Div Trans
SO 8th Inf Bde
SO 9th Inf Bde
SO 76th Inf Bde

3rd Division

War Diaries

Divisional Train

S. S. O.

January to 30th June

1916

WAR DIARY
or
INTELLIGENCE SUMMARY
(Erase heading not required.)

Army Form C. 2118

Place	Date	Hour	Summary of Events and Information	Remarks and references to Appendices
GODEWAERS- VELDE	1/4/16		Hoisted old number Popperinghe road sign 1 D Office. Instructions received that an railways G.R.E. France 3rd week, attached 76 I.B. for returning.	
	2/4/16		Routine as usual. Instructions received that railways will exchange 8 camel train 5th week, owing to determining trucks of Gozenwaerts Brothers & trucks trucks from 6th down at Popperinghe Stn.	
	3/4/16		Routine as usual. Drilled D.S.S.T. re change of railhead.	
	4/4/16 – 5/4/16		Routine as usual — went Cassel train R.S.O. re meeting at Cassel tomorrow. Railhead at Cassel Stn. today. Meeting time 8.30 a.m.	
	6/4/16		Routine as usual. orders received that the 4 Sheep r.to/hairfoot Deeks will entrain Capt. J Erving in the 8th inst. at BAILLEUL for another area. Equipments S.S.O.	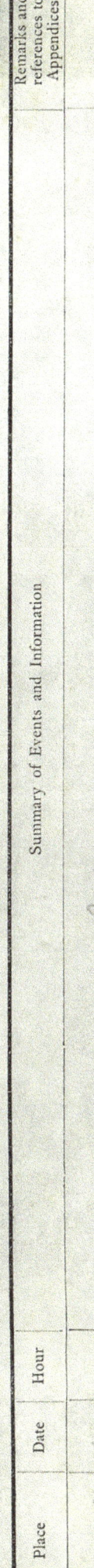

Place	Date	Hour	Summary of Events and Information	Remarks and references to Appendices
GODEWAERS VELDE	6/11/16	Continued	Supplies for requisitions with me were made to Army return, one days reserve on the 7th inst. Three wagon breaks with one's, one days supplies for consumption greater the loaded on lorries in the morning, and have to proceed to Bailleul on long hunt to be furnished by each batt of N Co, 2 men who will be furnished by each batt. Slow fuelled inst be responsible for their respective unit for the returns while they are dumped at Bailleul.	
	7/11/16		Returns as usual. No returns drawn by the 2nd Bde R.A.R.E since the 3rd inst. - as they expressed Captain their returns from another Division have been stopped. Moving them from Trithead - DADQMG informed. Hay known at Trithead today - 9th ult known.	
	8/11/16		Visited all dumps. Telephone to Office - So's instructions to each Brigade Supply Officers staff want 2 hours Authority to be temporarily station key return. Telephone DSGS, received from 10th to 6th for their 2 hours. Short return at Trithead today to the swallowing by bread furnaces. Hay drawn from the 9th inst.	Jb Dunn Capt RASC

WAR DIARY
or
INTELLIGENCE SUMMARY

Army Form C. 2118

Place	Date	Hour	Summary of Events and Information	Remarks and references to Appendices
GODWAERS VELDE	9/11/16	—	Visited all dumps. Poperinghe analysed, TD office. ADMS required. Numbers from divisions cured to refilled on Poperinghe – Reninghelst Road & on Poperinghe – Vlamertinghe Road. Did him each unit could take 2 divisions. Had an interview regarding for day from Divisions who had been through by Canadian Division, resulting forestry inquiries as the Napham where brought in and the Corps area. Overland received at and. Arranged with OC Supply Column there to arrange at my disposal for carrying Army registration Vehicles up to Brigade areas for distribution. Supplement sheet return.	
	10/11/16		Railhead returned to Godn - Arranged with Vandentronck Supply the Division with transport like Straw (oats) etc. Left ½ Divisional Train in Stoeps train – lorries helping Regiment for Reninghelst dumps – trailed sheets daily.	AMSavour Capt DO

WAR DIARY
or
INTELLIGENCE SUMMARY

Army Form C. 2118

Place	Date	Hour	Summary of Events and Information	Remarks and references to Appendices
G.HEADQTRS V.DE.	11/1/16		Visited all dumps. Poperinghe, overlapped & D.	
	12/1/16		Went Canal Bank, Ottawa, railway supply, Coal yard at Ottawa — coal, coke transferred to Poperinghe. Usual routine. Visited railhead. Lunch with Slavin (R. Transport) & Jones in neighbourhood of Shinworth. Unloaded about 30 cwts forage, 1 lorry. Lent 9 M. 2.9 Lorries to send up. Charcoal supply lively & fair. Received returns 85 lbs Shivers. Visited railhead. Stopped unloaded trucks as R.O. in place of D'Lattre. Unloaded all dumps – also 2 MR. Headquarters. Went up to P' touches.	
	13/1/16		8/6 gram. T.O. regulated extra supply tea, as men had tea in early morning. Met Lin Bernard who wanted for purpose of feeling them but knew they hope in early morning — nevertheless — given its men, except that they hope. No break return — historical — BL Signals transfered 8 No 16 as S.O. unless 7 Horses.	
	14/1/16		Usual routine — attended SSO's conference at DDQ & MT. Outputs. Instead of relating with 33155 — all supplementary gpa became — do — " 33163377. The real return the received weekly. Railhead railhead.	W.B. Cunningham SSO

WAR DIARY
or
INTELLIGENCE SUMMARY

Army Form C. 2118

Place	Date	Hour	Summary of Events and Information	Remarks and references to Appendices
GODUMARSWLDE	15/11/16		Usual Routine — Truck stands out. Arrangements made with Captsfod for issue from 19th S.B. high threat lorry cars. Bundles taken for unloading. Capt Winter trimble & supply clerk in field & Col Griffiths to No 2 Co. Pvt Albion from Div on to reguments & groups in lieu of short returns.	
	16/11/16		Routine as usual. The S.S. O's car is now the only car running in the town. No 2 Co's car returned broken up 6 weeks ago. Snap heel axle. No 3 Co's car returned 6 weeks ago. No 1 Co's still arrived a/o, all breakdowns — Nos 3 Co's cars have not yet arrived. It is in consequence very difficult for the S.S. O's to get through their work properly.	
	17/11/16		Routine as usual. Divisional Supply Column, Tilmoorde.	
	19/11/16		Routine as usual. Rations arrived as usual — were distributed to Brigade areas.	A. Knapp Capt A.S.C.

WAR DIARY or INTELLIGENCE SUMMARY

Army Form C. 2118

Place	Date	Hour	Summary of Events and Information	Remarks and references to Appendices
GODEWAERS VELDE	19/1/16		Routine arrival — W.O.R Car to Luppy. Col. Blore new cup. Put on front wheel — Went with Col Berry & Reninghelst (P.M)	
	20/1/16		Routine arrival. Went to Dickebusch & Voormezeele.	
	21/1/16		Routine arrival. 3rd S.A.C. complained the [? negro] Married form received it. attended conference amounted to 4 or 5 of one [?] who not particular officer that the R.A. received [?] the R.A. Cav. sent up Brickhouse by our Park Trans. at Norway [?] weight too [?] allowance for to allege shortage could be made — The question has always been referred to D. of T. who dislike [?] between Relatives that the Division as a whole receives its fair return of them, any a unit receives a little short of what it would be able to its level of uniform in Belgium & Flanders below, no extra allowance could be made. — It was also pointed out of conference that he was purchasing largely, shoes, hay, [?] Cape T [?] in extra [?] up [?] to be refund. [?] must [?] [?] (It would appear that the O.C. believes that there is certain shortage)	[signature] Off. S.C.

WAR DIARY or INTELLIGENCE SUMMARY

Army Form C. 2118

Place	Date	Hour	Summary of Events and Information	Remarks and references to Appendices
COURERS VELDE	22/1/16	—	Routine arrival – Saw Vanderbuche re arrival of Platoon returns from him. General slack up – Saw A.D.R.T. Hazebrouck re new Captain of getting supplies through local Contractors which it will be necessary to get an order of Transport Supplies before troops move up the Platoons from a station – at present the delay is getting this arrangement completion quickly – two men up on supply of Platoon. Vanderbuche has too many Rhen even the Transports arriving betimes.	
	23/1/16	—	Routine General. Went Steenvoorde. Revd Mr Shaw.	
	24/1/16	—	Routine arrival. Owing to letter of divisional Purchase Scheme which it is letter of Brigadier sufficient force & beffelden for the division by local purchase without the necessity of trying through a Breweries, Brig-Gen has him of purchase yesterday, beginning Purchasing Officer Dejong as his assistant yesterday – of Purvis (ct-Mastery, B/c of divisional . Plot of Breechope – ct Clothier). Ct Neale promoted ct Captain au S.O B–76th J Brigade. Captains as S.O B–76th J Brigade.	[signature]

Army Form C. 2118

WAR DIARY
or
INTELLIGENCE SUMMARY
(Erase heading not required.)

Instructions regarding War Diaries and Intelligence Summaries are contained in F. S. Regs., Part II. and the Staff Manual respectively. Title Pages will be prepared in manuscript.

Place	Date	Hour	Summary of Events and Information	Remarks and references to Appendices
GODWAERS VELDE	25/1/16		Routine as usual. Went Hazebrouck & Pshin, also bought 3 forks for horses and 1 bridle, and 7 bridle and 1 Van den broucke.	to see RTO re consignment casting being sent to Hazebrouck. Also finish Steenbecke to
	26/1/16		Routine General; Pushed two truen forage new Hazebrouck, 9 G wagons not in just been collecting forage from Strazeele, for divisional dumps: 3,800 kilos obtained altogether.	
	27/1/16		Routine onwared.— Went to Dickeldoom & Purchased from Mr Fortier, 1 truck vegetables & 1 truck forage for delivery to Godewaersvelde, also made arrangements for future delivery of Steenvoorde of forage.— Agreed with Mr Vandenbroucke to take 3000 kilos oats from Camel area. 9 G. wagons from train not in area today collecting forage. — 3,700 kilos forage obtained.	

Army Form C. 2118.

WAR DIARY
or
INTELLIGENCE SUMMARY.
(Erase heading not required.)

Instructions regarding War Diaries and Intelligence Summaries are contained in F. S. Regs., Part II. and the Staff Manual respectively. Title pages will be prepared in manuscript.

Place	Date	Hour	Summary of Events and Information	Remarks and references to Appendices
G.H.Q. W.A.C./S.S.M./b V.E.I.D.E.	28/7/16		Routine carried on. Daimler car turned today, also Vauxhall Car returned from workshop. Went to meet with Col. Stokes & representative of Py—. Officers Motor — The French being short of petrol have requisitioned a large quantity of they have from this area.	
	29/7/16		Routine carried on. Went to Casal (Dep. of S.T.) & Vicks Stores arrived at Wichura today for periodical dumps. Capt. Neale tells me at 5.6 today as S.O.	
	30/7/16		Routine carried on. Wires Q to cut 5 days coal supply, & so him how in stock to prevent inroads to take any more in cool fuel — went with Col. Stokes our 5th Army lines. Over something for forage, rations, written, Auxiliaries Motor, interviewed Manager in each place, obtaining information	

WAR DIARY or INTELLIGENCE SUMMARY.

Army Form C. 2118.

(Erase heading not required.)

Instructions regarding War Diaries and Intelligence Summaries are contained in F. S. Regs., Part II. and the Staff Manual respectively. Title pages will be prepared in manuscript.

Place	Date	Hour	Summary of Events and Information	Remarks and references to Appendices
GODEWAERS VELDE	30/11/16		Information also reaches of merchants who deal in forage in this area. The French Belgian authorities are requisitioning forage. The inhabitants of a certain place find it difficult to get their stuff. There has often been being occupied by troops. A certain amount of forage appears to be obtainable in this area. Resources examined.	
	3/11/16		2. Instructions received at midnight. Instructions received from O.O/ S.T that in view of forage shortage 2/16 and can be known as midnight in view of shortage by units drawing forage hitherto supply return.	J.E Sumner Capt S.S.O 11/th Division

T2134. Wt. W708—776. 500000. 4/15. Sir J. C. & S.

"S.D. III Div Troops" "S.D. Divl Train"

WAR DIARY
or
INTELLIGENCE SUMMARY.
(Erase heading not required.)

Army Form C. 2118.

III DIV TRAIN

Instructions regarding War Diaries and Intelligence Summaries are contained in F.S. Regs., Part II. and the Staff Manual respectively. Title pages will be prepared in manuscript.

Hour, Date, Place		Summary of Events and Information	Remarks and references to Appendices
Godawarsotte	1-1-16	Train arrived 4/k. Drew 8 a.m - 8 water. Rest units	
	2-1-16	Routine as usual	
	3-1-16	Routine as usual	
	4-1-16		
	5-1-16	Train arrive 7.30 a.m. Drew 4.500 to 8.25 a.m.	
	6-1-16	Routine as usual. Companies are endeavouring to get reasoned as to influences of concentration. There from forces. Drills officer to be quite marrated.	
	7-1-16	Routine as usual. Contents are also being received on to	

Army Form C. 2118.

F.D. H.Q. No Troop.

WAR DIARY
or
INTELLIGENCE SUMMARY.
(Erase heading not required.)

Instructions regarding War Diaries and Intelligence Summaries are contained in F.S. Regs., Part II. and the Staff Manual respectively. Title pages will be prepared in manuscript.

Hour, Date, Place	Summary of Events and Information	Remarks and references to Appendices
Godewaersvelde. 7-1-16 (cont)	Quantity weight of bale 3 lay.	
" 8-1-16	Raining incessant	
" 9-1-16		
" 10-1-16	Local purchases & droughts must up for reduced quantities sent up from Chocolate entries & on in Godewaersvelde.	
" 11-1-16	Routine in camp. Visit units.	
" 12-1-16	Routine as usual	
" 13-1-16	Lt. Stokes arrived from No. 3 Coy to take on duties as S.O. III Division.	

Signature

Army Form C. 2118.

WAR DIARY
or
INTELLIGENCE SUMMARY.
(Erase heading not required.)

Place	Date	Hour	Summary of Events and Information	Remarks and references to Appendices
GODAERSVALDE	13/6 4/76		Took over duty from Dr Neal as S.O. III Div. Troops. Refilling lorries arrived 7.15 A.M. Waggons 8 A.M. Refilling over 8.30 A.M. Sergt Wilson reported for duty once Corpl Griffiths transferred to Coy HQ Div. Indus. The lorries of the train were inspected by the O.D. S.O. T.T. Army.	
"	15/6 16/76		Morning routine as usual. Rum issue. Pictd. III Div D.A.C. Morning routine as usual. Gift of 5 cases chest Gadcar chocolate arrived at refilling point. Sent to Coy. Park & Supplies Column arriving & railhead GODAERSVALDE to be issued. Visited North trial house, to D.A.C. & & Bde Hqrs. Chocolate distributed.	
"	17/6		Morning routine as usual. Visit Indian chocolate distributed	
"	18/76		Refilling point visited by O.C. III Div. Rail & Major Pennet.	
"	19/76		Morning routine as usual.	
"	20/6		Morning routine as usual. Ordered mob. Medical officers detailed	
"	21/6		Routine as usual. Motor Lorry to report. Nothing to report. meet long eld as arriving. Complaint from III D.A.C. re shortage of forage. H.J.D. Notley Major S.O. III Div. Troops.	

WAR DIARY
or
INTELLIGENCE SUMMARY.
(Erase heading not required.)

Army Form C. 2118.

Instructions regarding War Diaries and Intelligence Summaries are contained in F. S. Regs., Part II. and the Staff Manual respectively. Title pages will be prepared in manuscript.

Place	Date	Hour	Summary of Events and Information	Remarks and references to Appendices
GODAERIVELDE	22/6		Morning centre as usual. Called on III D.A.C. reference their complaint. Billiard obtuse as lay return not due to negligence or to dept of S.O.	
"	23/6		Morning centre as usual. Met oberst. comdt of Belly's bn. Afternoon Divisional Purchasing officer	
"	24/6		Morning centre as usual, nothing to report.	
"	25/6		Morning centre as usual, carried our duties as S.O. III Div troops to Lt Parker have I came from P.O. 9 Inf. Bde.	

H. J. D. Stokes Major.

T2134. Wt. W708—776. 500000. 4/15. Sir J. C. & S.

War - diary.

Jan. 26. Lt. A.S. Parkin took over the duties of Supply Officer, III Divisional Troops.
Lorries arrived at the usual time. Issues as usual.

Jan. 27. Lorries arrived at usual time & were off-loaded by 8 oc. Issues as usual.
Refilling finished by 8.45 a.m.

Jan. 28. Usual issues. Refilling finished by 8.35 a.m.

Jan. 29. Lorries arrived at 7.30 a.m. & off-loaded by 8 oc. Refilling Point finished by 8.50.

Jan. 30. Lorries arrived at usual time. Refilling point clear by 8.45.

Jan. 31. Usual issues for everything.

A.S. Parkin Lt. ASC
S.O. Divisional Troops.

S.O.8th Inf Bde.

Army Form C. 2118.

WAR DIARY
INTELLIGENCE SUMMARY of Supplies
(Erase heading not required.)

III DIV TR/N

Instructions regarding War Diaries and Intelligence Summaries are contained in F. S. Regs., Part II. and the Staff Manual respectively. Title pages will be prepared in manuscript.

Place	Date	Hour	Summary of Events and Information	Remarks and references to Appendices
Boesschepe	1.1.16		Lorries arrived 7.10 AM. Refilling 7.45. over 8.35. Wraps issue of Rum to those in front area. Brigade in trenches.	
	2.1.16		Lorries arrived 7.15 AM. Refilling 7.45. over 8.45. Tobacco issue. Brigade still at the ed of the week. 6 days Forage All Ranks. Shines H.P. L D Cake Oats 64/19 83 82 543 48 26	
	3.1.16		Lorries arrived 7.10 AM. Refilling 7.45. over 8.45. Brigade were out of the trenches. Rations east wise of Pea Soup, charcoal etc.	
	4.1.16		Lorries arrived 7.5 AM. Refilling 7.45. over 8.45. Brigade to come out of trenches in evening. Issue of Rum Rage. The 7th Batt. The K. Shropshire L.I. draw 480 Iron Rations.	
	5.1.16		Lorries arrived 6.50 AM. Refilling 7.45. over 8.35. Iron Rations to be issued to Jacks in replacement, for two days supplies. 80 Iron Rations issued to The 10th Batt. The Kings Liverpool Infant today, for two days supplies for 42 Batt. The Scott Lanes, who return on Saturday 8/1	

K Stephens Capt ASC
O 8th Bde

Army Form C. 2118.

WAR DIARY
or
INTELLIGENCE SUMMARY. of Tipples
(Erase heading not required.)

Instructions regarding War Diaries and Intelligence Summaries are contained in F. S. Regs., Part II. and the Staff Manual respectively. Title pages will be prepared in manuscript.

Place	Date	Hour	Summary of Events and Information	Remarks and references to Appendices
Boeschepe	6.1.16		Lorries arrived 6.46 A.M. Refilling 7.45. Over 8.30. Insert for Rum for issue on Saturday	
	7.1.16		Lorries arrived 6.45 A.M. Refilling 7.45. Over 8.35. The 4th Battn the 4th Scots Lance drew their two days supplies one days procured. Larger & Hornsol drawn. The no days supplies. Into Long & the Station at which the Battn detrain there were dumped and a good place over it.	
	8.1.16		Lorries arrived 6.45 A.M. Refilling 7.45. Over 8.40. Issue of Rum to the Brigade as Brigade in Rest Area.	
	9.1.16		Lorries arrived 7 A.M. Refilling 7.45. Over 8.50. Issue of Tobacco. Strength of Brigade at the end of the week for drawing Cigarres. All Ranks. Animals Shires H.P. L.D. Cobs Mule Mules 56,651 67 82 65D 4D 19	
	10.1.16		Lorries arrived 7.30 Refilling 7.45. Over 8.35. Hy Ration reduced from 10 lbs to 6 lbs. The extra 4 lbs to be for Heavy draught horses to the purchased locally.	

K.T. Anderson Capt A.S.C.
S.O. 2 Bde.

Army Form C. 2118.

WAR DIARY
INTELLIGENCE SUMMARY of Supplies
(Erase heading not required.)

Instructions regarding War Diaries and Intelligence Summaries are contained in F. S. Regs., Part II. and the Staff Manual respectively. Title pages will be prepared in manuscript.

Place	Date	Hour	Summary of Events and Information	Remarks and references to Appendices
Boeschepe	11.1.16		Lorries arrive 7.30 AM Refilling 8 AM over 8.50. The Brigade proceed to the Trenches. Fresh ration drawn. Cocoa tendered instead received to the front line of men. Soup of Oxo cubes.	
	12.1.16		Lorries arrive 7.30. Refilling 8 AM over 8.60. Great difficulties experienced in obtaining sufficient forage locally owing that use of transport. Canteen, carrots, turnips & oatcake allowed to be purchased in lieu of hay.	
	13.1.16		Lorries arrive 7.30. Refilling 8 AM over 9 AM. Rum issued.	
	14.1.16		Lorries arrive 7.30. Refilling 9 AM over 8.55. Issue of candles.	
	15.1.16		Lorries arrive 7.25. Refilling 8 AM over 8.55. Issue of Rum to those units & rest men. oatcake issued in lieu of hay.	
	16.1.16		Lorries arrive 8.45. Refilling 8.15 AM over 9 AM. Gift of 11 Cwt of Chocolate from the Colonel. Tobacco also gift of Brigadier & the Col. of the rect. Ammle Shoe HP LD Cwt Rolls Oats.	
			5703 69 83 5215 39 19	K.O. Akien Capt Alfe S.O. Sup.

T2134. Wt. W708—776. 500000. 4/15. Sir J. C. & S.

Army Form C. 2118.

WAR DIARY
or
INTELLIGENCE SUMMARY. of Supplies
(Erase heading not required.)

Instructions regarding War Diaries and Intelligence
Summaries are contained in F. S. Regs., Part II.
and the Staff Manual respectively. Title pages
will be prepared in manuscript.

Place	Date	Hour	Summary of Events and Information	Remarks and references to Appendices
Boesclap	17.1.16		Lorries arrived 7.15 AM. Refilling 8 PM over 8.55. Issue of oat straw in lieu of hay. Shortage of charcoal.	
	18.1.16		Lorries arrived 7.30 AM. Refilling 8 AM over 9 AM. Issue of Rum to Brigade, as Baths return from trenches.	
	19.1.16		Lorries arrived 7.30 AM. Refilling 8 AM over 8.45. Carrots + troops issued in lieu of has. Refilling	
	20.1.16		Lorries arrived 7.20 AM. 8. AM. over 8.45. oat-straw issued. 10 gallons of paraffin for the use of Brigade. Attack received. Thus 10 gallons will be used in lieu to the Brigade HQ daily of Primus stoves.	
	21.1.16.		Lorries arrived. 7.10. Refilling 8 AM over 8.45. weather very wet.	
	22.1.16.		Lorries arrived 7.25 Refilling 8 AM over 8.50. Issue of Rum to the whole Brigade.	

K.F. Andrews. Capt. ASC
S.O. 8th Bde.

Army Form C. 2118.

WAR DIARY
or
INTELLIGENCE SUMMARY. of Supplies
(Erase heading not required.)

Place	Date	Hour	Summary of Events and Information	Remarks and references to Appendices
Boesghe	23.1.16		Lorries arrived 7.20. Refilling 8 AM. over 8.55. Tobacco issued. Brigade strength at the end of the week:- All ranks Ranks Shoes H.P. L.D. Cobs Mules Lees 55-54. 66. 82 309. 37 19	
	24.1.16		Lorries arrived 7.25 Refilling 8AM over 8.35. The Supplies drawn as Brigade includes Gun Battery, form it the first time. a separate unit.	
	25.1.16		Lorries arrived 7.20 Refilling 8.1AM over 8.45. Brigade proceeds to the tenth tonight. Issue of coca milk in lieu ration. Shortage of Charcoal owing half-ration issued.	
	26.1.16		Lorries arrived 7.20 Refilling 2AM over 8.45.	
	27.1.16		Lorries arrived 7.20 Refilling 8AM over 8.45. A Divisional Staff started for Forage Unit to recent Forage dump & draws from store. This will sort all units a considerable amount of work, as all Forage can be obtained at one place. Until other have red Local Farms etc.	M.T. Askew Capt/LEO O.SMQ

Army Form C. 2118.

WAR DIARY or INTELLIGENCE SUMMARY.

(Erase heading not required.)

Instructions regarding War Diaries and Intelligence Summaries are contained in F. S. Regs., Part II. and the Staff Manual respectively. Title pages will be prepared in manuscript.

Place	Date	Hour	Summary of Events and Information	Remarks and references to Appendices
Boeschepe	28.1.16	7.30	Lorries arrived. Rifles 8 ATT over 8.45. Unit drew Forage from the Divisional Forage Depot for the first time.	
	29.1.16	7.26.	Lorries arrived. Rifles 8AM over 8.45. Issue of Rum. Letter says that we are not in the trenches.	
	30.1.16	7.25	Lorries arrived. Rifles 8AM over 8.55. Tobacco issue. Strength Bungr at the end of the week. All ranks Animals: horses HD LD cobs mules 5817 70 75 508 37 28.	
	31.1.16.	7.30	Lorries arrived. Rifles 8AM over 8.45. Nothing of note occurred, weather cold.	

K.G. Andrews. Capt ASC
S.O. Lysope

S.O. 9th Inf. Bde.

Army Form C. 2118

WAR DIARY
INTELLIGENCE SUMMARY
(Erase heading not required.)

Instructions regarding War Diaries and Intelligence Summaries are contained in F.S. Regs., Part II. and the Staff Manual respectively. Title Pages will be prepared in manuscript.

Place	Date	Hour	Summary of Events and Information	Remarks and references to Appendices
BOESCHEPE	1/11/16		Service commences 7.30 a.m. Offertory taken by 7.45 a.m. Felling commences 7.55 a.m. Service concluded. Reflecting finishes 8.35 a.m. Other ranks of a manual.	
"	2/11/16		Service commences 7.15. Service as above, finishes as usual. Routine as usual	
"	3/11/16		Service commences 7.30 a.m. Offertory taken by 7.45 a.m. Felling commences 7.55 a.m. Finishes 8.50 a.m.	
"	4/11/16		Service commences 7.0 a.m. owing to orders from HQ. Routine by usual. Service closes 8.50 a.m.	
"	5/11/16		Service commences 7.0 a.m. Offertory taken by 7.20 a.m. Felling commences 7.55 a.m. Finishes 8.30 a.m. Routine as usual	

E.W. Head
Captain

Army Form C. 2118

S.O. 9th Inf Bde.

WAR DIARY

INTELLIGENCE SUMMARY

(Erase heading not required.)

Instructions regarding War Diaries and Intelligence Summaries are contained in F.S. Regs., Part II. and the Staff Manual respectively. Title Pages will be prepared in manuscript.

Place	Date	Hour	Summary of Events and Information	Remarks and references to Appendices
BOESCHEPE	7/1/16		Aeroplane sounded 7.0 a.m. Offenders taken by 17. 30 mm Kelly commenced 7.45 a.m. Our line not reached till 9.15 a.m. (Scotch) Enemy aircraft seen. Enemy artillery active on ment. Eastern lines. Enemy bringing up to Blockhouse to ment. by water carriages on horses to 3rd army area. Source no ment. including neg takes. Rapidly finishes 8.50 a.m. Otherwise no ment.	
"	8-1-16		Aeroplane finishes 7.5 a.m. Reffelly as ment.	
"	9-1-16		Aeroplane commences 7.0 a.m. Offenders taken in 1y 7. 30 mm Kelly commences 7.50 a.m. Source as ment. (onlight convoys 15 mill wes.) his Offenders(?). Refeeli finishes 9.0 a.m. Otherwise as ment.	
"	10-1-16		Reffelly as ment. Weather hindered Offenders observations tile 10.30 to 6 the first showance to further matter. Konw as ment.	

E.M. Mart Captain

Army Form C. 2118

WAR DIARY
or
INTELLIGENCE SUMMARY
(Erase heading not required.)

S.O. 9th Inf. Bde.

Place	Date	Hour	Summary of Events and Information	Remarks and references to Appendices
BOESCHEPE	11-1-16		Lorries arrived 15 beer, Offloaded oleo by 7.45 am. Refilling commenced 7.50 am. Lorries arr. meat & bread by 8.15 am. Refilling vegetables finished 8.50 am. Return to rail head as usual.	
"	12-1-16			
"	13-1-16		Lorries arrived 5.30 am ambulance – no horse but about 400 lbs extra stores. Aeroplanes & Canteen (put 2½ divisions car out) at 10/1/16. Lorries arr. meat Refilling commenced 7.50. Finishes 8.55. Return to rail for 13th unit. Through last 3 days drivers & officers	
"	14-1-16			
"	15-1-16		Lorries arrives 7.35 am. Refilling commenced 8.0 am. No meal also extra forage obtainable. Refilling finishes 9.0 am. No lorry loads of forage & bread as Corps Res for move tomorrow.	

EW Wood
Capt ASC

WAR DIARY
INTELLIGENCE SUMMARY
(Erase heading not required.)

Army Form C. 2118

S.O. 9th A& B [?]

Place	Date	Hour	Summary of Events and Information	Remarks and references to Appendices
BOESCHEPE	16/1/16		Lorries arrived 7.40 am (including 3 lorries what stood 14th Bn). Offloaded delay by 8.10 am. Rations e[n]trained 8.15. Same as usual including fresh vegetables plus what stores to supplement deliveries yesterday. Also gift of chocolate. Rations finished 9.10 am. Other routine as usual.	
"	17-1-16		Routine as usual	
"	18-1-16		Routine as usual	
"	19-1-16		Lorries arrives 7.20 am. Offloaded delay by 7.45 am. Rations commenced 7.50 am. Same as usual 7.15 am. Finished 9.10 am. Arrays lorries to entrained at finish to General tomorrow. M.F.O. Other routine as usual	
"	20-1-16		Lorries arrive 7.25 am. Offloaded delay by 7.50. Same as usual including fresh vegetables. Rations finished 8.55 am. Also 1 lorry load of stores down to supplement deliveries to outposts [?] Other routine	

J.W. Neal Capt. OC

WAR DIARY or **INTELLIGENCE SUMMARY**

Army Form C. 2118

S.O.9 & R.2a

Place	Date	Hour	Summary of Events and Information	Remarks and references to Appendices
BOESCHEPE	24/1/16		Lorries arrives 7.15 am. Officers detailed by J.H.R. Rately. Commences 7.30 am. Lorries as usual. Delivered to vegetable. Rationing finished 8.30 am.	
"	25/1/16		Routine as usual	
"	26/1/16		Routine as usual	
"	27/1/16		Lorries arrives 7.30 am. Officers ordered by J.H.R. Rately Commences 7.30 am. Lorries as usual. Rationing finishes 8.30 am.	
"	28-1-16		Routine as usual. R.O. (Lieut. A. Parker) left to take over duties as S.O. III Div Qrs. Lieut over Supper of Parking appointment as R.O.	
"	26-1-16		Routine as usual	

C.W. Neal
Capt. A.C.

Army Form C. 2118

WAR DIARY
INTELLIGENCE SUMMARY
(Erase heading not required.)

S.O. 9th Infantry Bde

Instructions regarding War Diaries and Intelligence Summaries are contained in F. S. Regs., Part II. and the Staff Manual respectively. Title Pages will be prepared in manuscript.

Place	Date	Hour	Summary of Events and Information	Remarks and references to Appendices
BOESCHEPE	27-1-16		Convoy arrived 7.30 a.m. Offloaded delay by 7.55 a.m. Relay commenced 8.0 a.m. Same as usual — obtaining vegetables. Riddling finishes 8.50 a.m. Bivouacs above spares in Boeschepe.	
"	28-1-16		Convoy arrived. Refilling carts moved to 2nd unit WRE & ACC. Supper on Dis charge store Guise to Infy units. 32 at Carbide tank over R.O. delte.	
"	29-1-16		Routine as usual	
"	30-1-16		Convoy arrived 7.30 a.m. Offloaded delay by 7.55 a.m. Refilling commenced 8.0 a.m. Same as usual. Convoy departing 9.0 a.m.	
"	31-1-16		Routine as usual	

E.M Leod. Capt
S.O. 9th Infy Bde

S.O. 76th Inf Bde

Army Form C. 2118.

WAR DIARY
OR
INTELLIGENCE SUMMARY.
(Erase heading not required.)

Instructions regarding War Diaries and Intelligence Summaries are contained in F.S. Regs., Part II. and the Staff Manual respectively. Title pages will be prepared in manuscript.

Hour, Date, Place	Summary of Events and Information	Remarks and references to Appendices
HOOGGRAAF WESTOUTRE Saturday Jan 1st 1916	Company billeted in Square G.32.a (Belgium Sheet 28) Car completely broken down — a new one to be supplied which may be a month or more in arriving — MP Wrote to Brigade HQrs. re price of Lewis Supplies for Machine Guns Emplacements — MP	Brigade Group Strength on 1st All Ranks 6026 Horses 19/lb 121 15/lb 146 12/lb 699 10/lb 50 6/lb 19
Sunday 2nd	A return of all Supplies in the Corps area to be made — Each Requl. dairying Officers allotted a certain area — MP	
Monday 3rd	Detailed A.S.C. & G.C.M. at Cheshire R.E. Cg. billets. Visited units. MP	
Tuesday 4th	Purchase of Stores for gun position for 3rd Siege Batt. MP	
Thursday 6th	Gloxo in lieu of Chalk — Ratn 1/28 of a tin. MP	
Sunday 9th	Cocoa + Condensed Milk issued in lieu of 1/15 Pea Soup Ration for those in the trenches — MP	Brigade Group Strength Jan 8 All Ranks 5793 Horses 19/lb 157 15/lb 103 12/lb 698 10/lb 32 6/lb 21
Monday 10th	Hay ration at Refilling Point reduced to provide for 10.6.6lb — Conference with S.S.O. in connection with same — MP	
Tuesday 11th	172 Turn: Cy RE to have an extra 3c/lb y Candles pr day they working a late issue of 80lb — MP	
Wednesday 12th	Authority to purchase the following additional commodities to meet the reduction in the Hay Ratn — MP Carrots, Turnip + Linseed Cake — MP	Basil Mearns Capt ASC S.o 76 Brigade

Army Form C. 2118.

WAR DIARY
or
INTELLIGENCE SUMMARY.
(Erase heading not required.)

Instructions regarding War Diaries and Intelligence Summaries are contained in F.S. Regs., Part II. and the Staff Manual respectively. Title pages will be prepared in manuscript.

Hour, Date, Place	Summary of Events and Information	Remarks and references to Appendices
HOOGGRAAF WESTOUTRE Thursday 13th Jan	Shortage of Charcoal. Half issue to be made & a Reserve kept. Estimate of Quantity of Oat Straw or other Forage required from Railhead each during time of reduced Hay Ration 2 tons – MP	Brigade Group Strength out 15th All Ranks 5987 Horses 1966 171 15466 93 12466 622 10466 49 6466 19
Friday 14th	Sgt. Winter Supply Clerk interchanged with L/Cpl Griffiths of Divl. Troops. Stock taken of Supplies Equipment. MP	
Saturday 15th	New Return of Supply Personnel sent in. 172nd T/m Coffee agree to have in addition to the daily issue, 2 cases of Candles per week. Supply Personnel 2 deficient – Pte Greedy having gone to the Base Pte Kelly being in Hospital – MP	
Sunday 16th Monday 17th –	Issue of Chocolate given by the Colonies Trinidad, Grenada + St Lucia. 1 Box of 12 tabs to 12 men. MP Authority for 30 Bdes RFA t Horse to ten per week for tr thps – 5.50 will issue same – In future receipt for Supplies purchased which are handed in after the last day of a Period, are liable to be disallowed. No Supplementary Returns to be sent in. MP	
Tuesday 18th –	5 gallons per day Paraffin to be issued to Brigades HQs for "Primus" Stoves in the Trenches – MP	
Wednesday 19th –	Authority for "the" issue of 4 Cwt of Coal p the Company ASC for Shoeing. MP	W Reeves Capt ASC So 76 Brigade

Army Form C. 2118.

WAR DIARY
or
INTELLIGENCE SUMMARY.
(Erase heading not required.)

Instructions regarding War Diaries and Intelligence Summaries are contained in F.S. Regs., Part II. and the Staff Manual respectively. Title pages will be prepared in manuscript.

Hour, Date, Place	Summary of Events and Information	Remarks and references to Appendices
HOOGGRAAF WEST OUTRE January. Friday 21st	Four Lorry loads of Wheat Straw brought to Refilling Point yesterday issued today. This 3,200 kilos was brought for the Brigade by R.O. Div: T.R.S. is to be so shown in Return of Supplies Purchased with the monetary value at 6f.100 kilo. — MT	Brigade Coys Strength n 22nd All Ranks 59/78 Horses 19/66 172 13/Hy 30 17/Hy 68 } 683 15/Hy 49 6 Mo 19
Saturday 22nd	Return of Supplies Purchased to be brought on to Refilling Point on Dec 16 — 22nd — 17 of the month. MP	
Sunday 23rd	I am to be transferred to No. 2 Gtt 8 Ammunition Park — 2/Lt Hindr. Requisitioning Officer, is to take over Supply Duties, temporarily in addition to his own — MT	
Monday 24th	Handed over to 2/Lt Hindr. MP	
	(Sgd) Newsum Capt ASC So 76 Brigade	
Tuesday 25th —	Capt Pearson leaves St Omer — duty his quarters of front-arrive at Bump — Handed over to Capt J.D. Wade (the last) —	
	WStevens 2/Lt ASC for So 76 Inf Bde	

Army Form C. 2118.

WAR DIARY
or
INTELLIGENCE SUMMARY.
(Erase heading not required.)

Instructions regarding War Diaries and Intelligence Summaries are contained in F. S. Regs., Part II. and the Staff Manual respectively. Title pages will be prepared in manuscript.

Hour, Date, Place	Summary of Events and Information	Remarks and references to Appendices
HOOGGRAAF Westoutre Wednesday 26th	Taken over shelters of "D" Co "Field" from 2/Lt Hindi	
" Thursday 27th	Routine as usual. Two lorries went down early to Poperinghe attempt made before dawn to proceed R.E. and 5th Divisional Cavalry supplies sent by route as phase 1 Heavy relaxation from 10p.m to 4 a.m. prevented Coys achievement "B" to "A" feld huts relieved by one Coy moving to obtaining of supply.	
" Friday 28th	Routine as usual	
" Saturday 29th	Routine as usual	
" Sunday 30th	Lorries arrived 7.50 a.m. late owing to fog & smoke of morning	
" Monday 31st	Lorries sent to water as arrangement. Returned to 4.16 hrs. Return as usual.	

(73989) W.4141—463. 400,000. 9/14. H.&J.Ltd. Forms/C. 2118/10.

WAR DIARY
or
INTELLIGENCE SUMMARY.
(Erase heading not required.)

Army Form C. 2118.

S.S.O. III DIVISION
Feb 16

Place	Date	Hour	Summary of Events and Information	Remarks and references to Appendices
GOUROCK SVELDE	1/2/16		Routine as usual. D/Stokes to Steenwerck re purchase of hay, reported he was unable to get any past our rail. Horse transport commenced loading at Neuhout today supplies for 2nd troops, this has proved to relieve lorries for other supply work and deep supply for 2nd troops kept by Supply Column in reserve.	
	2/2/16		Routine as usual. Hay return for division to do from today 3rd mid inclusive — difficulties to obtain by local purchase getting very severe in area — D/Stokes securing 14 purchase of hay from Steenwerck — hay rations being potatoes are also at /Stokes. Arrangements made with OC Supply Column that the supplies for troops will be drawn by lorry from Steenwerck unless otherwise ordered.	

Place	Date	Hour	Summary of Events and Information	Remarks and references to Appendices
GODEWAER-SVELDE	3/3/16		Routine as usual. Information received that no invasion will take place even starting from tomorrow - Attended Conference from that date of move would be struck, no details yet available as to when R.E. RA reinforcements will arrive. Lt Colonel Anderson returned from Audriug reported that OC Details there was furnishing all keys in huybench of Audriug who could obtain most of this invasion. He also reports that O field T 5th corps sent to supply Col. has negotiated for supply (army) Unfortunately from his Headquarters at Sherwoode- Martin reported to the Division (P).	before ado SEO III Drou

Army Form C. 2118.

WAR DIARY
or
INTELLIGENCE SUMMARY.
(Erase heading not required.)

Instructions regarding War Diaries and Intelligence Summaries are contained in F. S. Regs., Part II. and the Staff Manual respectively. Title pages will be prepared in manuscript.

Place	Date	Hour	Summary of Events and Information	Remarks and references to Appendices
GODEWAERS VELDE	4/7/16		Went O offis. Supply Column also to MOULLE to arrange interview SSO 17th Division re arrangements for move knowing our supplies, it was suggested that each Division would find troops as they arrive in III Division area. This was afterwards cancelled it being decided that the 3rd Bgd would find all its own units throughout the move. Second Brettaleich 2 more frails supplying us at EPERLEQUES & Reserve animal unit rulein & one at WAEMERS CAPPEL in L rest park when units going by road could pick up rations to take them into EPERLECUES. Nullhead changed Strik — bye pouvant dept for interview throughts when 2nd army HQC at Lassa this leave prechary	
GODEWAERSVELDE	5/7/16		Nullhead at CASSEL. SURJRetn HENRY BATTEN Advanced parties 76th I.B. 4/S Camp. Droyal Artichokes Phone left by train from Pop: Poole to Aubrey & Arques. No 3 CRASC left by march stepping at the camps for night. No 3 CRASC Returns fut writern for resumption of march. Units SSO 17th Down delayed of units being transferred to Divisions. Went CASSEL supply column.	J. Coleman Lt Col SSO III Div

T134. Wt. W708—776. 500000. 4/15. Sir J. C. & S.

Army Form C. 2118.

WAR DIARY
or
INTELLIGENCE SUMMARY.
(Erase heading not required.)

Instructions regarding War Diaries and Intelligence Summaries are contained in F. S. Regs., Part II. and the Staff Manual respectively. Title pages will be prepared in manuscript.

Place	Date	Hour	Summary of Events and Information	Remarks and references to Appendices
GODEWAERS-VELDE	6/7/16		(7th K.S.L.I.) 10 MT in tractors (Lieut Gow) 1 st Stephen Hands. 13th King's D'port (Lieut Gow) & 8th B'ffs to S.G. Allenbrooks Rail & RE by train. Blocks came from Pop't Godew. Squatson N.H. & A/Col G by road via L area — No 3 G arrived ENCLESQUE from Lezen. HiR. M.E. dump in Eperlecque. Went to W'M'kers CAPPEL. Visited SIGTR stores — Went to Office & Supply column. Saw Capt Shelbourne 7/17th Divisn. Spent have full details of full transfers from 3rd to 17th division. Have duly returned by us. 7th Refresher class by rail for Calais. Arrived by us to STORES, 8/arrived.	
	7/7/16		9th DB HQrs & 4 buttns to Boeschere by train, but 17 Grs by bus. Mounted Section RE & 3rd Sig ORE by road to L area. All returned for Conscription 8th. Went Office & Supply column. No 1 & 2 G left by road for L area & Nos 3 & Nos 4&5 F'Amps. Hants & 17th Division	
	8/7/16		Sent return not from Canal by lorry to artillery training school Reckerghem for Conscription 9th inst. Arms wanted blocks distribution to returned with Coming K'Supps Col. New bus card out following morning write notices for Conscription 10th inst. —	J. K........ B.G. E.S., III Divn

T2134. Wt. W708—776. 500000. 4/15. Sir J.C. & S.

WAR DIARY
or
INTELLIGENCE SUMMARY.

Army Form C. 2118.

(Erase heading not required.)

Place	Date	Hour	Summary of Events and Information	Remarks and references to Appendices
GOMMECAPS RIDGE	September 8/9/16		9th & 3rd Rn Negros, 2 Bn R Warks, 2 Bn Bdk Watch, 8th KRRC, 8th KOYLI Rgt & subalterns, 9 th Bgde M.G.Coy, dismounted parties R.E. Sanders, Son, by train struck down from Pop - Essex - Marched to 11.E Bethune Ca. 14 and report 7 walkers /11 d BAPC by road for 2 miles, attained convoy Gros 9 arrived. Helges tram left side for MOULLE — nulla slits at GOMMES-CAPPEL. Also sent to EPERLECQUES, must everything in order. Purchased harness chains from CASSEL & WATTEN. (see cash accounts) & road R.H.A. horses etc.	
MOULLE	9/9/16		Reached billing at WATTEN — supplies for 7b.R.R 9.R 79 K. LR. 2 led chemfred on EPERLECQUES, Supplies for R.H.A. & M.V. etc. sent by lorries & B etc. Scraps. (No! Gr dump water at Osborne) road reviewed. 2 lorries can R.3rd this through by road to Z — returned area. 10.15 in ints. Tracker GOMMECAPS-CAPPEL Supply Col.	
	10.—		14 gro R.A. 1 (sec ratio) Supplies by road to Z area from Bonetique - 9 th OR drunk. moved from EPERLECQUES to Main Calais-Stome Road J36 a.6.1 (Sheet 7 N.E) & 76.B.B to HOULLE Q.5.c.1.4 (Sheet 27 N.S.E) — Col. appointed WATTEN.	[signature]

T2134. W. W708—776. 500000. 4/15. Sir J. C. & S.

WAR DIARY
or
INTELLIGENCE SUMMARY.

Army Form C. 2118.

Place	Date	Hour	Summary of Events and Information	Remarks and references to Appendices
MEULLE	11/3/16		Remainder 3 B. H. & Regt. RTA moved to the area. Lt Bn. O'Brien resumed a Interp returns up to conscription 14th Krübrés No 1 Co A.S.C. left Bourop for the area. Have received O office new Camps.	
	17/3/16		DAO & M rd Co left Bourolype for the area. Supply Clerk at WEMAERS-CAPPEL Sheed & Copenhia hoveware all supplies up war Yannes No 1 Co proceeded to NORDEYNES all RTA units are clearing 9th JR for rations will arrive No 6:	
	1.30Mc		Supply situation normal all units transported for return to further refilling points. No 16. report on RACCON S.E. move Schoepenhay, all mid feed storepeace muse 20th yamme N Co's review morethen any well Any return at Wilhelm this morning up to 20 m. fr. here. Truck down arrived at WATTEN. Honeod of bread transport.	
			Went CASSEL (POTSTO). Conveyance difficulty experienced in buying refitable to the area. Been Dunion fring well cleared. Weath reported B.O.E from.	Marry Capt 830. II Am

Army Form C. 2118.

WAR DIARY
or
INTELLIGENCE SUMMARY.
(Erase heading not required.)

Place	Date	Hour	Summary of Events and Information	Remarks and references to Appendices
Mon 377 VGS	14/9/16		Routine as usual. Have consulted with Col Berry PS Plcham re shortage of vegetables in France Command Area — Attended Conference at Q with DQMG respecting move of Division to its new supply arrangements discussed.	
—	15/9/16		Received instructions at 5.30 pm that the 76th Inf Bgde would move to at once to the Rivinghed area — more due to General attack — gave instructions to SSQ & to buyers as to h of rations & rations for consumption. Various points shown in this morning looked into. Return to 18 Artois, Supply keepers & SSO [?] & returned to Supply Column M[?], purchased for 76th & 13 Kt at fault. Arr 6 — train arrived from dump at 7 pm. Turned off rations 9 pm for HARDIFORT. From there to Rinchpletem B[?]per ([?] attached units RE + 7 Australian) finished entraining at 9.15 pm — return to Bouvincour Corning town station on train & remained hard all evening. — All attached units transferred 8th Div for returning intrasd SSO I[?] Sir J.C.&S.	W[?] Capt SSO

WAR DIARY
or
INTELLIGENCE SUMMARY.

Place	Date	Hour	Summary of Events and Information	Remarks and references to Appendices
MOULLE	16/3/16		Instructions received that 76th S.B. were to hold as chopuel the 5th Corps. The O.C. to report for instructions at Corps Hd qrs 11 am — have Arund Park ascertains that 76th S.B. would unison with 17th Division Rear S.B. Division proposed about returns (as far) fm 19th and transport Orders issued that 8 & 9th S.Br. must likewise holdease off at such an arrangements were accordingly. Lord at 3pm the troops (That Corps) was cancelled from the 76th S.B. would for today so into traveler for 30. 11 deep then return from front —	
	17/3/16		Routine as usual — 76th S.B. in trucks on 17th Division front —	

Army Form C. 2118.

WAR DIARY
or
INTELLIGENCE SUMMARY.
(Erase heading not required.)

Place	Date	Hour	Summary of Events and Information	Remarks and references to Appendices
Woelle	15/7/16		Orders received at 8 a.m. that the 40th Bgde. R.T.H. would leave by D.G.14 am rail via WITTEN & HENGELS-CAPEL for ST. OMER — Supply wagons loaded for Consumption 19th & detailed by road under Lt Welsh. Head up Brigade at HAZEBROT. Supply lorries with rations Consumption 20th. Sent & HAZEDIPAT to refill into Supply wagons there & then & forward train 17th Divn Supplied at GRESTRE. SSO 17th Divn advised arrangements made & had ordered return for trains Consumption 21st inst. 6 p.m. Instruction received that R.Reding Field AR.E. would retrain from St Omer at 9 pm for 17th Divn — Arranged with Supply Col to send lorry with rations Consumption 29th Amm. & Hesitation Hands into GS wagons. If not, this was done. — Return for Consumption required 24 hours. the Board at Aviethere — Return form constable to 17th Divn Supply Col. SSO 17th Divn informed. It afterwards transpired that the Reding Rifle dept behind 49 men 9th & 1 horse — these men attached RA & Horses for returning Hampers.	[signature] GOC 17th Divn 880

Army Form C. 2118.

WAR DIARY
or
INTELLIGENCE SUMMARY.
(Erase heading not required.)

Instructions regarding War Diaries and Intelligence Summaries are contained in F. S. Regs., Part II. and the Staff Manual respectively. Title pages will be prepared in manuscript.

Place	Date	Hour	Summary of Events and Information	Remarks and references to Appendices
MOULLE	19/5/16		Orders received that the 56 Siege Bty (9th S.Br.) will leave for 17th Division tomorrow by train. Necessary arrangements made.	
	20/5/16		56 Field Co RE left by 5pm train from Boursin, conveying rations for consumption 21st. Rations to consumption 22nd Sept by lorry from Watten to 17th Divn S.Col at Boeschepe. SSO 17th Divn informed by wire. — Arranged if Staff Captain Capt who agreed therefore to issue Staff Buckets, arrangements now made to send the dump in Bourmigny Coal, quantity about 30 tons at a time for issue to whole of RA in the Division, lorries being to use their transport coming into Wordergreen for coal. — Information received that the 1/4 Gordon Highlanders (Pth S Br) will leave this division for the 51st Division (3rd Army), on the 23rd inst; also the rations for consumption 24th incld. SSO 51st Divn informed by wire of arrangements made, also Through France.	address T Divn

WAR DIARY
or
INTELLIGENCE SUMMARY.
(Erase heading not required.)

Army Form C. 2118.

Place	Date	Hour	Summary of Events and Information	Remarks and references to Appendices
MOULLE	22/7/16		Refilled Supply wagons a/Fontaine during the afternoon with Rations for Consumption on training. Evening today.	
	23/7/16		A/Fontaine left by train from St Omer at 3pm for 3rd Army area — Capt Hale returned from leave today. Weather cool & showery.	
	24/7/16		Routine as usual — Weather very cool.	
	25/7/16		Routine as usual. Orders received that another Supply Bgde will leave for 17th Division at an early date.	
	26/7/16		8th Supply Bgde leave via 2nd train together with detachment 158 men RAMC Messing Supply arrangements made.	
	27/7/16		Went to Foucarmelle interviewed SSO 17th Division reference move 8th Supply Bn. Took Capt Andrews & O'Hickey (NO3 6) with me on for as 9th Bn left there to St N. Popeninghe by rail arrangements arrived their in their Co — Canal Saw the S&T OS re Coal were informed which there that the 8th Supply Bn move had been cancelled – Telephone	McKenzie Capt II Corps SSO

WAR DIARY
or
INTELLIGENCE SUMMARY.
(Erase heading not required.)

Army Form C. 2118.

Place	Date	Hour	Summary of Events and Information	Remarks and references to Appendices
Houlle	Continued 27/1/16		Telephoned R.T.O. Poperinghe hundred Capt Aurelius & hookers Nissen & WOTTEN regain this Company. Owing to them instructions received telems by horse transport from railhead starting from tomorrow him WATTEN must necessary Cup arrangements with C.C. Supply Column - bread fresh meat & (hot turned over days from tomorrow at railhead.	
	27/1/16		Lorries dumped supplies for consumption 1.3.16 at 4 p.m. for 8th in Bn &c in order to enable Supp wagons away loaded.	
	28/1/16		Horse transport provided railhead horses supplies for divnl S/o 17th I.B. in cell 83 wagons - working commenced at 9 a.m. Everything about 10.45 a.m. Supplies handed to Regtl groups was ready to second thro' for wagons by train 7 Oh Rmy - Central Champ were formed at J 36 C 6 a.1 on main Calais road, transport about 12 noon, refreshing Commenced at 5 p.m.	Schinrrings 880 III Div

Army Form C. 2118.

WAR DIARY
or
INTELLIGENCE SUMMARY.
(Erase heading not required.)

Instructions regarding War Diaries and Intelligence Summaries are contained in F. S. Regs., Part II. and the Staff Manual respectively. Title pages will be prepared in manuscript.

Place	Date	Hour	Summary of Events and Information	Remarks and references to Appendices
MOULLE	1/3/16		Routine. Horse transport of reinforcet, 16 O.R. wagons for 8th Inf Bn & 3 for 9th S. Bn & 40 for time troops, drawing finished in 1 hr 50 minutes. — 8/c Inf Bn dumped at Eperlecques & 9th & Suicide or Central dump. Host Grade with 8 APwg 8 ten DDST about new rations — orders received that the 8th Inf Bn with PAMC attachment will move by train for Poperinghe early Tomorrow morning — Convois with Suppl. Consumption 2.3.16 dumped in Eperlecques, Supplies loaded into Supp Wagons. — Convois with rations for Consumption 3.3.16 have tomorrow for attachments 17th Field Amb. — SSO 17th train arrived by wire of arrangements made.	J.P. Cunningham SSO Lynn Ditton

S.O. III Div. TROOPS

Army Form C. 2118.

WAR DIARY
INTELLIGENCE SUMMARY.
(Erase heading not required.)

Instructions regarding War Diaries and Intelligence
Summaries are contained in F. S. Regs., Part II.
and the Staff Manual respectively. Title pages
will be prepared in manuscript.

Place	Date	Hour	Summary of Events and Information	Remarks and references to Appendices
GODEWAERSVELDE	1/2/16		Lorries arrived at usual time. Off-loaded by 8 o'clock. Refilling Point finished by 9 o'clock.	
"	2/2/16		Routine as usual.	
"	3/2/16		Lorries arrived at 7.35 a.m. Off-loaded by 8 o'clock. Refilling commenced at 8.15 a.m. & finished by 9.20 a.m.	
"	4/2/16		Usual times for lorries & refilling. Issues as usual.	
"	5/2/16		The Supply Officer, Lt. A.S. Parker, A.S.C, was detailed to proceed to WEMAERS-CAPPEL to take charge of a Divisional Store, as the Division were moving back into rest. 2/Lt Osborne took over the duties of Supply Officer. Issues as usual.	
BOSCHEPE	6/2/16		Lorries arrived at 12. P.M. Refilling at 3 P.M. Issues as usual.	
"	7/2/16		Lorries arrived at 12 P.M. Routine as usual.	
"	8/2/16		Routine as usual.	
"	9/2/16		Refilling at 3.20 P.M. Issues as usual.	
"	10/2/16		Lorries arrived at 11.30 a.m. Routine as usual.	
"	11/2/16		Two days supplies issued to Divn Amn Column & XI ordered not to be in force & move into Rest area	

Osborne 11/2/16
for LOIII DivT Tps

Army Form C. 2118.

WAR DIARY
or
INTELLIGENCE SUMMARY.
(Erase heading not required.)

Instructions regarding War Diaries and Intelligence Summaries are contained in F. S. Regs., Part II. and the Staff Manual respectively. Title pages will be prepared in manuscript.

Place	Date	Hour	Summary of Events and Information	Remarks and references to Appendices
WIMMERS-CAPPEL	12/2/16		Lt. A.S. Parker rejoined No 1. Company who had marched in the night before & took over the supply duties from Lieut. Osborn. The Company moved to La Recousse on the main Calais - St Omer Road.	
La Recousse	13/2/16		Lorries arrived at 8 a.m. 9 were off-loaded by 8.30 a.m. Lorries as usual including Tobacco. Refilling Point finished by 10.15 a.m.	
"	14/2/16		Lorries arrived at 8 a.m. Off-loaded at usual time. Usual Times 9 wanes.	
"	15/2/16		Lorries arrived at 8 a.m. Off-loaded by 8.30 a.m. Refilling commenced at 8.45 a.m. 9 wans cleared by 10.15 a.m.	
"	16/2/16		Routine as usual. Fresh vegetables were issued this morning to units unable to purchase for themselves.	
"	17/2/16		Lorries arrived at usual time. Lorries 9 Limes for Refilling as usual.	
"	18/2/16		Lorries arrived at 8 a.m. Off-loaded by 8.30 a.m. Refilling commenced 8.15 a.m. & cleared by 10 o'clock.	
"	19/2/16		Routine as usual.	
"	20/2/16		Routine as usual. Usual issues including Tobacco & cigarettes.	
"	21/2/16		Usual times for Lorries & Refilling Point.	

A.S. Parker
Lieut. A.S.C.
S.O. III ⁄ III Div. L⁄s

Army Form C. 2118.

WAR DIARY
or
INTELLIGENCE SUMMARY.
(Erase heading not required.)

Instructions regarding War Diaries and Intelligence Summaries are contained in F. S. Regs., Part II. and the Staff Manual respectively. Title pages will be prepared in manuscript.

Place	Date	Hour	Summary of Events and Information	Remarks and references to Appendices
La Recousse	22/3/16		Routine as usual. Refilling Point commenced 8.25 a.m. & cleared by 10 o'clock. 40th Bde R.F.A. left Divisional Troops.	
"	23/3/16		Usual games issues.	
"	24/3/16		Routine as usual.	
"	25/3/16		Lorries arrived at usual time. Issues as usual. Refilling Point cleared by 10 o'clock.	
"	26/3/16		Usual Routine.	
"	27/3/16		Lorries arrived at 9 o'clock. Off-loaded by 9.30 a.m. Refilling commenced 9.50 a.m. & cleared by 11.10 a.m.	
J.36.c. Sheet 27.B	28/3/16		Owing to heavy snow & the state of the roads, the lorries did not arrive at the usual Refilling Point, the Horse Transport went to Railhead at WATTEN & off-loaded at J.36.c. (Sheet 27.B). Refilling commenced at 2 p.m. & was finished by 8.30 p.m.	
"	29/3/16		Refilling at J.36.c. Usual issues. Arrangements have been made to have lorries to help unload the wagons on Refilling Point on their return from WATTEN, as before it was impossible to clock the various commodities.	

A. Rathbury Lt. A.S.C.
S.O. III Div. Troops

S.O. 8th Inf. Bde.

Army Form C. 2118.

WAR DIARY
or
INTELLIGENCE SUMMARY. Of Supplies.
(Erase heading not required.)

Feb /16.

Place	Date	Hour	Summary of Events and Information	Remarks and references to Appendices
Beschope	1.2.16		Lorries arrived 7.20. Refilling 8 a.m. over 8.45. Brigade lorries out of the trenches. Issue of Rum. All units drew out straw from Div Forage Store, to supplement the Army ration.	
	2.2.16		Lorries arrived 7.25. Refilling 8 a.m. over 8.45. Nothing of note occurred.	
	3.2.16		Lorries arrived 7.25. Refilling 8 a.m. over 8.45.	
	4.2.16		Lorries arrived 7.30. Refilling 8 a.m. over 8.35. Division to move on the 5th. Arrangements with the 8th Bde. to issue on the 5th at ... the next great to the station near the various Battns entrain.	
	5.2.16		Lorries arrived 7.10. Refilling 8 a.m. over 8.50. Supplies sent as arranged. The Battns where they are offloaded were placed under a guard. The Battns on their arrival taking their supplies and loading them on the train. The S.A.A. wagons arrived with K.O.York.L.I. Capt R.A.S.C. D.O. Supplies

Army Form C. 2118.

Instructions regarding War Diaries and Intelligence Summaries are contained in F. S. Regs., Part II. and the Staff Manual respectively. Title pages will be prepared in manuscript.

WAR DIARY
or
INTELLIGENCE SUMMARY. J.S. Hopkins

(Erase heading not required.)

Place	Date	Hour	Summary of Events and Information	Remarks and references to Appendices
Boesehape	5.2.16 cont.		The A.S.C. company, ex H5. The 8th Rde 5 Days then supplies on the 6th in the Square at EPERLEGUES	
EPERLECUES	6.2.16		Lorries arrived on the 5th inst. Refilled Lidday. Units refill at. Then Baggage wagons ex Supply wagons travelling by road have not yet arrived. Tobacco issue. Take over Coal Dump from 17th Division. Brigade Strength at the end of the week. All 19/19, 36 ft. Divns 29. H.D. 39. L.D. 243 Cdts 25. S.M. 24.	
	7.2.16		Lorries arrived on the 6th inst. Refilled Lidday. Railhead WATTEN. A grand placed over the supplies in the Square at night.	
	8.2.16		Lorries arrived Lidday on the 7th inst. Offloaded in the Square and placed over the tea at night. Refilled Lidday.	
	9.2.16		Lorries arrived on 8th inst. Refilled. 9 p.m. eve 10 AM. 3000 Kilos of mixed vegetables received	
	10.2.16		Lorries arrived 6.30 AM Refilled - 7.30 AM eve 8.30. All units issued extra fuel allowance to units, but not sanctioned by the Division	R.I. Anhurt. Cpt. ASC. D.O. Y Rde.

T-2134. W^t. W708—776. 500000. 4/15. Sir J. C. & S.

Army Form C. 2118.

WAR DIARY
or
INTELLIGENCE SUMMARY. J. J. Giffin
(Erase heading not required.)

Place	Date	Hour	Summary of Events and Information	Remarks and references to Appendices
Epelecque	11.2.16		Lorries arrive 6.45. Refillers 7.15. over 8.40. Extra bacon sent up in lieu of Bttn. bread. all unit drawing their extra allowance of 2 lb oats in lieu of 4 lb hay. The shortage of hay for L.D. is causing great difficulties for local purchase as the local supply is limited.	
	12.2.16		Lorries arrive 7.30. Refilling 8 A.M. over 9 A.M.	
	13.2.16		Lorries arrive 9 A.M. Refilling 9.30 A.M. over 10.20 A.M. Brigade Dhies 9th at the end of this week. All a/MGS 53.55. Dhies 85. HO. 47. L.D. 542. Cdr. 11. S.M day 15.	
	14.2.16		Lorries arrive 8 A.M. Refilling 8.30 over 9.30. Free pay return of 10 lbs of L.Bses. great lack of pageant to be purchased locally.	
	15.2.16		Lorries arrive 8 A.M. Refilling 8.10 over 9.20. 76th Bde go back to the Trench lines to saddle are. 82 Bde take over. battn. trek there, Divisional Cyclists, 142nd & 73rd Fd Amb.. T.A. and Sig unit for feeling of supplies. K. Andrews Capt RFA S.O. J Bde

Army Form C. 2118.

WAR DIARY
or
INTELLIGENCE SUMMARY.
(Erase heading not required.)

Instructions regarding War Diaries and Intelligence Summaries are contained in F. S. Regs., Part II. and the Staff Manual respectively. Title pages will be prepared in manuscript.

Place	Date	Hour	Summary of Events and Information	Remarks and references to Appendices
EPERLECQUES	16.2.16		Lorries arrive 8 AM Refilling 8.30 over 9.30. Nothing of note found.	
	17.2.16		Lorries arrive 9AM Refilling 9.30 over 9.25. Great difficulty in keeping up regular supply of vegetables, all being hung up by small arms fire.	
	18.2.16		Lorries arrive 9AM Refilling 9.30 over 9.30. unit short of Fwr. Ratios. The quarter-depot & the Nursery had any to refrigerator. One to the Red Beef Tins. All day the selling threw tons of xxxxx cake backing then went all.	
	19.2.16		Lorries arrive 9AM Refilling 8.30 over 9.20.	
	20.2.16		Lorries arrive 9AM Refilling 9.30 over 10.30 Tobacco Issue	

Strength at the end of the week.

	All ranks.	Horses.	H.D.	L.D.	Cobs.	Small ares.	Cars.	M.C.		
	5991	1114	87.	723	80.	15			E. Andrews Capt AFC 2.0. AFRA

Army Form C. 2118.

WAR DIARY
or
INTELLIGENCE SUMMARY.
(Erase heading not required.)

Instructions regarding War Diaries and Intelligence Summaries are contained in F.S. Regs, Part II. and the Staff Manual respectively. Title pages will be prepared in manuscript.

J S Apples

Place	Date	Hour	Summary of Events and Information	Remarks and references to Appendices
EPERLEGUES	21.2.16		Lorrie arrive 8 AM. Refilling 8.30 over 9.30.	
	22.2.16		Lorrie arrive 8 AM. Refilling 8.30 over 9.25. Snow began to fall. Very cold.	
	23.2.16		Lorrie arrive 9 AM. Refilling 8.30 over 9.30. Heavy frost. Snow & morning. Brigade sports in the aftn.	
	24.2.16		Lorrie arrive 8 AM. Refilling 8.30 over 9.30. Weather still very cold. All units to be asked if a larger proportion of fresh meat need be prepared in lieu of preserved. Letters received in con. of	
	25.2.16		Lorrie arrive 8 AM. Refilling 8.30 over 9.35. Another heavy fall of snow during evening.	
	26.2.16		Lorrie arrive 8 AM. Refilling 8.30 over 9.30. Orders to note received on the 25th. Dates Refilling to take place tomorrow. 27.2. Supply wagons to travel free with ten tonnes (?) of pea soup in lieu do. A day supply of vegetables to be cancelled to be taken	K.S.Potatoes Cart Pte. 20 S.P.R.

WAR DIARY or INTELLIGENCE SUMMARY.

Army Form C. 2118.

(Erase heading not required.)

Place	Date	Hour	Summary of Events and Information	Remarks and references to Appendices
EPERLEQUES	27.2.16		Lorries arrived 9 A.M. Refilling 9.30. Issue of Tobacco. Units drew two days supplies. Lorries arrived in the afternoon. Rifle 2.30 P.M. all preparations complete. Charcoal, whale oil, vegetables, pea soup issued, the orders to move cancelled, tea fatter active.	
	28.2.16		Every truck have received a two days supply of rations, on the 27th Feb. No supplies issued. Orders to be staying to	
	29.2.16	10 hours arrived	Owing to thaw Roads in an impossible condition for mechanical transport. those hardest supplies wagons had direct from Rustrend Gables to move accrued rations. A wire sent to Supply Column Lorries arriv. at 3.15 P.M. roads improved. Supply wagons loaded & despatched to units. Pale troves arriving on the morning of 1.3.16 The strength at the end of the month.	

K.T. Andrews Capt ASC
S.O. 8th Divs

WAR DIARY
or
INTELLIGENCE SUMMARY
(Erase heading not required.)

Army Form C. 2118

S.O. 9th Inf. Bde.

Place	Date	Hour	Summary of Events and Information	Remarks and references to Appendices
BOESCHEPE	1/7/16		Outpost duties as usual. Officers relieved by 7.15 am. Relief commenced 8pm, first detachments. Relieving finishes 8.50pm. Otherwise no want of note.	
	2/7/16		Routine as above	
	3/7/16		Service as usual 7.30am. Clean by 1st. Relieving commenced 8 o'clock. Service routine as usual.	
	4/7/16		Routine as usual	
	5/7/16		Outpost duties 7.30am. Officers relieved by 1st. Relief commenced 8 o'clock. Relief finishes 8.50pm. Outpost arrives 3.30 pm with rations for 1st Bn. Relieving commences 8.15 pm. Service as usual.	
	6/7/16		Relieving commences 8.15am. Service as usual with rations. Relieving finishes 9.15am. 11.30am Officers defend at 12.35pm. 2.5 relief commenced 3.30pm. Service as usual. Relieving finishes 4.15pm. 10.15pm all wagons, except one, proceeded to deliver supplies to move off in the morning	E.W. Wright Capt. a/c

Army Form C. 2118

WAR DIARY
INTELLIGENCE SUMMARY
(Erase heading not required.)

S.O. 9th Divisible

Place	Date	Hour	Summary of Events and Information	Remarks and references to Appendices
MERRIS CAPPEL	11/7/16		Capt Nugent & Lieut S Love & Rusell Owen proceeded to Poperinghe the St Omer & Boulogne Road. On the Road Lts Gwalia & Stallings were handed over & were then sent to all units in before transment. Supply men marches empty from BOESCHEPE.	
QUEMBERGUE	8/7/16		Supply wagons in marks empty.	
"	"		Ratios at EPERLEQUES & supplies deliveries to went nearest men. Also refilled MT lorries stores & Buckshots.	
"	"	10/7/16	Lorries arrived at new reget MANNECOVE. Trail SE of NORDAUSQUES at 7.30 a.m. Unloaded & loaded by 6.30 a.m. Refill commenced 8.30 hours. Lorries arrive at Refills. Lunches 9.30. Loaf over coal yards on specialled points.	
"	"	9/7/16	Lorries arrived 7.40 a.m. Offloaded & delivery by 8.5 a.m. Refill commenced 8.20 a.m. Lorries were individually despatched. Vegetables also vehicles sent to 23rd & 4th Bde. R.F.A. Refills.	
			Lorries 10.20 a.m.	E W McNeal Capt R.A.S.C.

WAR DIARY
INTELLIGENCE SUMMARY
(Erase heading not required.)

Army Form C. 2118

S.O. 9th S.f. Bde.

Place	Date	Hour	Summary of Events and Information	Remarks and references to Appendices
QUEMBERCE	17/7/16		Lorries arrived 7.30 am. Offloaded taken by S.O. Refilling Establishment commences 8.15 am. Lorries to unusual unloading. Street vegetables. Refilling finishes 9.30 am.	
	13/7/16		Lorries arrived about 9 am. Offloaded at 9.30 am. Duties as usual.	
	14/7/16		Lorries arrived at 6 am instead of 7 men as stated. Duties as usual. No vegetables procurable. Refilling finished at 9 am. O.C. Carlisle R.O. arranged for lunch supply of vegetables and purchased 2000 kilos of potatoes for billets.	
	15/7/16		Lorries arrived at 8.30 am very late. All supplies meet and unusual as usual. Vegetables issued. Refilling finished by 9.30 am.	
	16/7/16		Lorries at 8.15 am clear by 9 noon. Refilling over by 9.15 am. Steady as present arrival. Unusual issued. Issue of above hay purchased heavily.	

E.W.S [signature]
Capt. A.S.C.

Army Form C. 2118

S.O. 9th Infantry (?)

WAR DIARY
of
INTELLIGENCE SUMMARY
(Erase heading not required.)

Instructions regarding War Diaries and Intelligence Summaries are contained in F.S. Regs., Part II. and the Staff Manual respectively. Title Pages will be prepared in manuscript.

Place	Date	Hour	Summary of Events and Information	Remarks and references to Appendices
QUERRIEU	17/2/16		Weather fine for April. Lorries arrived at 8.15 am. Refilling as usual.	
	18/2/16		Lorries refilling finished by 9.15 am. Weather fair. Lorries at hand time. Refilling nearly 9.15 am. Reduced transport issued to 8th Field Ambulance – other issues as usual.	
	19/2/16		Weather fair. Lorries at usual hour. Refilling as usual. 16 Company sent three wagons to ALDERSHOT for vegetables.	off (?)
	20/2/16		Weather fine. Lorries arrived at 9/15 am. Refilling as usual.	
	21/2/16		Weather fine. Lorries arrived at 8.15 am. Refilling as usual. 58th Coy R.E. left to join 19th Division temporarily.	
	22/2/16		Weather fine. Lorries arrived at 8.15 am. Refilling as usual.	
	23/2/16		Lorries arrived at 8.15. Refilling as usual. Snowed during the day. Captain Peat returned to duty from leave.	
	24/2/16		Lorries arrived at 8.15 am. Refilling as usual. Sent wagons to Achiers (?) to fetch vegetables. Weather fine.	

E.M. Head (?)
Capt A.S.C.

Army Form C. 2118.

WAR DIARY
or
INTELLIGENCE SUMMARY.
(Erase heading not required.)

C.O. 9th Suffolks
For 16

Place	Date	Hour	Summary of Events and Information	Remarks and references to Appendices
QUEMBECOURT	27/7/16		Lorries arrived 8.15am. Rolls call commences 8.45am. Issued as usual. Artillery shelled 9.15am	
"	28/7/16		Routine as usual	
"	29/7/16		Lorries arrived 9.15am. Companies relieved by 9.30am. Reliefs commenced. Rations etc. rations by 10.8 am. Other routine as usual	
"	28/7/16		Proceeded to railhead with 23 waggons to load direct from train. This procedure considered inadvisable by the train as train went entirely up the road. Rations [?] to unload rapidly commences to the trucks. Did not pads supplies. Rapidly commences to the trucks. Rang lot the transport in charge to continue only their own lot. Line transport which left supplies. Lorries as usual	
"	29/7/16		Ration [?] loaded at railhead Shiek [?]head to have two trains supplies at [?] at railhead point to unload the [?] etc. First line transport units to commence at 8 pm	

M. Weale
Capt. RASC

SENIOR SUPPLY OFFICER
3rd DIVISION.
MARCH 1916.

Army Form C. 2118.

WAR DIARY
or
INTELLIGENCE SUMMARY.
(Erase heading not required.)

Instructions regarding War Diaries and Intelligence Summaries are contained in F. S. Regs., Part II. and the Staff Manual respectively. Title pages will be prepared in manuscript.

Place	Date	Hour	Summary of Events and Information	Remarks and references to Appendices
MOULLE	1/3/16		Transport loading at Railhead this morning - 23 wagons for 9th L.F.A. & 28 for 2nd Div. Ypo. The yard at WATTEN Stn is a good one for loading - plenty of room to turn in system working very well. 8th Sup. Coln left for Pop. by train supply wagons army returns convey from sid - return convoys from 2nd Div by lorries to Caestre (arriving 17th) our S. Col SSO 17th Divn informed temporarily under Armie Command drawing at Reinhem again.	
	2/3/16		Roads in normal condition	
	3/3/16		further trip west Louvigny - attached units up behind by 8th Div. Wheeled 9th Dett for returning.	
	4/3/16		Orders received that numerous divisional convoys commence to move up to line on 6 trains.	per Lieuten. Orde SSO 3rd Div.

T2134. Wt. W708—776. 500000. 4/15. Sir J.C. & S.

WAR DIARY
or
INTELLIGENCE SUMMARY

Army Form C. 2118.

Place	Date	Hour	Summary of Events and Information	Remarks and references to Appendices
Moville	14/3/16		Orders received that 2 Battns of In Bgde will leave today. Return for consumption 6th sent on supply wagons returned. On lorries with return cars 7th sent to Creeslough forewarned from SSO Letterkenny warning message. Arrangements attempted - Saw SSO 7th Refuse coal & M.T. 100 tons wheat in western area barrows on the erection between that stack is up to Reminghled have had trouble with O.C. supply blumin on supply wagons. Visited O Office + O C refuses more Quillam the government from thenial.	
	15/3/16		Reminners 17th got into site left by train supply wagons carrying rations to walking returns ft 8th sent caretis by lorries. Sent Capt Peak to Caretes Munsel over lorries figures to Column Supply Officer in turnover working to Letterkenny. Supplies for 7th Ambulance sent overseas capers to much 1st day on March through Lorries. — 105-106 CRC Married from 75th Dev Moville courted. — Ohr S.W. Borthern Premier Partn	McKenry SSO M.B.

Army Form C. 2118.

WAR DIARY
or
INTELLIGENCE SUMMARY.
(Erase heading not required.)

Instructions regarding War Diaries and Intelligence Summaries are contained in F. S. Regs., Part II. and the Staff Manual respectively. Title pages will be prepared in manuscript.

Place	Date	Hour	Summary of Events and Information	Remarks and references to Appendices
GOMMECOURT WOOD	7/3/16		Negro Division & Negro train left for new Rtery. Pushed on Gommecourt. Supplies also sent through N area for units working through N area. Lorries furnish bookings. Coal at trouble - storming key well. Returning.	
	8/3/16		Position previous to stop at Wemaers-Capell & took after one of returning troops leaving through N area. Suffolks sent to Cassel. W Capell hold area & Brackets Neuve trenches in Winnezeele, for 8.9th & 76th Bttln Inspection.	
	9/3/16		Noon 7th left for W.Capell today. 4nd 730 gun RFA & T mortar batts left Winnezeele for Cassel. Supplies to Cassel & Wemaers W.Capell.	Winnezeele Class 550 111 Divn

Army Form C. 2118.

WAR DIARY
or
INTELLIGENCE SUMMARY.
(Erase heading not required.)

Place	Date	Hour	Summary of Events and Information	Remarks and references to Appendices
GODEWAERS VELDE	10/2/16		Leaving Section 423 30th Regts RFA left N area for line. Supplies for ammunition Col to Capel. Refilling for Latheroulee unit. Sus Hers today for bad time. All unit started the normal transfer movement attaches (transferring to 9th In Bn. to returning). Supplies for following units transferred from 17th Division drawn from rail this today for first time. 2nd Duyham R.E. 172nd Divnl Sig Coy R.E. 6th Labour Battn Bus Coy., Belgian Artillery (transport lines), 7th Labour Battn, 3rd M.M. Gun Co. 30th Fd Ambs. Issued wood fuel rations. Also fr 1 Regt R.H.A. T.M. batteries belonging 17th Divn (about 1,750 men) 22nd Regt. R.F.A. D.A.C. besides 116 Month Camb House. Bread issue depot left N area (nine for N area today) — ammunition	
	11/2/16		423 and 30 Regts left N area for line. Supplies drawn full today.	

Capt. SEO 11th Bron

WAR DIARY
or
INTELLIGENCE SUMMARY.
(Erase heading not required.)

Army Form C. 2118.

Place	Date	Hour	Summary of Events and Information	Remarks and references to Appendices
GODEWAERS-VELDE	12/3/16		105 + 106 C.R.E. S.W. Bouldens Pioneer Buttn rifled twice before morning for 257 men not known missing - 220 ozt ammunition 7th Pioneer Buttn Yorks Lanc found from 17th Divn returned by us from Ourenmptiem 15th inst - Rope and Wiring SHQ Meeting C.C. 2nd Bgde Tom N area Minor I Supplies and Wiremen Capul for new line totley.	
	13/3/16		Order DDGST 2nd Army Cruerone Road 6 to him dining & focus word for 1 week - Ceckupp and totley - Conference of Roo Peos. Re wiring up at WO 3313 78th sec Bgde theochine guns fromised to prince teddy from England. Considerable difficulty in reference to obtaining portalir at wider before the cupps to getting pumice - water reported d.s.l. Train 2nd Army - oil can finished at Bailleul Arrivals 1/2 3rd Rogel Reuthers, M.I.H. Sewed against from N area Whis - Who completed ths move of the Division.	J. McKaing CEO

WAR DIARY
or
INTELLIGENCE SUMMARY
(Erase heading not required.)

Army Form C. 2118.

Place	Date	Hour	Summary of Events and Information	Remarks and references to Appendices
Godwinsroad	14/3/16	-	Refilling Situation normal. Returned Bus Co Offr. detained by 17th Division — No notice of transport for returned from 5th Corps. Wrote 76th Inf Bgd refusing from G.S.D to G.27.B. Wrote 27 Div complaining of arrangements made for bread. The troops & lorries by hand transport at railhead truwaresd. Interview with Telugu drawing from railhead unit. Interview Officers at Carotti.	
	15/3/16	-	Horse transport brand the drawing at railhead from Tolley. Unable to get sufficient supply Indian vegetables from railhead. Shortage in fresh vegetables which are still deficient.	
	16	-	Worked RTH from 76th Inf. exchange with 30th Bgd for rationing purposes. Flesh Supply refilling at uns dump from today. Vans started overloaded to Kinama & potatoes. Unable to obtain supplies to as the flesh has been opened then by	
	17	-	24th & 30th Divisions. Correspondence in consequence of this	February Capt

T2134. Wt. W708—776. 500000. 4/15. Sir J. C. & S.

WAR DIARY or INTELLIGENCE SUMMARY.

Army Form C. 2118.

Place	Date	Hour	Summary of Events and Information	Remarks and references to Appendices
GODEWAERSVELDE	17/5/16	Continued	Officer finding went off to find the free of potatoes in the area & unable to find any were unable. Water reported to O.C. train. Train 17th down trying potatoes in own area, there were taken by Lt Stephen to issue 7 Subalterns by order of O.C. train.	
	18/5/16	-	Wired D.A.D.R.S.T. with G.B Army reference potato shortage. Received permission to buy if necessary up to 18/- per 100 kilos for potatoes till with rations 10/lins. Best for him thereby up to Steenbeck. 2000 O.S. Rations 7300 petrol tins of gas they up to Steenbeck. Grete Rouge Negro autowar forward. (returns to wait an lorries unit petrol tins for company generals)	
	19/5/16		While in Poperinghe Do wired two hostile aeroplanes croise were tripping & bombs, however & done. Guns fired Anti aircraft fire on potatoes - Batlocks on arriving in base conditions upon sent to Poberinn R.S.O.	55/O Feb

Place	Date	Hour	Summary of Events and Information	Remarks and references to Appendices
GODEWAERS- VELDE	2/3/16	7.00	C.R. 1330 filled two lend batches at Hqs Central. 1st Regt arrived, & 1/Ct. have been up to hand supplies over. Vauxhall car broke down this morning at Boeschepe, sent in Workshop – wanted to O.C. Train but supplies urgent Newport available at Poperinghe – telew new Truck attachment R.E. from the division from Steenvoorde sent for Rations (Prisoners) and to Dunkerque re potatoes C.I. stores taken to new hospital at Bailleul.	
	2/3/16		Went Canal re potato supply. Arrival reports were available at Dunkerque. Went Bailleul re arrangemt supplies of harvest cakes at troopers along until further orders – Price 2¼sof. for loaf. Worked HOUPLINES - BAILLEUL new hospital hence an Hill Woods trefoilen new rations stored there. Found 63 coves in good condition, proceeded from there to the Bluff & inspected 75 coves ammunition stored in dugouts near Spoil Bank, all in good condition. Was accompanied by Capt Hunter from S.O.S. I.T.	Appendices See

Army Form C. 2118.

WAR DIARY
or
INTELLIGENCE SUMMARY.
(Erase heading not required.)

Instructions regarding War Diaries and Intelligence Summaries are contained in F.S. Regs., Part II. and the Staff Manual respectively. Title pages will be prepared in manuscript.

Place	Date	Hour	Summary of Events and Information	Remarks and references to Appendices
GOSNOGES VIC AC	Continued 22/3/16		Officer – Staff Officer 76th Inf Bn finished out the trail caneles for the Centering the frozen Harbor Traction & the landing of the 10th coming off then Causing the ration became too meagre for food – with troops hundreds of Officers.	
—	23/3/16		Sent instructions to Capt. Officer to proper matters Presenting of Mess's by units – Arranged Blanc Samp rations from British to to homes. 23 men leaving for Murman. dupot. Situations the news from Bougaine answered. Sent rates to universe engeteles Jell Supt. Services brought by Strikans on leps Beto. Telegrams ODC. T. gone for extensive of Leroy. God merchant. Calvin unsafe to leave him. Peters Baleg.	
	24/3/16		New Bridge marched 5+6 days for the to hold wire fitting for two sent up in stock breakers/workshop partially extend but two dubrovno of fitting work for the moment. prices ranged from 21 f to 8.5 D – Conditionally hot than we are keeping as present in this area.	J. Dunphe SD

WAR DIARY
or
INTELLIGENCE SUMMARY

Army Form C. 2118.

Place	Date	Hour	Summary of Events and Information	Remarks and references to Appendices
GODEWAERS VELDE	25/3/16		Orders received from Q to send up 1500 COCOA rations to 76th Inf. Bde. Owing to mist, transport carried out by Supply Col. SSO 2nd Canadian Div here working over area blocked over by this Divn.	
	26/3/16		2 Lt RARE left today returned for Consumption 28 thous. etc. for 5 days returned up to 1st Inst. Canadians also DOULLENS. Q ordered data returned up to last from Vaudricourt. Stenworth ordered 50 tons straw in bales from Bee Cocoa ruit sent Q office in reserve. Sent Anderson Stenworth Wheatfinker.	
	27/3/16		Although this division in Elbi front last night. Princpl 3 Brigades engaged — Bee a ruit got to same ruen last y/o but were to to 4th N Zelve.	
	28/3/16		New Fanteer Puckerton	
	29/3/16		Wheat were to go to ORESTRE to entrenchment. Troops of Relievere — ordered. Relieves left own retain for two battns up by bngd's — new remitted at Elets	[signature] Capt SO

Army Form C. 2118.

WAR DIARY
or
INTELLIGENCE SUMMARY.
(Erase heading not required.)

Instructions regarding War Diaries and Intelligence Summaries are contained in F. S. Regs., Part II. and the Staff Manual respectively. Title pages will be prepared in manuscript.

Place	Date	Hour	Summary of Events and Information	Remarks and references to Appendices
Bolarum (continued)	2/8/16		So 2nd I.P. Division furnished 100th as 7.7 Cavalier go on obtained through wire to S/Capt Coh 76th Inf — as described at 6.30pm. Oct 16. 6.15.10 p returned by Capt Campbell with Canteen profits. M. Thind 706 once berth hire of MT.O. — Major Smith had off for wire MT.O. — Je in. Heard Engrns. (Chambers) re Rocks etc Return. — Another mentions of Engrns informs receipt the Capt of Sooero offered him So Op Ln Cutter are running meantime — Wrote upstairs to O.C.rein arranged to furnish from parties of Sickestown to be based on tours CA Off per 100 rested, relieving B Coy men in afortnight. attemph with tORT M transport Rthurs. Nuithence at Crechi from today.	
	30/8/16			Signature SO/

Army Form C. 2118.

WAR DIARY
or
INTELLIGENCE SUMMARY.
(Erase heading not required.)

Instructions regarding War Diaries and Intelligence Summaries are contained in F. S. Regs., Part II. and the Staff Manual respectively. Title pages will be prepared in manuscript.

Place	Date	Hour	Summary of Events and Information	Remarks and references to Appendices
Codwere Wood	3/8/16	—	Paid fatigue parties for Infantry fatigue work in Rouen by army. DOST wire P5917. 27/3/16. Fuel winter fuel to continue until 30/9/16. S/1157/16. 873/16. As from 3/4/16 tent rations held W. 60th Front 2570 P.m. 157% R+S (Officers) or Pork rations. Show quiet. Wire sent Divisional HQ ordering that 7th yorks leave Division tomorrow. Pneumatic leave for 17 stations to arrive CRS 2.4.16. Necessary arrangements made.	J Morris Capt SSO 2nd Divn

WAR DIARY
~~INTELLIGENCE SUMMARY~~
(Erase heading not required.)

Army Form C. 2118

SUPPLY OFFICER.
III DIVISIONAL TROOPS.
MARCH 1916.

Instructions regarding War Diaries and Intelligence Summaries are contained in F.S. Regs., Part II. and the Staff Manual respectively. Title pages will be prepared in manuscript.

Place	Date	Hour	Summary of Events and Information	Remarks and references to Appendices
J.36.c Sheet 27.B La Recousse	1/3/16		Refilling at usual place. Times as usual. Supps came up & were issued to the various units.	
"	2/.		Routine as usual.	
	2/3/16		Lorries arrived at 2.00 p.m. were off-loaded by 2.30. Refilling over by 3.45 p.m.	
	3/3/16		Refilling Point still at J.36.c. Sheet 27.B. All petrol Tins were taken away by lorry.	
	4/3/16		Routine as usual.	
	5/3/16		Refilling Point changed again to La Recousse. Lorries arrived at 1.30 & were off-loaded by T.S.O. Lorries as usual.	
	6/3/16		Routine as usual.	
	7/3/16		Visited 30 Odd. R.F.A. at TOURNEHEM. Also III D.A.C.	
	8/3/16		Visited III Brig. Hd Qrs at NORDAUSQUES.	
	9/3/16		Lorries arrived at usual time. Refilling Point finished by 9.35 a.m.	
	10/3/16		Routine as usual.	
	11/3/16		Routine as usual.	
	12/3/16		Company left La Recousse for WEMAERS-CAPPEL. Sh. 30.9.3 Sheet R.7A	

Army Form C. 2118.

WAR DIARY
or
INTELLIGENCE SUMMARY.
(Erase heading not required.)

Instructions regarding War Diaries and Intelligence
Summaries are contained in F. S. Regs., Part II.
and the Staff Manual respectively. Title pages
will be prepared in manuscript.

Place	Date	Hour	Summary of Events and Information	Remarks and references to Appendices
	13/3/16		were also billeted here.	
NearBoschepe	14/3/16		Company arrived at GODEWAERSVELDE. Position the same as before. Refilling Point changed to cross roads near BOSCHEPE. Lorries arrived at 8.20 & were off-loaded by 9 o'clock.	
	15/3/16		Horse Transport drew supplies from Railhead instead of Lorries.	
	16/3/16		Routine as usual. Horse Transport drew supplies from Railhead as before.	2/Lt Parkin L.C. S.O. VIII Div. No. 17.3.16.
	17/3/16		Lt A.H. Mackay took over supply officer's duties from A.S. O'Brien. Routine as usual.	
	18/3/16		I done when an supply officer from A.S. O'Brien. Routine as usual.	
	19/3/16		Routine as usual.	
	20/2/16		Routine as usual. The refilling point changed back to Godewaersvelde at the same place as before.	
	21/3/16		Routine as usual.	
	22/3/16		Routine as usual. Supplies came up a new route if will.	
	23/3/16		Routine as usual	
	24/3/16		Routine as usual	

Army Form C. 2118.

WAR DIARY
or
INTELLIGENCE SUMMARY.
(Erase heading not required.)

Instructions regarding War Diaries and Intelligence Summaries are contained in F. S. Regs., Part II. and the Staff Manual respectively. Title pages will be prepared in manuscript.

Place	Date	Hour	Summary of Events and Information	Remarks and references to Appendices
	23/3/16		Routine as usual.	
	24/3/16		Routine as usual. Tobacco issue.	
	27/3/16		Routine as usual. Third Sin. S.A. 4/s arr. Three 9fg mn strength, & be retained by 8" Bde.	V.
	28/3/16		Routine as usual.	
	29/3/16		Routine as usual.	
	30/3/16		Supplies came up & refilling point by M.T. arriving 7.30 am. Refilling over by 8.30 am.	W/m S.O. fr. 3.30

WAR DIARY
or
INTELLIGENCE SUMMARY.
(Erase heading not required.)

Army Form C. 2118.

SUPPLY OFFICE 8th I. Bde. 3rd DIVISION
MARCH 1916

Place	Date	Hour	Summary of Events and Information	Remarks and references to Appendices
EPERLECQUES	1.3.16		Brigade leaves rest area. No Rifles today. ours to go & issue yesterday. A.S.C. Coys. loves for Hts. Jus position for Rifles Post chan.	
OUDERDOM	2.9.16	10. A.M.	Lorries arrive. Rifles at res. post'n 10.30.. Roads in a very bad condition, weather cold & wet	
	3.3.16	8.30 P.M.	Lorries arrive. Rifles 9AM. 9.45.AM. Issue of Rum occurred, the Russian trucks the 8th R.Rs are temporarily attacked are in the habit of receiving 5 issues of Rum per week.	
	4.3.16	8.15 AM	Lorries arrive. Rifles 9AM. 9.35 AM. Brigade to have at the trenches. Rum Sop as usual for 2 sons fires, weather very cold	
	5.3.16	8.15 AM	Lorries arrive. Rifles 9 AM over 9.50. Tobacco issue also morning. Charcoal issued. Brigade Strength at the end of the week for feeding & spars.	
			All ranks Stores Heavy Draught Light Draught Cobs Mules	
			4186 52 39 299 11 9	

K.T. Andrews Capt/RSC
S.O. 8th Bde.

Army Form C. 2118.

WAR DIARY
or
INTELLIGENCE SUMMARY. 1st Supple
(Erase heading not required.)

Instructions regarding War Diaries and Intelligence Summaries are contained in F. S. Regs., Part II. and the Staff Manual respectively. Title pages will be prepared in manuscript.

Place	Date	Hour	Summary of Events and Information	Remarks and references to Appendices
OUDERDOM	6.9.16		Lorries arrive 8.15. Refilling 9.A.M. over 9.40. Issue of Pickles secured up to just one. Great difficulty experienced in obtaining a sufficient supply of vegetables at the price fixed. Weather still very bad.	
	7.9.16		Lorries arrive 8.15. Refilling 9.A.M. over 9.40. Snow again this evening. The right Rum is being issued in addition to Rum Ration for men in the trenches.	
	8.9.16		Lorries arrive 8.15. Refilling 9 A.M. over 9.45. Several old units attached for feeding purpose to-day left to-night.	
	9.9.16		Lorries arrive 9.30. Refilling 10.30 A.M. owing to a very bad condition of our long stretched transport delay of whole convoy. Several units very badly cut up owing to severe weather.	
	10.9.16		Lorries arrive 8.15. Refilling 9 A.M. over 9.45. Convoys received orders to rest on the 11th but stamped area.	
	11.9.16		Lorries arrive 8.15. Refilling 9 A.M. The lorry containing the groceries failed to put in an appearance owing to engine difficulties until 11.30 A.M.	G. Herbert Capt A.S.C. S.O. Supplies

Army Form C. 2118.

WAR DIARY
or
INTELLIGENCE SUMMARY.
(Erase heading not required.)

Instructions regarding War Diaries and Intelligence Summaries are contained in F. S. Regs., Part II. and the Staff Manual respectively. Title pages will be prepared in manuscript.

Place	Date	Hour	Summary of Events and Information	Remarks and references to Appendices
OUDEDOM (cont)	11/2/16		The Riflers was thus delayed for some considerable period. The east of the wagons was at length unloaded into them. The company proceed to old area but owing to these fields being occupied by the troops being the company had to pitch camp about a mile away for the night.	
BOESCHEPE	12/2/16		Riflers in old position on the summit of BOESCHEPE hill. None. Ammt 8.20. Rifles 9 A.M. over 9.50. Tobacco issue Brigade strength at the end of the week Gee ranks Silures. Heavy Draught 1 Draught Cats. S. Ones. 5731 87 65 538 11 9.	
	13/2/16		Louis arrivt A.M. 8.20. Rifles 9 A.M. over 9.50. Vegetables becoming very scarce almost impossible to purchase at the price.	
	14/3/16		Louis arrivt 8.20. Rifles 9 A.M. over 9.50. Bugots & drums out of the ranks with the exception of the machine gunners of 1 Battn. of 2 companies.	
	15/2/16		Louis arrivt 8.30. Rifles 9 A.M. over 9.55. Vegetables full. Tulienne wanted for to take them please.	

K. T. Andrews Capt RR
S/O 2 Rifle

Army Form C. 2118.

WAR DIARY
or
INTELLIGENCE SUMMARY.

(Erase heading not required.)

Instructions regarding War Diaries and Intelligence Summaries are contained in F. S. Regs., Part II. and the Staff Manual respectively. Title pages will be prepared in manuscript.

Place	Date	Hour	Summary of Events and Information	Remarks and references to Appendices
BOESCHEPE	16.3.16		Lorries arrived 8.20 AM. Refilling 9AM over 9.50. Issued oil cake Issued to all units to supplement their ration. Owing to Belgian decree that no hay is to be purchased in Belgium no has otherwise.	
	17.3.16		Lorries arrived 7.45 AM. Refilling 8.30. Over 9.25 AM. Vegetables shot no Tienne available at CAESTRE Until confirm that vegetables are available for local purchase. Let any to Belgium decree no potatoes can be bought in Belgian area.	
	18.3.16		Lorries arrived 7.45. Refilling 8.20 over 9.20 nothing of note.	
	19.3.16		Lorries arrived 7.40 AM. Refill 8.30 Over 9.55. Totals Troops strength started after week Light Draught Heavy Draught Cobs - S. Mules All 90 Kg	

5722   95   936   90   11   9 Officers 20 ORRs

Army Form C. 2118.

WAR DIARY
or
INTELLIGENCE SUMMARY.
(Erase heading not required.)

Instructions regarding War Diaries and Intelligence Summaries are contained in F.S. Regs., Part II. and the Staff Manual respectively. Title pages will be prepared in manuscript.

Place	Date	Hour	Summary of Events and Information	Remarks and references to Appendices
BOESCHEPE	20.3.16		Lewis arrive 7.50 am Repelling 8.20 eve 9.30 call arrive too very bad wintr see the socks ette on o split open, several ets tasted from each sack.	
	21.3.16		Lewis arrive 7.45. Repelling 8.20 eve 9.25. Severe until shot of two Patrol sent round to find out exact shortage of unit	
	22.3.16		Lewis arrive 7.15 Repelling 8.20 eve 9.25. all eyes Patrol one sent to Division enemy to bury of vessels for campt hati the trenches.	
	23.3.16		Lewis arrive 7.15 Repelling 8.20 eve 9.30. Sergt Yelling Head Clerk called away to 4th Army	
	24.3.16		Lewis arrive 7.15 Repelling 8.20 eve 9.15. health very bad heavy snow storm Juny Repelling	
	25.3.16		Lewis arrive 7.40 Repelling 8.15 eve 9.15. health improved Julienne arrived in sufficient quantity for me days complete issue.	

K. Athens Capt. H.Q.e
20 J.B.L.

T2134. Wt. W708-776. 500000. 4/15. Sir J. C. & S.

WAR DIARY
or
INTELLIGENCE SUMMARY.
(Erase heading not required.)

Army Form C. 2118.

Place	Date	Hour	Summary of Events and Information	Remarks and references to Appendices
BOESCHEPE	26.3.16		Lorries arrived 7.40. Refilling 8.15. over 9.15 AM. Tetanus Brigade strength to end of the week. All ranks. Shires. Heavy Draught. Light Draught Off. Rule Rules. 6176. 93. 85. 923. 11. 9.	
	27.3.16		Lorries arrived 7.35 AM Refilling 8.15 AM over 9. AM. Lorries arrived 7.35 AM Refilling 8.15 AM over 9.5 AM Rather [?] at second weather improving.	
	28.3.16			
	29.3.16		Lorries arrived 7.40 AM Refilling 8.15 over 9.5 AM. great difficulty experienced in obtaining a sufficient supply of potatoes.	
	30.3.16		Lorries arrived 7.40 AM Refilling 8.15 over 9 AM weather very fine winds dry.	
	31.3.16		Lorries arrived 7.40 AM Refilling 8.15 over 9 AM. Brigade strength at the end of the month. All ranks. Shires. Heavy Draught. Light Draught. Off. Rule Rules. 5368. 91. 68. 927. 11. 9.	

WAR DIARY
INTELLIGENCE SUMMARY
(Erase heading not required.)

SUPPLY OFFICER
9th I. Bde. 3rd Army Form C. 2118.
S.O. 9th Inf. Bde.
MARCH 1916

Place	Date	Hour	Summary of Events and Information	Remarks and references to Appendices
QUENIBER G.E.	1/3/16.		Supplies loaded direct on to horse transport at railhead (WATTEN) in bulk. Supplies were dumped at Brunel Rgfell. Civilian organised by units to man/kit 1st line transport & commencing at 3 o'clock. Guns items as usual	
"	2/3/16.		Routine as for 1st inst. above	
"	3/3/16.		Lorries arrived at railhead refilling point at 6.15am. Offloaded & taken by 8.40am. Rations issued. 8.45. Lorries are usual (Ration trucks) 9.30am. Routine as for Days inst.	
"	4/3/16.		" " " " "	
"	5/3/16.		Lorries arrived 8.15am. Offloaded & taken by 8.40am. Ration refill commenced 8.45am. Leave no about ambulating took up with 5 wagons to North's Div. Supply Dump directed direct to Ques to return with the units. Lorries arrived & refilling at 3 O.m. Rations at 3.30pm to all units received referred to their units to nearly total men 1 still waggon reported to their men 6th inst.	
BOESCHEPE	6/3/16.		4 to ASC lorries of supplies for refilling Bde at 8am to at 12.40pm	

E.M. West
Capt. ASC

WAR DIARY
INTELLIGENCE SUMMARY.
(Erase heading not required.)

Army Form C. 2118.

S.O. 9th Rifles

Place	Date	Hour	Summary of Events and Information	Remarks and references to Appendices
BOESCHEPE	7-3-16		Lorries arrived 8.30 am. Rifles detailed to party B.8 Station. Rifles commences 9.0 am. Lorries 9.45 for Station. Parade from hut as usual.	
"	8-3-16		Lorries arrives 9.10 am. Rifles detailed by 9.40 am. Rifles commences 9.10 am. Other routine as usual	
"	9-3-16		Lorries arrived 9.0 am. OT Rifles detailed salon by 9.35 am. Rifles commences 9.50 am. Large parties of Lovers as usual for preliminary take up the Rifles parades 11.0 am. took over flats from M.G.Sect. D. Coy, Oc G.O.C. arrived much interested.	
"	10-3-16		Lorries arrives 9.0 am. Reveille sounded 9.45. Parades 11.0 am. Parade as usual until midday relief took up the parade and arrived owing to severe weather. Other routine as usual	
"	11-3-16		Lorries arrives 8.30 am. OT sounded relay by 9 am. Rifles parades 10 am. Same to normal. Other routine as normal	

E.M.Paul Capt AA

Army Form C. 2118.

S.O. 9 L.I.H.

WAR DIARY
INTELLIGENCE SUMMARY.
(Erase heading not required.)

Instructions regarding War Diaries and Intelligence Summaries are contained in F. S. Regs., Part II. and the Staff Manual respectively. Title pages will be prepared in manuscript.

Place	Date	Hour	Summary of Events and Information	Remarks and references to Appendices
BOESCHEPE	17-3-16		Reveille at 5.30 am. Affiliated labour by 7.50. Rifle Exercises 9.15. Leave as usual except for 1st October. Also rifles went to attached for feeling on ammunition the supernumerary at D.A.C. Rifles during the day as usual.	
"	18-3-16		Reveille at 5.30 am. Affiliated labour 7.10 am Retain commences 9.20 am. Rifles usual attached to all D.C. Pte Ratcliffe furlough 11.20 am. States went on as usual.	
"	14-3-16		Reveille at 5.30 am. Routine as usual	
"	15-3-16		Routine as usual	
"	16-3-16		Reveille at 5.30 am. Cavalry 9.0 am. Rifles commence 9.10 am. Leave as usual. Report Pte Radcliffe 10. & others returns as usual.	

E.W. Weir
Capt. A.V.C.

Army Form C. 2118.

WAR DIARY
or
INTELLIGENCE SUMMARY.
(Erase heading not required.)

S.O. 9th [Bde?]

Place	Date	Hour	Summary of Events and Information	Remarks and references to Appendices
BOESCHEPE	17-3-16		Reveries expires 5.7.45am. Offsaddled orders by 8.15am. Stables commences 9.10am. Horses also fed. Horses exercised (for men that go) Retallie punches 9.30am. Others rev time as usual. Lieut Penny took over as [?] by R.O. from 2nd at Carlisle.	
"	18-3-16		Run time as usual	
"	19-3-16		Run time as usual	
"	20-3-16		Horses supplies to general services by mount also fed vegetables. Horses Cafe. Other men time as usual	
"	21-3-16		Run time as usual	
"	22-3-16		Reveries arrives 5.7.45am. Clean by 8.25am. Retallie commences 9.30. Horses as usual also Sunday's Cafe (for two Sundays till vegetables cease). (& feed to mens). Retallie punches 9.30am	
"	23-3-16		Reveries expires 5.7.45am. Clean by 8.10am. Retallie commences 8.45am. Stables 9.30am. Supplies as usual ( )	

E.W.N.? Capt
a/c

Army Form C. 2118.

WAR DIARY
or
INTELLIGENCE SUMMARY.
(Erase heading not required.)

Instructions regarding War Diaries and Intelligence Summaries are contained in F.S. Regs., Part II. and the Staff Manual respectively. Title pages will be prepared in manuscript.

S.O. 9th Lgt Bde

Place	Date	Hour	Summary of Events and Information	Remarks and references to Appendices
BOESCHEPE	24-3-16		Lamies arrives 7.45am. Off loaded & delom by 8.10am. Refilling commences 8.35am. Empties 9.10pm Leave as usual, also frest vegetables & James Cake	
"	25-3-16		Routine as usual	
"	26-3-16		Routine as usual	
"	27-3-16		Lorries arrives 7.40am. Clean by 8.15am Refilling Commences 8.35am. All emties off, 24th muk. Off Routine as usual	
"	28-3-16		Routine as usual	
"	29-3-16		Able test at about 900 metres (some strength was Other mentioned as usual) Casualties.	
"	30-3-16		Lorries arrives 8.40am. Off loaded & delom by 8.10am Refilli arrived 8.40 and leaves 9.20am as usual, with fresh vegetables & James Cake. Refilling finishes 9.20 am. Other as usual.	
"	31-3-16		Routine as usual	

E.M. Neal. Capt RCE
S.O. 9th Army Bde.

SUPPLY OFFICER.
76th Inf. Bde., 3rd Division

Army Form C. 2118.

WAR DIARY
or
INTELLIGENCE SUMMARY.
(Erase heading not required.)

Army Form C. 2118.

MARCH. 1916.

No. 764 Supply Bde. —
Instructions regarding War Diaries and Intelligence Summaries are contained in F.S. Regs., Part II. and the Staff Manual respectively. Title pages will be prepared in manuscript.

Place	Date	Hour	Summary of Events and Information	Remarks and references to Appendices
OUDERDOM — VLAMERTINGHE H.14. Sh.28.	Wed.y March 1st	40M u 43	2nd Trench Mortar Battery move from their billet valise out period for their rations. Demand of J.A.E H.33/6. — Wired 17th Divl Supply Column for Sliding Baker car on loan from 9th Bde (4 Coy) Routine as usual. —	
	Thursd.y March 2nd		Reply sent to S.S.O. III Divn as desirability of larger issue of biscuits — JFM & Bread to PM — Biscuit — Lorries arrive 9am — Usual routine — Wired 17th Divl S.C. for second time for Sliding Baker Car. —	
	Friday March 3rd		Lorries 9am — One lorry having broken down (meat) did not arrive until 11am — Going for Sliding Baker car not from 17th D.S.O. — 94 gallons rum received which was not demanded — Order by S.S.O. to make double issue to Units intending going into trenches. —	
	Sat.y March 4th		Lorries 9am less me Oat lorry 9.45am — Complaints sent to S.S.O. III Divn S.S.O. 17th Divn regarding shortage of JFM & Bread met while attached to 17th Divn. Routine as usual. —	Bear Emp'ty following Charge 573/16 AR. 46 SO HD 139 SD 10963
	Sunday March 5th		Lorries 9am Refill 9.45am Letter rec'd from DDSF II Army stopping local purchase of hay in British area (Zoo hay had been available for last six months) —	78th Mtr 10963

H. Kinmarsh Lieut RSC
S.o. 76th Inf. Bde.

T2134. Wt. W708—776. 500000. 4/15. Sir J. C. & 8.

Army Form C. 2118.

WAR DIARY
or
INTELLIGENCE SUMMARY.
(Erase heading not required.)

SD 76K Cay/Bde

Instructions regarding War Diaries and Intelligence Summaries are contained in F. S. Regs., Part II. and the Staff Manual respectively. Title pages will be prepared in manuscript.

Place	Date	Hour	Summary of Events and Information	Remarks and references to Appendices
Dudendam			Warm & bright	
H.14 Sheet 28				
	Monday 6th March		Routine as usual. —	
	Tuesday 7th March		37 Field Coy RE, 111 E Riding RB advance me that they have 5 days for Godwaersveldt. 105 & 106 Coy RE arriving during morning for relocation stating that their ration are to draw from reo. — Confirmed later by acting SSO III RD (Gotha) who arrived here during afternoon. — Adopted Pioneer Batln S.W.Borde. will estimates rations strength of 900 & 100 LD horses. Rations for all three units arrived during the afternoon by Supply Column. — Wales SSO III RD & Coy Train & Rodwaersvelde and arranged for E Riding RE & 36 Coy RE to draw from GA Bot. —	
	Wednesday 8th March		Temperature 10.30 am owing to bad weather lorries being ditched. 100 Ration Broad sheet — Studs Bater Bos taken by Supply Column for again.	
	Thursday 9th March		Ration of parcels read on dump 10 p.m. — Lorries 9 am Park Carapp. Ration dan below firm in — did not arrive for ration — Routine as usual. —	
	Friday 10th March		Refill as usual at 11.14. — SSO Lin Ratison read for 8 Kings Own Regt. after dump move to G.32 a cold farm with came up the ground as Welever by Bryan as before going hut at Feby 8th. Bee ground trucks for Congo Several sent up to Coff Belac court. Bel Transport thus distributed Trench rations. — Batn Average Sech arrive at 4 pm for rations —	

[signature]
SO 76K Cay Bde

WAR DIARY or INTELLIGENCE SUMMARY

Army Form C. 2118.

W.D. 76th Inf. Bde.

Place	Date	Hour	Summary of Events and Information	Remarks and references to Appendices
HOOGRAAF.	Saturday 11th March	G.32.a (?28)	Lorries arrive G.32.a at 9.15 am. Refilling delayed until 10.45 am owing to block in traffic. Rations received. "Rums grown daily from men in trenches together with full ration of tea & sugar. 76th Bde Trench Mortar answerbook for rations (99 men) stating that they had been detached from 17th SWB Sid from reserve. — No vegetables recd. Enter of Ordnance made to supply us also Sub. Purchasing officer — visited G.O. School re arranged for their rations the next by R.W.clok Waggons —	
	Sunday 12th March		Lorries arrive G. 5 am. Refill 10.30. — 1 Pack Squadron units fed in addition to those yesterday. M 3rd H.Gro Granades School, S.S.60y R.E., 7 Field Ambulance. Salvage boy. — Sen 76th Bde Trench Mortar Span. Orders received from S.S.O. that 105 boy R.E., 106 boy R.E. — Swab Beavers (Pioneers) were to be refilled again to-day that supplies would arrive from S. Column at 5 pm. — Orders sent out to find the units W.W. then to come into ration at once — All arrived during evening & nearly morning. — No vegetable ration Demanded for rations 7th Yorks Lanc. (Pioneer Batn) AR.893 the fed on 14th inst —	Tracing thur ff thun ff Road kings AR 5550 HD 207 LD 1378

J.K.M---- Young M.S.C.
S.O. 76th Inf. Bde.

Army Form C. 2118.

WAR DIARY
or
INTELLIGENCE SUMMARY.
(Erase heading not required.)

76 H of Supplies

Instructions regarding War Diaries and Intelligence Summaries are contained in F. S. Regs., Part II. and the Staff Manual respectively. Title pages will be prepared in manuscript.

Place	Date	Hour	Summary of Events and Information	Remarks and references to Appendices
HODGRAEF.		G.32.R.		
	Monday 13th March	9 am	Visited S.S.O. during afternoon. Belgian Artillery (previously fed by this Bde) included in demand for filling 14h. – Remain in Sece regarding rendering of W.3313 (Supplies Purchases) – Arrangements made that R.O. should himself take returns in mornings of 18th 19th 22nd 10th March. – Drew received that no vegetables (Potatoes) were to be purchased which were grown in Belgium. – 76 + Mortar Battery did not arrive – Lorries left 3rd am 7 Mortar Battery did not arrive for rations detected for 3316. (Demand for rations) Fed 7th York Lancs Regt. (Rations Galls) Only 210 lb. Salmon received of anise demand of 600 lb. – Item allowance of 14go issued –	
	Tuesday 14th			
	Wednesday 15th	8.10 am	Lorries. Refill 9 am R.O. took W.3313 (Supplies Purchases) arranged 13.415/1.C. to S.S.O. office to be checked with Field Purchasing officers. A/c from which officers came from vegetables had been received during the period. – Only 320 K. Potatoes recd. from DPO. out of Bat. allowance allotted by SSO as 900 K. – 1000 K. Potatoes received from Gordon OUDERDOM	

A.H. Hewitt 2/Lt. RASC
DA 76th Bde Supplies

T2131. Wt. W708–776. 500000. 4/15. Sir J. C. & S.

Army Form C. 2118.

WAR DIARY
or
INTELLIGENCE SUMMARY.

(Erase heading not required.)

Instructions regarding War Diaries and Intelligence
Summaries are contained in F.S. Regs., Part II.
and the Staff Manual respectively. Title pages
will be prepared in manuscript.

Place	Date	Hour	Summary of Events and Information	Remarks and references to Appendices
HOOGRAAF G.32.a.5.5	Thursday 16th		Increasing difficulty in obtaining vegetables owing to recent order prohibiting purchase in Belgium & region. Potato local price 17-18 frs per 100 K against 13 fr fortnight previously. — Hay/oats 8.35 — Other ration lorries 9.45am — Issued to 2/1st Field Ambulance mule ration from S.S.O. 2/3 rations which had been supplied to men of officers 1/4 Field Ambulance demanded rations for 30th Bde R.F.A. in lieu Jack Bde R.F.A. — Orders received that refilling point must be changed at once. — Refilling point chosen on BOERINGHE — RENINGHELST Road at G.27.b. (sheet 28) — Lorries 7.30am Refilling point as arranged yesterday — Report	
	Friday 17th		8.35 — Lt. H.V. Barcey from No.2 Coy/176 Bde as Requisition Officer. Visited units of Brigade Group.	
	Saty 18th		Lorries 7.30am Refill movement — Visited most units of Bde Group — worthwest of Reffier — Received orders to report to H.Qrs. 4th Inf Divn on duty as Dirt Enclosing Officer — Handed over supply officers duties temporarily to 2nd Lieut Caldeau — Bo in ward Troops. Capt 30th Bde R.F.A. in lieu Jack Bde R.F.A.

J.M. Hurst Lt RFA
D.S.O. 76th Inf Bde | |

Army Form C. 2118.

WAR DIARY
or
INTELLIGENCE SUMMARY.
(Erase heading not required.)

76 Inf. Bde. Supply Bde

Instructions regarding War Diaries and Intelligence Summaries are contained in F.S. Regs., Part II. and the Staff Manual respectively. Title pages will be prepared in manuscript.

Place	Date	Hour	Summary of Events and Information	Remarks and references to Appendices
HOOGRAF.	18/3/16		Lt. A.S. Parkin took over the duties of Supply Officer 76. Inf. Bde. temporarily from Lt. Hund, who reported to Hd-qrs. of Train for duty.	Starting Strength 76 Bde Sup Coln 19/3/16 AR 5365 HD 203 LD 1011
	19/3/16		Lorries arrived at 7.20 a.m. were off-loaded by 8 o'clock. Usual ones.	
	20/3/16		Lorries arrived at usual time. Barbed oats were reported to have put itself into the sacks the ordinary oats. Germans are supposed to have put itself into the sacks	
	21/3/16.		Visited Bde Hd Qrs at WOODCOTE HOUSE. Saw the Staff Captain, who stated they went moving that night to GORDON TERRACE, owing to WOOD COTE HOUSE being heavily shelled the day previously.	
	22/3/16		Lorries arrived at usual time. Off-loaded by 8 o'clock. 50 lbs of Bacon was short on the Refilling Point. Lorries as usual. Oats-sacks in bad condition.	
	23/3/16.		Routine as usual. The deficiency of 50 lbs Bacon of the day before was made good. The following units were visited:— 9/Kings own. 10/R. Welch. 58/Bty R.F.A. R.E. 7/3rd Amb. Yorks 9 Lancs Regt. 30 Bde R.F.A. Amm Col. 30. Bde R.F.A. Hd Qrs./Gordon Highlanders. 129 & 130 Batteries of the 30 Bde R.F.A. 9 Camp Commandant III Div.	
	24/3/16.		Lt. Hund resumed duties of S.O. 76. Inf. Bde. Brigade came off trenches to-night.	

A S Parkin Lt.
a/S.O. 76. Inf. Bde.

Army Form C. 2118.

S.O. 76th Infy Bde

WAR DIARY
or
INTELLIGENCE SUMMARY.
(Erase heading not required.)

Instructions regarding War Diaries and Intelligence
Summaries are contained in F. S. Regs., Part II.
and the Staff Manual respectively. Title pages
will be prepared in manuscript.

Date	Hour	Summary of Events and Information	Remarks and references to Appendices
HQ RAAF March	G.32.a.5.5.		
Friday 24th		Return to 76th Bde resumes duties as S.O. 76th Infy Bde - Lt Parkin returns to Divisional troops - Visited D.P.O in hospital at Hazebrouck -	
Saty. 25th		Lorries 7.10am - Complaint regarding the bad state of what Oat Sacks arrive at Ryveling point sent to S.S.O. (9 out of 10 sacks contain large holes causing great wastage of oats - Visited Young Officers School -	Hazebrouck J.Bde. Card v.8/1/1.6 AR 5685 H.D. 205 L.D. 1004
Sunday 26th		Routine as usual - Oat Sacks again very bad 180 torn at Supply Bde. - This Brigade did not send for their Cocoa & Milk received. Letter on instructions from S.O. for 9th Supply Bde. - ration as arranged -	
Monday 27th		Lorries 7.15am Routine as usual. Donation issued to D.H.Q. for German Prisoners - 9th Brigade sent for Extra milk rations -	
Tuesday 28th		Visited Units of Bde Group - 138 rations issued to D.H.Q. for German Prisoners (Taken by 9th Bde) 2nd Corporal in base Oat Sacks forwarded to S.S.O. Issued 250 rations & envy garments to Bde forge	H J Stevens 1/Maj. S.O. 76th Infy Bde

Army Form C. 2118.

To 76 H Inf Bde

WAR DIARY
or
INTELLIGENCE SUMMARY.
(Erase heading not required.)

Instructions regarding War Diaries and Intelligence Summaries are contained in F. S. Regs., Part II. and the Staff Manual respectively. Title pages will be prepared in manuscript.

Place	Date	Hour	Summary of Events and Information	Remarks and references to Appendices
H Qrs RAF Maud	Wednesday 29th	G. 32 a 5.5	Leave 7.10 am - rifle P.15 - visited Old Red Ann - Nordagres Hoeke - Sergnes for Rennes rest for O.C. Trees - Wandtree HAC Battle on extending hill for Oliver purchased in England 1915 - and find that they have left St Omer - Moutaubert? War Socks continue transmiring, bad condition -	
	Thursday 30th		Routine as usual - visited 7H Reg.t Belgian artillery at the trench of Bayonette Camp - visit Fortier, Ouderdom -	
	Friday 31st		Visit Fortier, Ouderdom with SSO barrage for purchase of potatoes - show for Jermain - Rifling a arrival Battacks improve in quality - visited Fortier, Ouderdom close on Contact Pr 50000 Kilos Potatoes, 100000 Kilos Straw - Bur Mourney Barrack for outstanding bill for purpose Oake - Impress of completes the account - letter to my name lost new of 16 Rennes by 1st Rennes on 1st April - Newredan - received regarding matter for keeping accounting of Byls received passes flints in Rifling Point -	

H Hilmen Lt R.E.C.
S.O. 76th Inf Bde

31/3/16

SENIOR SUPPLY DEPOT
3rd DIVISION
APRIL 1916

WAR DIARY
or
INTELLIGENCE SUMMARY.
(Erase heading not required.)

Army Form C. 2118.

Instructions regarding War Diaries and Intelligence Summaries are contained in F. S. Regs., Part II. and the Staff Manual respectively. Title pages will be prepared in manuscript.

Place	Date	Hour	Summary of Events and Information	Remarks and references to Appendices
GODEWAERS- VELDE HH	1/4/16		Operation orders for move of 3rd Division to hines 5th Corps front area received. Move to start from first week. Orders received that Completed 76th & 9th Inf. Bgde lead for rest area tomorrow.	
	2 —		HQrs 9th J Bgde, 1st R.S.F., 4th R. Fus, 11th R.F. to Zelw, 2 mg Coys etc, 76th Bgde to hand 1st R.S. Fus. Co. left for rest area today. 150 details from 4th R. Fus & 1st Gun. 1st R.S Fus. left behind as working party. The attached 76th Dn Bgde. No to G.A.S.C. left Helys. Camps at x3 a 7.8. Artillery front X10D 3.7 owing to tactical situation impenal OOT previously cancelled. Units know best when possible. Refilling in rear area c. 13 pm — two artillery trolley to [?] for return:	
	3 —		8th J. Bgde Staffs 151 N Zelw both 1st Gordons march to rest area — attacked Helys (Brun) 1st R.E. to 7 Alve today, 8th Foot huds to Milletow 4th r.l. F. to Selle. Pars to 2nd Canadian Bivt Down M Lunger f [?] 15 — IC 17 & Bruneh C. Bar Co. to 10th Lalun Battn 7 thee Belg fes. Units failed a Lunops Station — details 7/ for Diosson CSO Lut Brigs Transport arranged.	

Army Form C. 2118.

WAR DIARY
or
INTELLIGENCE SUMMARY.
(Erase heading not required.)

Instructions regarding War Diaries and Intelligence Summaries are contained in F.S. Regs., Part II. and the Staff Manual respectively. Title pages will be prepared in manuscript.

Place	Date	Hour	Summary of Events and Information	Remarks and references to Appendices
G. OUTTERS VILDE	4/4/16		Refilling 7 lorries 3/pa 76th & 8th Rifles at 3 pm returned midday & tomorrow morning - 9th AS on wash	
	5		1500 Rube cartridges arrived at midnight, Purchase quantities of cartridges - Complete distribution by S.B.L. 2000 × 8 sm, 2000 tryth. 1500 Rifle & 1000 sps - Huntzwithdrawn M Potatoes & Flour; train lifepa 8 FLETRE, P.26 TERRIE.	
FLETRE	6		173 Remaining Co. 6th Eastern Battn, 7th Belgian Artillery, Bn.6 Co, 17 a/craft Gurkhas refilled today with 2nd Canadian Divn also with Joliot - he spoke for first time 7 we Btry 7TM & TM battery, attached 5th Infantry Division - Humma ran convoys at Bressope & Reninghels ASSO 2nd Canadian Divn also took over from him convoys at BAILLUL his convoy has agree as training several depts, water in dispute rate little later. - took over from 50th divisn 27 two coal at EECKE. - Put Sgt Rewlings I/C coal yard at Bailluel with guard attached 1 man from Borachip barracks 20. 8th Suffolks - Army Cine Hoth attm EECKE coal. Saw RTO rSO Bailluel	Unclear signature S.S.O. Inspector

At Ent: T. Y. Buketeir.
T.2134. Wt. W708—776. 500,000. 4/15. (SirJ.) J. C. & S.

Army Form C. 2118.

WAR DIARY
or
INTELLIGENCE SUMMARY.
(Erase heading not required.)

Instructions regarding War Diaries and Intelligence Summaries are contained in F. S. Regs., Part II. and the Staff Manual respectively. Title pages will be prepared in manuscript.

Place	Date	Hour	Summary of Events and Information	Remarks and references to Appendices
FLETRE	7/4/16		Artillery move cancelled, guns remain in position until further orders.	
	8/4/16		Major Ramsgate [?] with Capt Veal saw CRA reference artillery move, unable obtain any definite information. Handed over by matters to SSO to Capt Veal, preparatory to going on short furlough.	Minimum Appx SSO Instruction

T2134. Wt. W708–776. 500000. 4/15. Sir J.C. & S.

WAR DIARY
or
INTELLIGENCE SUMMARY
(Erase heading not required.)

Army Form C. 2118.
SENIOR SUPPLY OFFICER
3rd DIVISION

Place	Date	Hour	Summary of Events and Information	Remarks and references to Appendices
FLETRE	9-4-16		Finished refilling points to supplies. Walk to looking at BAILLEUL. Walk to G.R.A. concerning R.F.A. moves. 85 Bde (with 1 Sqn) moved at ailers. No 1st train last evening from the source. No at ailers 2nd train this afternoon. Arrival of 2nd Division forbids this afternoon's movement.	
" "	10-4-16		Waited refilling points to supplies. Southerly tonight to Armentières + silence. Division to tomorrow LUMBRES. but no further. By train to HARDIFORT then onto. Studied the send of Supply indents to this — by no takings on/tonm.	
" "	11-4-16		Visited refilling points assembled. Potatoes — pork. Also 2 trucks for the armoured front of Garrison. Visited Staff Captain G.R.A. re. ammunition, R.F.A. moves, Supply of C. Is — to Sub-divn. Visited C.O. 3rd Divn. re R.F.A. moves.	

WAR DIARY
or
INTELLIGENCE SUMMARY.
(Erase heading not required.)

Army Form C. 2118.

Place	Date	Hour	Summary of Events and Information	Remarks and references to Appendices
FLETRE	12-4-16		Visited artillery points unmolested. Eight team stations inspected. Chosen to have Brewster guns kept up by R.E.D. with my orders. In trial of vertical compass Device elementary in phone. But have Grand Chiswick to two in positions in BAILLEUL in guns taken. Lens send the 50.0 to guns to more in afternoon to unhorsed.	
"	13-4-16		Visited artillery from to unhorsed. R.E. are now to completed attack O.C. Guff Col. were to Francisch front ? see to Concrete Pl.	
"	14-4-16		Visited artillery points. Sir Unrouched to unhorsed front. Visited Lionel & tan Poles tanks to an in Battle Cows. Last time in BAILLEUL to observation. Promises to take Julienne on Road tango Courage. Infantry took up position to Land. Must be dotong. Infantry Supply to be Supplementary. & was unable to notice.	

E.M.Hedge
Major

Army Form C. 2118.

WAR DIARY
or
INTELLIGENCE SUMMARY.
(Erase heading not required.)

Instructions regarding War Diaries and Intelligence Summaries are contained in F. S. Regs., Part II. and the Staff Manual respectively. Title pages will be prepared in manuscript.

Place	Date	Hour	Summary of Events and Information	Remarks and references to Appendices
FLETRE	15-4-16		Visited resibilling point to windhead. Checked & signed the 9/6/33/12 opermen to el Bristoot.	
"	16-4-16		Visited resibilling point, coal yards, windhead. Eugst Coy (other) potatoes & peas & beans & ones thro' RavensSpeak. S. BAILLEUL. Received advice that WOIC Batty been due to report for training with 2nd Can. Div. Wires Coy attacking shoes & ordered woods at Bulhens out to ECRE grand.	
"	17-4-16		Visited refilling point to windhead. 40 tons of coal at railhead. A.O.C. Capt. Hull. gave division on 18th May on assembly graduated station demo to rattached to 9th Bde group.	

Army Form C. 2118.

WAR DIARY
or
INTELLIGENCE SUMMARY.
(Erase heading not required.)

Instructions regarding War Diaries and Intelligence Summaries are contained in F. S. Regs., Part II. and the Staff Manual respectively. Title pages will be prepared in manuscript.

Place	Date	Hour	Summary of Events and Information	Remarks and references to Appendices
FLETRE 18/7/16				
	19/7/16		Routine as usual. O.O. 74 (Issued) re move from to KEMMEL front. Minwoork — move to Cauruaghe on 21st inst. 2 trench stores arrived at midnight one for 76th so Bogla & one for Brum'ships. Hvt Onderdonk refunded to fit Castle returned.	
	20/7/16		Saw SSO 50th Division re lorries for Minis Road game to thus Brum — Hvt DD7B, T Cassel re local purchases. 2 Pdr R/Costs + 7M TS & T Chedrig RE Stonewore factory, transferred to 8th Sea Bogle for return. — S/M 7 Hartlinne transferred to between from 9 Mt B.&Ts. Sea Bogle.	
	22/7/16		M. 3 Co. Read Division left for Houvrien Telery refilling point TM 34853. Conf at TM 33 C 5 w. Chedrig 7 G. 8th Bogle Belgian 8th 7 Antrim, RS 7 & Vo, 8/Cypothro & Houveran 7 delay. Very hot day.	
	23/7/16		from T delay w/Bty R 379 & T McBeal drew rations from 50th Divn in old area — 9th Bogle M.Guard to Bruns and Telery.	/Melvinge [?] 880

Army Form C. 2118.

WAR DIARY
or
INTELLIGENCE SUMMARY.
(Erase heading not required.)

Instructions regarding War Diaries and Intelligence Summaries are contained in F.S. Regs., Part II. and the Staff Manual respectively. Title pages will be prepared in manuscript.

Place	Date	Hour	Summary of Events and Information	Remarks and references to Appendices
FLETRE	24/4/16	—	H/R Islno, 13/Kings Liverpool & C.orE. H.E. Ricketts R.E. & Temporarily attached 85th Bgde from 76th for rations, while working in neutral 2 Irishman returned, one Cent D/Sind Ibo, & Cent 5/8/Sgt Sew 5/28/T & fly tops rifles - Sent Stenwords references more 17/07 & 86 R/777 Instrs. for fly tops for use) Excursion.	
	25/4/16		55 S.A.3. & Cage. 14 & 7 Ambles & Westfahlen 9th In Rgle Hqrs to Boulogne. No 6 & Cent SA 3.8 Refilling from M34.C.11. Post Z. Sent Hqrs Westaluit, Irwin Hqrs to CROIX DE POPERINGHE, attached to 6 Company for rations. Sent (9136) Infanterie Fund Gordon, headwound arrived, sent to 8th In Rolfs. Sent SBD STA.min, returned privates - wind cannal.	

T2134. Wt. W708—776. 500000. 4/15. Sir J. C. & 8.

Army Form C. 2118.

WAR DIARY
or
INTELLIGENCE SUMMARY.
(Erase heading not required.)

Instructions regarding War Diaries and Intelligence Summaries are contained in F. S. Regs., Part II. and the Staff Manual respectively. Title pages will be prepared in manuscript.

Place	Date	Hour	Summary of Events and Information	Remarks and references to Appendices
Croix du POPERINGHE	25/4/16		1340 pprx ho 1/N.Felns, 6 Oxen, Lauding Sa troostrate 1510W7 ho 18t Fordnos. Gunfrmns atta for returns from services to 9 A.R. Bde - pending arrival of 7 J Co. ASC	
	27/4/16		10th KNT ho 18t Fordnos Stores. 13th B.R.E. AT arrived at Bailleul today from this division. no returns to tomorrow were omplying because they with 2 day returns.	
	28/4/16		6 Ruling RE 76th Subspt Hhyro, 7th Foundue, the B 79 SC buoro one Foley — w.o.c. Camp M 33 C.S.V.— Referred from S 3 Central between 5.0 hrs emergency from Section. We arranged as required. — 3 Lwich Strens arrived at Northwood. 8th K'Oun, 8 of Support W Cort Rly. Arrived into coat yards at Bailleul today to S.D.s. division (370 tons). Floor man york ad, C. Clyster, Coat, October the Ref (1x 5.1x 8 hrs) from SD.Ca. Brits. — 76th Subspt Hhyro moved back to C oat today morning to Shellery of Privarl Camp.	
	30/4/16		Advance echelon FM 7th trens ones Today	

A.D. Winch.
SS.O.S. 5

50. DIV. TROOPS
APRIL 1916

S.A. Div. Troops
Army Form C. 2118.
3rd Div.

WAR DIARY
or
INTELLIGENCE SUMMARY.
(Erase heading not required.)

Place	Date	Hour	Summary of Events and Information	Remarks and references to Appendices
Estaminet	1st May 1916		Routine as usual. We have on our strength now 17 units. Three Batteries are in action.	
"	2 "		Routine as usual.	
"	3 "		Routine as usual.	
"	4 "		Routine as usual. The S.S.O. has now moved to Station, in the evening I went over to see him & the following units were added to his Group strength. 8" Bde H.G. Bty, 20" Bde R.F.A., 41" Bde R.F.A., 30" Bde R.F.A., 5" Howitzer sect., 14/2 Field Amb., 7 Field Amb., 3" Siege Grenade school, 41st Workshop Unit, 56 by R.E., 4/1 E. Riding R.E., 4/2 J.M. Battery, making a total of 20 units.	
"	5 "		Troops on leave arrived 8.15 am. The refilling took place as anticipated, & the refilling point was clear by 9.45 am. A second refilling took place at 3pm.	
"	6 "		Routine as usual. The 56 by R.E. arrived & located at our area, this is the last item we mention then, they are on the strength of 50" Bde.	
"	7 "		Routine as usual. Think eight units arrived. The 3 Sam Div. & Earthwater R.E. taken off strength.	

WAR DIARY
or
INTELLIGENCE SUMMARY.
(Erase heading not required.)

Army Form C. 2118.

Instructions regarding War Diaries and Intelligence Summaries are contained in F. S. Regs., Part II. and the Staff Manual respectively. Title pages will be prepared in manuscript.

Place	Date	Hour	Summary of Events and Information	Remarks and references to Appendices
Sstrumoutre	8th Aug	10 p.m	Routine as usual. Refilled with 3, Units. All Batteries in action. Withdrew the distribution of 9.2" Heavy Ration endorsed by me.	
"	9th "	"	Routine as usual. Refilling not 30 units, A.O.B. H.Q.R.2 Signal Cy. & 8" Old Battn. by below SAA strength.	
"	10th "	"	Routine as usual. Refilled with 25 Units 7 lorries drawn from or for the last time, afterwards to be retained by 2 Garrisons in Città	
"	11th "	"	Routine as usual. The W. Ind. Horse have relieved by th' East Lanes. their mules being sent to new area by lorry.	
"	12th "	"	No refilling. Slow tour of Ordnance received from railhead lorries. there were parked in the enemy.	
Sletie.	13th "	"	Refilling 26 Units, lorries arrives 8 a.m. Afterwards moved to new area just outside FLETRE.	
"	14th "	"	Lorries came up 8.15 en a next area. W. Refilling point W.S.c 7.6. near FLETRE. In afternoon visited Units in new area.	
"	15th "	"	Routine as usual. Refilling at 8.30 a.m 26 Units.	

Army Form C. 2118.

WAR DIARY
or
INTELLIGENCE SUMMARY.
(Erase heading not required.)

Instructions regarding War Diaries and Intelligence Summaries are contained in F. S. Regs., Part II. and the Staff Manual respectively. Title pages will be prepared in manuscript.

Place	Date	Hour	Summary of Events and Information	Remarks and references to Appendices
Station	16 Aug	10 pm	Routine as usual. Refilling 5.30 am. O.O.T., H.Q.A.I., typed copy & A.O. Tipts added & altered.	
"	17 "	"	Routine as usual. Refilling 5.30 am. 30' limit. R. & R. from draw to the last line.	
"	18 Aug	"	Routine as usual. 2 g limits.	
"	19 "	"	Routine as usual.	
"	20 "	"	Routine as usual.	
"	21 "	"	Routine as usual.	
"	22 "	"	Routine as usual.	
"	23 "	"	Routine as usual.	
"	24 "	"	Routine as usual.	
"	25 "	"	Routine as usual. The 14th Field Amb., recharge bay., R.E.H.Q., 3 argued bay." 3 Div # 9 draw for the last Turn.	
"	26 "	"	Routine as usual. 25 limits refill at 8.30 am. O.O.T. draw for the last Turn.	
"	27 "	"	Routine as usual. 2 24 limits refill at 5.30 am.	

T2134. Wt. W708—776. 500000. 4/15. Sir J. C. & S.

Army Form C. 2118.

WAR DIARY
or
INTELLIGENCE SUMMARY.
(Erase heading not required.)

Instructions regarding War Diaries and Intelligence Summaries are contained in F. S. Regs., Part II. and the Staff Manual respectively. Title pages will be prepared in manuscript.

Place	Date	Hour	Summary of Events and Information	Remarks and references to Appendices
Ellis	28th	10 p.	Routine as usual.	
"	29 "	"	Routine as usual.	
"	30 "	"	Routine as usual.	

T2134. Wt. W708—776. 500000. 4/15. Sir J. C. & S.

S.O. 8th J.Bn
S.O. 8th Inf Bn
APRIL 1916
Army Form C. 2118.

WAR DIARY
or
INTELLIGENCE SUMMARY.
(Erase heading not required.)

Place	Date	Hour	Summary of Events and Information	Remarks and references to Appendices
BOESCHEPE	1.4.16		Lorries arrived 7.45 AM Refilling 8.15 A.M. over 9 P.M. Great shortage of petrol from Petrol's Army.	
	2.4.16		Lorries arrived 7.40 P.M. Refill 8.15 AM over 9.15 P.M. Tobacco issue. Shortage of Brigade at the end of the week. All rank Shoes H.Q. I.D C.T.R Small Arms 5235 91 68 927 11 9	
	3.4.16		Lorries arrived 7.45 PM Refilling 8.15 AM over 9.5 AM Brigade cooks at off the trenches. With a new turnout a staff two days supply of rations issued to the unit. Lorries arrive at 2 P.M.	
	4.4.16		Lorries arrived at 2 P.M. Refill 9.30 P.M. over 4.15 P.M. Units now have six days rations in hand. A & C Coy RFA attached from the 15th Inst. All RFA & RE attached for feeding purposes to the school S.O. Divisional Troops.	
	5.4.16		One Refilling Company notes from area. Refilling Point close until new Brigade settled in their new area.	K.Andrews Captain S.O. 8th Bn

Army Form C. 2118.

WAR DIARY
or
INTELLIGENCE SUMMARY.
(Erase heading not required.)

Place	Date	Hour	Summary of Events and Information	Remarks and references to Appendices
SCHAEXKEN	6.4.16		Lorries arrived 7.15 AM Refg took place in New men. Unit was rationed as follows :— 8th Bde HQ. 2nd Battn. The Royal Scots. 7th Battn. The Kings Shropshire L.I. 8th Battn. The East Yorks. 10th Battn. The Kings Liverpool. Cheshire Field Coy R.E. Trench Mortar Battery. 7th Battn. R.F.A. 8.35 AM Refilling over.	
	7.4.16		Lorries arrived 7.15 AM Refg. 7.45. over 8.35 AM The 10th Kings Liverpool Regt. took the place of the 1st Royal Scot Fusiliers took their place. Three tons white carrots received	
	8.4.16		Lorries arrived 7.20. Refg 7.45 over 8.30 AM three thousand kilos potatoes arrive at Refg. front & lorries. Considerable trouble with renewing of all empty sacks, as great difficulty experienced in obtaining sufficient quantity of the same.	
	9.4.16		Lorries arrived 8.15 am Refilling 8.45. Capt Andrews proceeding on leave & was relieved by Lieut Rogers who also saw Indent of R.O.	
	10.4.16		Lorries arrived 8.15 Refilling 8.45. Arrangement was made by the S.S.O for Potatoes to be delivered by train on account of local	

A.E.E. Rogers Lt A.S.C.
for S.O. 8th Bde.

WAR DIARY
or
INTELLIGENCE SUMMARY.

Army Form C. 2118.

Place	Date	Hour	Summary of Events and Information	Remarks and references to Appendices
SCHAEXKEN.			Shortage. R.O. prohibiting the purchase of same in Belgian Area	
	11.4.16		Lorries arrived 5.15 a.m. Refilling 5.45. Units were again reminded to return sacks otherwise potatoes would have to be issued loose	
	12.4.16		Lorries arrived 5.15 a.m. Refilling 5.45. Visited units	
	13.4.16		Routine as usual	
	14.4.16		Lorries arrived 5.15 a.m. Refilling 5.45. Visited units	
	15.4.16		Routine as usual	
	16.4.16		Lorries arrived 5.15 a.m. Refilling 5.45. Total supply strength All ranks 3418, Horses 77, Mules 54, HP 20, LD 528, Carts 20	
	17.4.16		Routine as usual	
	18.4.16		Lorries arrived 5.15 a.m. Refilling 5.45. Went to Noon to discuss matter at which all OC Coys & SO's attended. Captain Andrews returned from leave & resuming his duty as S.O.	
	19.4.16		Lorries arrived 8.10 a.m. Refilling 8.45. At 9.30 a.m. potatoes arriving by rail, short weight. This matter to be looked into. K.A. Harris. Capt. A.S.C. S.O. ASC	

WAR DIARY or INTELLIGENCE SUMMARY

Army Form C. 2118.

Summary: 7/S. Rifle [Brigade]

Place	Date	Hour	Summary of Events and Information	Remarks and references to Appendices
SCHAEXKEN	20.4.16		Lewis gunners 8.15 A.M. Rifles 8.45 ove 9.25 AM Units combine from the new area. Trench where located O.P.	
	21.4.16		Lewis gunners 8.20 AM. Rifles 8.45 OK 9.30 AM beattu Died	
	22.4.16		Lewis gunners 8.15 AM. Rifles 8.45 ove 9.30 AM H Company lve into new area. 2 Trip by Batt's. New Rifle Post Settled	
CROIX DE POPERINGHE	23.4.16		Lewis gunners 8.45 A.M. Rifles 9.10 A.M. ove 9.45 AM Rifles new area for first line. Several units for 50th Division G be attached to feeding stations for 25th Int. Feeling strength at the end of the week:- all ranks Shire HQ. L.D. att Small Arm 4099. 99 48 501 29 2	
	24.4.16		Lewis gunners 8.45 Rifles 9.10 AM ove 9.45. Two long loads of rest straws for Gotha arrival at Dump.	
	25.4.16		Lewis gunners 8.45 Rifles 9.5 AM ove 9.50." New unit attacked outside for first line.	

W.T. Arthur Capt A/
2 Gds

Army Form C. 2118.

WAR DIARY
or
INTELLIGENCE SUMMARY.
(Erase heading not required.)

Instructions regarding War Diaries and Intelligence Summaries are contained in F.S. Regs., Part II. and the Staff Manual respectively. Title pages will be prepared in manuscript.

Place	Date	Hour	Summary of Events and Information	Remarks and references to Appendices
CROIX DE POPERINGHE	26.4.16		Lorries arrive 8.20. A.M. Rifles 8.50. A.M. over 9.50 A.M. 1h 10z Potatoes arrive 1 3 lbs wasted.	
	27.4.16		Lorries arrive 8.25 A.M. Rifles 8.50 over 9.45 A.M. Letter very Rt. large demand for creosote, any Troops being left in the coys.	
	28.4.16		Lorries arrive 8.25 A.M. Rifles 8.50 over 9.45. G. Sacks potatoes received from Railhead it was found that the were sent to come old shot this matter is being looked into. First issue of G.O.M. Syrup received.	
	29.4.16		Lorries arrive 8.20 A.M. Rifles 8.50 over 9.50 A.M. Large demand for triple soda any gas attacks.	
	30.4.16		Lorries arrive 8.20 A.M. Rifles 8.50 over 9.55 A.M. Tobacco issued. Strength of the Brigade O. feely & lifted at end of the month all ranks. Shires H.Q. 1 D. cths.	
			5685 93 61 552 22	

W. Ayhers Capt.
S.D. off.

Army Form C. 2118.

WAR DIARY
or
INTELLIGENCE SUMMARY.
(Erase heading not required.)

Instructions regarding War Diaries and Intelligence Summaries are contained in F. S. Regs., Part II. and the Staff Manual respectively. Title pages will be prepared in manuscript.

S.O.9th L.Bde

Supply Officer
9th L.A. Bde

Place	Date	Hour	Summary of Events and Information	Remarks and references to Appendices
BOESCHEPE	1-4-16		Lorries arrived 7.45am. Officers det. delayed by 8.15am. Refilling commenced 8.35am. Lorries as usual. Refilling finished 9.15am. Otherwise as usual.	
METEREN	2-4-16		Lorries arrived & unloaded 7.45am at 7.45 et res refilling point at BOESCHEPE. Refilling at 8.30am. Left for Bn. 7th D.A. at 10.70. The vehicles of No.2 & 3rd A.O.P. left without difficulty, sent to left behind in res. artie. Cpl & 1 Art. one plicion replace to reach on to new billet. Cpl. & 1 wheeler to make return to afternoon as usual 3rd Div. bn. between hrs. 7 & 11.30am Conditions II A.S.C. draw.	
"	3-4-16		Lorries arrive 5.30am. Refilling commences 5.8.30am. Lorries as usual. Reloading finishes 9.0. Also rejoined 15 Rus. 10 Rw.Les. Drivers. 3rd Cyclists sent up for H. Pde. Returned 3.15 met.	
"	4-4-16			
"	5-4-16		Rout as usual	

G.M. Dearl Capt. A.S.C.

Army Form C. 2118.

S.O.9 [illegible]

WAR DIARY
INTELLIGENCE SUMMARY.
(Erase heading not required.)

Instructions regarding War Diaries and Intelligence Summaries are contained in F. S. Regs., Part II. and the Staff Manual respectively. Title pages will be prepared in manuscript.

Place	Date	Hour	Summary of Events and Information	Remarks and references to Appendices
METEREN	6-4-16		Lorries arrives 7.15am. Offloaded by 7.45am. Refuse commences 8.30am. Lorries as usual. Rations [illegible] R.E. 9.0am. Played a [illegible] Lambeth [illegible] to the 9th R.B. 1st R.B. [illegible] Royal Regt [illegible] Riles from R.A.S.C. I then [illegible] [illegible] as usual.	
	7-4-16		Routine as usual	
	8-4-16		Routine as usual	
	9-4-16		I took over Supply duties from Capt. Veal to-day. Lorries arrived at 6am. R/filling took place at 8.30am. Men as usual. R/filling finished at 10.15am.	Myself Capt Veal
	10-4-16		Lorries arrived at 8.15 A.M. Offloaded and clear 8.40am. R/filling at 8.45. Men as usual. R/filling finished at 9.30am.	
	11-4-16		Routine as usual.	
	12-4-16		Routine as usual.	

[signatures]

Army Form C. 2118.

S.O. 9th Bde

WAR DIARY
INTELLIGENCE SUMMARY.
(Erase heading not required.)

Instructions regarding War Diaries and Intelligence Summaries are contained in F. S. Regs., Part II. and the Staff Manual respectively. Title pages will be prepared in manuscript.

Place	Date	Hour	Summary of Events and Information	Remarks and references to Appendices
Mahren	13/4/16		Routine as usual.	
	14/4/16		Routine as usual. A.O.O. 3rd Div. H.Q. & H.Q. 3rd Div. Signal Coy R.E. & H.Q. R.E.	
	15/4/16		Others omitted from 3316 tonight. They will be put by Div. Troops Coy on 17.	
	16/4/16		Routine as usual.	
	17/4/16		Routine as usual. Davies as usual saw A.O. 2, 3 Div. H.Q. Signal by R.E. & H.Q. R.E. who arr'd from Div. Troops Coy to stay.	
	18/4/16		Routine as usual. Left. That returned this afternoon & 9 hundred men supply duties to him.	
	19/4/16		Rushes arrived 8.15 a.m. Offloaded stolen by 8.40 a.m. Rifles commences 8.45 a.m. Arrivals 9.30 a.m. Others as usual	
	20-4-16		Routine as usual	
	21-4-16		Routine as usual	
	22-4-16		9 at 2nd Lieut magan left for 8th Bde after refusing & delivering supplies. Other duties as usual	

Army Form C. 2118.

WAR DIARY
INTELLIGENCE SUMMARY.
(Erase heading not required.)

Instructions regarding War Diaries and Intelligence Summaries are contained in F. S. Regs., Part II. and the Staff Manual respectively. Title pages will be prepared in manuscript.

S.O.9 =

Place	Date	Hour	Summary of Events and Information	Remarks and references to Appendices
METEREN	23-4-16		Lorries arrived 6.30 am. Loading commenced 6.50 am. Leave in normal, including fuel. Vehicles to Refilling Points 9.30 am. M.E.T.s. engines hides supplies to meet trains, butter uncertain arrival	
"	24-4-16		Lorries assumed normal. Refilling finished 9.30 am. to Regt.Prov.& B3= Kirkford Regt. Munitions. Supplies 7/2 to pre burden. Decided 94 - 585 Meat & Salvage to be retailing 94	
BAILLEUL	25-4-16		Refilling continued normal. Men, Lorries, were not had following marries or who were were able to delimeers noticed now to unemployment refilling point working mess by 10.15 by 10.45 am. Limit —(BAILLEUL—LOCRE R/S	
"	26-4-16		Lorries arrived 8.30 am. Offloaded solving by 6.45 am. Regt.Res.in more even, loaves no normal misshipment. Vegetables, butter urgent as normal	

EM Shead
Captain

Army Form C. 2118.

WAR DIARY
INTELLIGENCE SUMMARY.
(Erase heading not required.)

Instructions regarding War Diaries and Intelligence Summaries are contained in F. S. Regs., Part II. and the Staff Manual respectively. Title pages will be prepared in manuscript.

S.O. 9th Bde.

Place	Date	Hour	Summary of Events and Information	Remarks and references to Appendices
BAILLEUL	27-4-16		Lorries arrived as yesterday. Repairs on to pontoons as usual.	
"	28-4-16		Lorries arrived P.M. Offended solely by E.O. Source and unloading of pontoons ready 10th R.W.F. &c. Pontoons (27/6 B.R.E.) completed 9.50am.	
"	29-4-16		Repairing pontoons as usual	

E.W. Neal Capt R.E.
S.O. 9th Inf. Bde.

SD 76th Bde.
APRIL 1915

Army Form C. 2118.

WAR DIARY
or
INTELLIGENCE SUMMARY.
(Erase heading not required.)

Instructions regarding War Diaries and Intelligence Summaries are contained in F.S. Regs., Part II. and the Staff Manual respectively. Title pages will be prepared in manuscript.

Place	Date	Hour	Summary of Events and Information	Remarks and references to Appendices
HOOGRAFT		6.32 b.5.51		
	Saturday 1st April		Refill Unit arrived. - Ration 7th Yorks Lancs Regt drawn for last time. Issue 43 T. Mortar Battery whose rations were drawn up by 10th Royal Welsh Fusrs Boffrs. - Paid into Field Cashier V Corps balance in Regularising % say 5s. 6½ ps. no further receipt in settlement.	
	Sunday 2nd April		76/1 T. Mortar Battery's ration (437 M.S.) taken by 8 Kings Own Rlanes Regt. who paid this & and are unbroken up to date that they were in latest this Battery. These rations were returned by this Unit who states that they were unbroken by this Battery. Men and & Paymasters R. Bans. - Refill 10th R. Welsh Fusrs, 2 R. Suppliers. 76 Bde Machine Gun Coy for the first time as they have to-day for 9th Brigade Rat Area. These Units are attached temporarily to 76th Brigade for rations. — These Units are replaced by Units of 9th Brigade eg. Northumberland Fusrs. — & 12th West Yorks Regt. Coy 9 Corps orders that Fresh Vegetables are not to be issued with M.R. Rations received. (DS.T. S/403/6 d 29/3/15) 60% F MEAT. 15% Meat Ration (3 days P money) 25% P. MEAT. 15% Fresh Beans. (4 " ") Alteration in Pack train from 2nd april. 1lb F.M. 3/4 lb (Nominal) P.M. 1 tin M.V., 1/3 lb Pork Beans.	Scale – A.R. S/01. - Shum 109 M.D 79 L.D 84¼ Obs 24 Males 19 Hrs 1072 Leading String M 741/6 84/6 of Brigade on Camp
	Monday 3rd April		Refill Brigade as usual. Was Suffolk Regt. 10th R. Welsh Fusrs. 76th Brigade Machine Gun Coy. — In place of these Units the following were relieved. – 1st Northumberland Fusrs & 4th Royal Fusrs. — 12th West Yorks Regt together with two detachments of 1st Norsthumberland Fusrs & 4th Royal Fusrs.	

1 SD drawn each of Royal Scots Fusrs & 4th Royal Fusrs.

H. Wood ¼/M.S.
SD 76th Bde

Army Form C. 2118.

H.Q. 76th Inf Bde
Instructions regarding War Diaries and Intelligence
Summaries are contained in F. S. Regs., Part II.
and the Staff Manual respectively. Title pages
will be prepared in manuscript.

WAR DIARY
or
INTELLIGENCE SUMMARY.
(Erase heading not required.)

Place	Date	Hour	Summary of Events and Information	Remarks and references to Appendices
WESTOUTRE				
HOOGRAEFF G.32.c.5.5.	Monday 3rd April (contd)		refilling kept to join 9th Brigade — In addition to crowning their own rations, this Unit drew rations for 1 Coy. 10 Gordon Hldrs (170 OR) who had left for Rest Area. Received Copy of 10th Somerset field message — Relieving the T.M. Battery taken received by 8th Batt. Kings Own Rgt — Telegram from 38th Q received at midday acknowledging 48 rations to be sent to 3 D. & T Grenade School Roningheld before 3 pm. — These rations were delivered by 11.30 am — Supply Column arrived 3 pm with Brigade rations for conveyance. Sh. Coys — Refill at 9 pm — no on free refilling — Coln Northumberland Fus. & 6 London Wh. 3 D. & T HQrs drew for last time having left for rest Area today. —	
	Tuesday 4th April		Supply Lorries arrived 2.45 pm — Refill 3 pm — Instructed 17 A Arraigh Rd. & 7th Rgl Regn. Artillery that they were to refill from Supply Stores & 2nd Canadian Division. — Sent lorry load of Vegetables to new Camp in rest Area. —	
	Wednesday 5th April		No refilling. Leave Hoograaf at 9.45 am. Arrive Camp at Q.27.6.2.9. (Sh.28/4) EECRE - Camp on Roads outside a EECRE - GODWAERSVELDE Road about 1 Klom outside EECRE. Take over from 50th Division 2 lorries Coal. - Visited Bde HQrs at THIEUSHOUR. Q.35.6.4.4 Located units of Brigade to address their new Refilling Point viz Q.21.d.5.2. (1) Royal Welsh, 2 Suffolks (2) 76 T.M. Battery 6 T.O.C.	

H.P. Pleuts Lt Col OC
76th Bde

Army Form C. 2118.

S.S. 76th Inf Bde

WAR DIARY
or
INTELLIGENCE SUMMARY.
(Erase heading not required.)

Instructions regarding War Diaries and Intelligence Summaries are contained in F. S. Regs., Part II. and the Staff Manual respectively. Title pages will be prepared in manuscript.

1916

Place	Date	Hour	Summary of Events and Information	Remarks and references to Appendices
EECKE		O.Q.M.G. 2 (Refilling Point) Q 27.b.2.9 (Camp)		
	Thursday 6th April		Lorries arrive at new Refilling Point 7.0 am. Refill 8.30 am. Lorries off. Units of Brigade Group — Empronts from envelopes loaded arrive to	
	Friday 7th April		Took charge of Brigade Bomb Dump — Order to 3316 1/1 W. Riding R.E. Raid for truck carts reached from Emelien, Oudendom. 1/1 W. Riding R.E. — Fetched 16 latrine seats from farm at FLETRE in orders J.S.S.O.	
	Saturday 8th April		Lorries 7 am. Refill 8 am. Field Ambulance 1/1 W Riding R.E. — The latter arrived at 8th Bde after refilling. — Under orders of S.S.O. forwarded Calais bottles and outstanding claim for Col. from Viceroy Calais 20 tons oats supplied to troops in January 1915 — 696 frs. — Receipt stamped & passed through Inspect a/c of S.H. 76th Bdes. Regional Officer Billeting requirement for Brigade areas & King Own Plans 44 Inskiffler 75 Worcesters 120 (The latter arriving without any rations for conveyance 9 kl) — Refrom Reserve — 3100 R Calais (Corr) received by rail from GONTIER Oudersdom	AR 2802 Brigade Supply 9/4/16 Shins 78 5/5 M.D 3.3 3½ LJ 2.3 G/5 10 8½ R Mules 10
	Sunday 9th April		Routine as usual — Sent from reserve Lorries B. T. Motors 111 terrain detailed on Scale — Received at terminal Rail Train 17 Sacks — 800 k. Potato also 86 Balva Straw for forage — purchased from GONTIER, Oudendom. —	

H.H. Hewent Lt. Col.
S.O. 76th Inf Bde

T2134. Wt. W708-776. 500000. 4/15. Sir J. C. & S.

Army Form C. 2118.

No 76th Ind Bde
[signature]

WAR DIARY
or
INTELLIGENCE SUMMARY.
(Erase heading not required.)

Instructions regarding War Diaries and Intelligence Summaries are contained in F.S. Regs., Part II. and the Staff Manual respectively. Title pages will be prepared in manuscript.

Place	Date	Hour	Summary of Events and Information	Remarks and references to Appendices
EECKE		Q21 & 52 (RP) Q27 & 29 (Camp)		
	Monday 10th April		Limbers 7.30am. Repelt & 15am Charges in rations take effect at Railhead viz Jam 3g in lieu of 4g. – Ordered MFR 12 men per tonnes of 16 – 9/600 Pr Men 50 men per week (instead of lambs) Motivation – 1 man per tin. Pork & Beans ration. 3 men per tin. – Visits limits of 75th Bn Camp & Issue 14 Brs Visited Garden Jam for luch of Pickles (9/10d) regulates the bill for C'monts in hand for 100's of men. – Transportance 6300R suit 6600R repaired.	
	Tuesday 11th April		Received 18 Sacks (900st) Potatoes at Std Post Train together with 5200R purchased from Lambin, Ouderdom – 2/Lt. H.V. Pearce (R.Q) to Hospital at Mont Noir. –	
	Wednesday 12th April		Two lorries of Potatoes received at Std Post Train – About 3 weeks supply Everything now in hand including 3 days supply of Iron Rys. – Visit Canteen Ouderdom Jay Jam for 20,800 R Potatoes received on	
			of 50,000 R ordered. –	
	Thursday 13th April		Limbers 10am in lieu of 7.30. Std stone by 35th Colliford for Station – All leave stopped – 114 – 240 km Ration issued to cart & polus to Gardeur the engineers	

[signature]
Lt/Col
76th Inf Bde

Army Form C. 2118.

No 2611 ...

WAR DIARY
or
INTELLIGENCE SUMMARY.
(Erase heading not required.)

Instructions regarding War Diaries and Intelligence Summaries are contained in F.S. Regs., Part II. and the Staff Manual respectively. Title pages will be reprinted in manuscript.

Place	Date	Hour	Summary of Events and Information	Remarks and references to Appendices
EECKE		Q.21.d.5.2 (R.P.) Q.27.b.2.9 (Camp)		
	Friday 14th April		Losses from Rifle & 8.30 a.m. 33 L.inf Batterie moved to No 2 Coy III Bn Transport. Routine as usual. – Inclusive of 3rd of Brigading RE in 33.6 of Infantry –	
	Saturday 15th April		Lieut. H.S. King R.E. Nov. nobrown having been added to the Brigade at Railhead. — Lieut 76th Trench Mortar Batterys (attached 149th of L Bde)	
	Sunday 16th April		4.15 pm. Inoculated for 69 men only of 1st Inf Suffolk, as the remaining 637 proved not to be fit to go to the digging. Arrangements made with the for the Front Line (the 7rd in 17th by 8th Bde (ie for Campagne for 18th) Routine as usual. – Ordered moved [illegible] by ready force at	Regmly heading Returned offg AR 2643 Shires 87 HD 50 LD 315	485 CofR 23 Trades 10 Beginning fading in the evening
	Monday 17th April		a few hours motion – Suffolk Regt (637 men) leave for a 6 y.tt. – (for digging) Routine as usual. – Units of Brigade Guards – Tent Beds received for 3 inf Suffolks when all to be for thirty men at a time — Returned to Coke in the evening —	
	Tuesday 18th April		Allied attacking Ron as normal air Rd by 15/2 B.O.th Division Battery 2/107 north the 2 inf Suffolks on leave – 10th Riveland (400) leave for a 6 y.tt.	
	Wednesday 19th April		Visit Bde HQr & aux Brigades (A.E.& Eusted) — Visit London Dudendorfo's party for further 30,100 & stake received in 8th [illegible] at Ballend Station — Lind. Unet of Bde has accompanied SDERR Mahal [illegible]	

H.P.[illegible] 14th Bde
Lt.Col. H. Hooday [illegible]

Army Form C. 2118.

WAR DIARY
or
INTELLIGENCE SUMMARY.
(Erase heading not required.)

To 76th Dy/y Bde

Instructions regarding War Diaries and Intelligence Summaries are contained in F. S. Regs., Part II. and the Staff Manual respectively. Title pages will be prepared in manuscript.

Place	Date	Hour	Summary of Events and Information	Remarks and references to Appendices
EECKE	Q 21 d 5 ± (R.P.) Q 27 b 2.9 (Coys)			
Thursday	20th April		475 men of 1st Gordons leave after refitting to be fed by 8th Bde in 21st. Front line of Brigade Group. Gen Paton covered 7 Field Ambulance (220) L.J. Supplies 11.	
Friday	21st April		Relieve all Bde Units except 1st Gordons (475) the Gord by 8th Bde. Routine as usual. West all units of Bde Group & H.Q.	
Saturday	22nd April		Routine as usual. Inspection of Units of Bde in new area received from 8th Div. 8 Sp.t. train. 520 men of Kings Own Pioneers leave to be fed by 8th Bde.	
Sunday	23 April		We all think of Bde has K.O.R.L. (580) & 11th E Riding note left in 21st of new area — Gen 14 men of 8th which is to be left behind until Bde moves to new area. Easter Day. 8 Kings from Pioneers fed by 8th Bde.	
Monday	24th April		Fed all units. Pivotes Bexsty tall units of Brigade Gp.	
Tuesday	25th April		Routine as usual. Lecture at Brigade H.Q. by A.D.M.S. & O.M.S. J Brigade Supplies L.o.M.: R.A.M.C. T.Knochreenhoek 2.30 pm Advent units I change in Cal scale very glad not 917 66 per Serving 195th Glam	
Wednesday	26th April		Routine as usual.	

H.W. Williams 2/Lt/MSC
f.o. 76th Inf Bde.

Army Form C. 2118.

WAR DIARY
or
INTELLIGENCE SUMMARY.
(Erase heading not required.)

Instructions regarding War Diaries and Intelligence Summaries are contained in F.S. Regs., Part II. and the Staff Manual respectively. Title pages will be prepared in manuscript. 1916.

Place	Date	Hour	Summary of Events and Information	Remarks and references to Appendices
EECKE	Q.27, q.29 (cent) Q.21, d.31 (R.F.)			
	Thursday 27th April		Led all units to 76th Bn Machine Gun Coy who leave by rail from 9th Bde — 1st London Yeo. & 10th Royal Welsh after refilling leave for new area where they will be supplied by 9th Bde until arrival of the Bde by rail in new area — Meat received from railhead very short in weight.	
	Friday 28th April		Refill Units less those to left on 27th for new area. — Leave after refilling. Officers men at GODEWAERSVELDE. — POPERINGHE near BAILLEUL (Moyenneville Sheet 28 M.32.b.5.5. Newe refilling point Danu Alert S.3 central. Refilled left behind in charge J. Olier.	
	Saturday 29th April		Lorries arrive 8.30am. Refill at 9am. All units 9th Bde. Coy pers. C Squadron N. Som Horse, 3 Tmt Cyclists, 3 Tim Motor Machine Gun Sect. — Meat again short in weight. Sheep averaged at 60 lbs weight, about 50 or so well average of about that weight. Expense provenue to S.O.O. Visited King's Own Pioneer, 10th Royal Welch Pans, 2nd Suffolks (London no Officer there) + Bde HQrs + 7th Field Ambulances —	
	Sunday 30th April		Routine as usual —	

H.H.Kent, Lt. A.S.C.
D.H. Aldridge, Bde. —

SS O.3420 1.5.16

Army Form C. 2118.

H.Q. 3rd Division

May 16

WAR DIARY
or
INTELLIGENCE SUMMARY.
(Erase heading not required.)

Instructions regarding War Diaries and Intelligence Summaries are contained in F. S. Regs., Part II. and the Staff Manual respectively. Title pages will be prepared in manuscript.

Place	Date	Hour	Summary of Events and Information	Remarks and references to Appendices
CROIX DE POPERINGHE	1/5/16		Divisions of P.P.A. left for new area today - No 1 to P.S.C to new area Camp M.3.c.B.6.7 refilling point M.3.D.7.d - Went overdown to purchase of provender.	
	2/5/16		107 Bde P.P.A. (Red Army Service) drew rations from CHESTER by arrangement of O.C. S.S.T	
	3/5/16		Battalion starting from tomorrow - Supply column drew the full P.M. ration today. 12 doses new rations issued today. Rations, fresh meat etc. exchanged in the usual P.M. the usual places to M.V. rations - Stores supplies will remain stored in the hospital until required for issue.	
	4/5/16		Horse transport drawing as subheck from this morning to require RS Camp. Thus allowing 6.15am until 7.30am.	
	5/5/16 6/5/16		Routine as usual. Kent Col. Clyde Read also Crossed the Major Bustin re Supply matters.	Major Crozier adjutant 880

T2134. Wt. W708-776. 500000. 4/15. Sir J. C. & S.

Army Form C. 2118.

WAR DIARY
or
INTELLIGENCE SUMMARY.
(Erase heading not required.)

N.O. 7th Division

Instructions regarding War Diaries and Intelligence Summaries are contained in F.S. Regs., Part II. and the Staff Manual respectively. Title pages will be prepared in manuscript.

Place	Date	Hour	Summary of Events and Information	Remarks and references to Appendices
CROIX de POPERINGHE	7/5/16		Instructions received that the North East Home Service Division Engineers for the 9th Army Corps, returns for Consumption 9th Field Ambulance by lorries this afternoon for issue to this unit. 5th Corps was also returns for Corn. 10th would be in charge of Lillers or for 11th at St Pol, with RSD of 11th place alongside Squadron. Supply officers from Police today for Bread Sects, supply for 16, 8 & 19 the Bgs. Plenta Bivouacs.	
	8/5/16		North Irish Horse left this morning. So 87. Supply People troops piece of Reinforce, as ground is the need no Camp to 8th Rgte.	
	9/5/16		Inspection Parade in Battalion for wasp Journals in course munitions Deficits. Complete Journals for 7/8 KSLI about went End of Regno Finfant forder (Books) the Parade burnigne better lost (144 lbs). Weather reported Improved troops.	SD

Army Form C. 2118.

S.A.O. 3rd Division

WAR DIARY
or
INTELLIGENCE SUMMARY.
(Erase heading not required.)

Instructions regarding War Diaries and Intelligence Summaries are contained in F. S. Regs., Part II. and the Staff Manual respectively. Title pages will be prepared in manuscript.

Place	Date	Hour	Summary of Events and Information	Remarks and references to Appendices
Croix au Poperinghe	10/5/16		Glasgow Yeomanry 144 A.R. 141 Coys. joined today from the 9th Division. The returned by us from Consumption Stations. —	
	11/5/16		B.A.C. Columns arranged with B.A.Column 30th Brigade RFA. exchanged temporary stores please with that battalion.	
	12/5/16		136 man & 189 horses supplies & established T.D.M.O. left for Calais taking 3 camp returns & transfer including ammunition statistic. Divn. guidelines received today for the rationing of troops.	
	13/5/16		Inspected all newly returned places in flying points by the support trenches, with the D.M.O.R.G. Went to D.R.P. 10.11.12 & 30. Instructions found returns correct and execution satisfactory. Visited battalions & Coppts of Highland troops. — Routine as usual	
	14/5/16 15/5/16 16/5/16		Glasgow Yeomanry left for 50th Division. returned for consumption strict. Purchased 30 kilos potatoes from various farmers. Stavrugh. While he visited battalions in bivouac area near Pop'ghe. J.C. Adam Capt. Coy.	

Army Form C. 2118.

WAR DIARY
or
INTELLIGENCE SUMMARY.
(Erase heading not required.)

Place	Date	Hour	Summary of Events and Information	Remarks and references to Appendices
Croix du Poperinghe	17/9/16		the extra supply for work cope, as present supply insufficient for work done in trenches.	
	18/9/16		Conditions from near arriving as outlined continues the bad – water trough to the activities of the R.S.O.	
	19/9/16		from foreign supply continues but require about 7,500 kilos which during from Infantry Eudurons. Supplied returned to Poperinghe bent to R&R Dump. Unmapped position in S Points in rights sector found no actions at Fort Victoria — made reference to the points going their fire. Visible between dumps 7 & 3 butter can after open with the morgue.	
	20/9/16		the R&R Dump	
	21/9/16		relief Infantry relief 7 3rd Division with 50 chairs, more to commence on 2 Division, duns with Orderly Berry Kent to O. SD Good train after 880 truces arranged in connection with the mess arrangements [signature] France.	880

WAR DIARY
or
INTELLIGENCE SUMMARY.

Army Form C. 2118.

Place	Date	Hour	Summary of Events and Information	Remarks and references to Appendices
Cour de Pipeinghe	22/5/16		Transport 10 time Cope from SS 50 th Division Copper through train to Pincer the Division Sam	
	23/5/16		4 K.R.Rfn, 73th Brigade had been 20th K.R.R. & 56 Reed 6, 7, 13 th Platoons Bivouac at La Clyte, as dispersed & & C 50 th Division, all dumies was full by return to No.	
	24 —		No. 4 R.E. left to not area Kelsey Camp x 4. c. 8. 3, shelling period x 6.2.3.7 Shell 7. — West 50 & f, J due busy & ———— Trail Sumbers	
	25 —		Went to Ouderdom Reeled Scaus 4/2 — 13th King Surpool left for out area this evening	
	26 —		10th R.W.Felrs, 1st R Scots kind area — Leving Help & FLETRE — 1st Sreyshire, 8th Exports, 8 x 7 6th Bgll let from Dieg & T.M Batteries to No. 4 area this evening —	
FLETRE	27 —		Divnl Hdgrs. R.E. to FLETRE. 7th 8th & 14 D 7 Kirkburns Fusileurs, No. Co A.S.C. to 1 Corps Camp at FLETRE (temporary). Artillery friens W.S.O.B.T. E. trailing of chubbers F.Q.R.E. from 50 th Division spaning —	Division arrived (Arbum copy) 230

Army Form C. 2118.

WAR DIARY
or
INTELLIGENCE SUMMARY.
(Erase heading not required.)

Place	Date	Hour	Summary of Events and Information	Remarks and references to Appendices
FLETRE	26/5/16		[handwritten entries - illegible]	
	29/5/16		[handwritten entries - illegible]	

Army Form C. 2118.

WAR DIARY
or
INTELLIGENCE SUMMARY.
(Erase heading not required.)

Instructions regarding War Diaries and Intelligence Summaries are contained in F. S. Regs., Part II. and the Staff Manual respectively. Title pages will be prepared in manuscript.

Place	Date	Hour	Summary of Events and Information	Remarks and references to Appendices
FLETRE	30/9/16		No 1 Coy to rest area, 7 WTR. Camp W.S.D.E.8. No 2 Co from W.S.D.E.8. to Q-7 b.2.9. refueling for M.T. with supplies for D.T. to 3 D.A. supply wagons refilled terminal rations for consumption 31st t. no future supplies in kingdom. – Runners between ½ batteries from line head area night 30/31.08. –	
	3/9/16		Horse, new Campbell all ranks in rest area –	Aslerup Capt PSO 3rd Bn

WAR DIARY
or
INTELLIGENCE SUMMARY.
(Erase heading not required.)

Army Form C. 2118.

S.O. 3rd br. troops
May 1916

Place	Date	Hour	Summary of Events and Information	Remarks and references to Appendices
Fletre	1 May		Refilling 7 am. 5 carts lorries in not over, 22 carts drawn rations	
Caestre	2 "		Routine as usual.	
Poperinghe	3 "		Routine as usual.	
"	4 "		Ration & forage arr now drawn from railhead, 5 hour transport at Brielle, 44 wagons were sent. Train arrived at Reftily front 7.30 am refilling took from 9 am to finished 10.15 am.	
"	5 "		Routine as usual.	
"	6 "		Routine as usual. 9 units approx to N. troops. N.J House, A.C.C. W.S.& L.& Inn, 5 Jan, bc, A.O.D. H.Q.R.E. Signal Coy, & Adjt. R.J. und alg.	
"	7 "		Routine as usual.	
"	8 "		Routine as usual. Ration of N.S. troops sent to Watou etc 4 lorries	
"	9 "		Routine as usual. Ration 30 units.	
"	10 "		Routine as usual. 3 proceed to England on leave tomorrow, liew Ration taken over from one	

To 3rd Glost Scotts

Army Form C. 2118.

Instructions regarding War Diaries and Intelligence
Summaries are contained in F. S. Regs., Part II.
and the Staff Manual respectively. Title pages
will be prepared in manuscript.

WAR DIARY
or
INTELLIGENCE SUMMARY.
(Erase heading not required.)

Place	Date	Hour	Summary of Events and Information	Remarks and references to Appendices
Crown de Peronne	9/5/16		Lt. Parkin took over the duties of Supply Officer from Lt. Mackay, who proceeded to England on leave.	
	10/5/16		Routine as usual. Wagons arrived from Railhead at 8 am & Refilling commenced at 8.30 a.m.	
	13/5/16		Routine as usual. Lt. Col. Berry visited the Refilling Point. 2 bales of Hay short.	
	14/5/16		Wagons arrived from Railhead at usual time & Refilling commenced at 8.35 a.m. The A.A.Q.M.G. 69th Div. visited the Refilling Point. Lt. Col. Berry, who was also on the Refilling Point, explained the system of Refilling, etc. to him.	
	15/5/16		Wagons arrived at Refilling Point at 8.30 a.m. the delay being caused at Railhead. Refilling started at 8th Gr & was clear by 10.15 A.M.	
	16/5/16		Refilling at usual time. 2 sacks of oats short from Railhead.	
	17/5/16		Must sieves for wagons from Railhead etc. The S.O. had to go to Refilling Point & clear the forage 2 cal wagons as there were deficiencies at Railhead. Sirouval. Troops all carried.	
	18/5/16		Routine as usual.	
	19/5/16		Lt. Mackay resumed the duties of Supply Officer.	

R Parkin Lt AsC
a/S O-n 3rd Div.
19/5/16

Army Form C. 2118.

WAR DIARY
or
INTELLIGENCE SUMMARY.
(Erase heading not required.)

Instructions regarding War Diaries and Intelligence Summaries are contained in F. S. Regs., Part II. and the Staff Manual respectively. Title pages will be prepared in manuscript.

Place	Date	Hour	Summary of Events and Information	Remarks and references to Appendices
Croix de Poperinghe	20 Aug		Routine as usual. Raining 29 units. 3 returned from leave last night & lost our ??? Carter.	
"	21		Routine as usual.	
"	22		The return today came of A artillery group of lorries, arriving at 6.30 am. artillery took place 7.45 am. & we finished 4.30	
"	23		Routine as usual	
"	24		Routine as usual	
"	25		Routine as usual	
"	26		Routine as usual	
"	27		Routine as usual	
"	28		Routine as usual. Artillery used lines, 22 unit drew the Lorries with men & not our own. Set of 9 - tripods Bde.	
"	29		Routine as usual. Rubin ??? in C.3 check ??? lost line.	
Sletta	30		We moved had A FLETRE first thing in morning, arriving at 7 am. a ??? lorries, Di bog ??? tea at 8.30 an artillery at 9 am. a	
"	31		Finished 10.15 —	

Army Form C. 2118.

WAR DIARY
or
INTELLIGENCE SUMMARY

(Erase heading not required.)

Place	Date	Hour	Summary of Events and Information	Remarks and references to Appendices
In the Field	1. 5/16		Lorries arrive 8.20 A.M. Refilling Infants Battalions in the Brigade	
	2. 5/16		Lorries arrive 8.20 A.M. Refilling as usual. First wagons for Fly-Papers received. Flies beginning to appear in native quantities	9.45 Visited all. Found everything satisfactory. 9.30 Rather as Sun is hot weather
	3. 5/16		Lorries arrive 8.20 A.M. Refilling. Also Potatoes drawn for store. Large quantities of unsought-for maggot many that consignment of carts, sent to the unit and during	9.45 Two thousand received for Hypo-soda. Refilling Point at
	4. 5/16		Horse transport draws Supplies from Railhead for first two wagons arrive Railhead at 6.A.M. and arrive Refilling Point at 7.30 A.M. Horses Exchanged. Refilling 8.A.M. Visited everything found correct	Over 8.45. All will

K.T. Ashens. Capt. FTE
S.O. 8th Rife.

Army Form C. 2118.

WAR DIARY
or
INTELLIGENCE SUMMARY

(Erase heading not required.)

Place	Date	Hour	Summary of Events and Information	Remarks and references to Appendices
In the Field	5/5/16		Transport arrived at Pepilly Point at 7.30. Refile 8.Am over	
		8.55.	The Kilt Balloon Sections, Road Staff, 24th D.A.C., S & Cable Section & Tunnelling Company are returned to the East time. One June Ray	
		9.00	Kit issued in lieu of Rum, all units notified to that effect.	
			The Summer allowance of fuel at present issued to all units is 1 lb wood + 1 lb coal for men, per diem.	
6/5/16		Refile 8.Am over	8.45 Am. Battery of Arts arrived. No more Pea Soup or cocoa to be issued to troops in the trenches	
7/5/16		Refile 8.Am over 8.50 am. Tobacco issue. Visited Brigade H.Q. and		
			the arranged purchase of cut of Rye grass as green fodder for the horses. 700 kilos purchased, at the rate of 4 fr per 100 kilos. Lieutenant Hay Rates	
			Brigade strength: Head of the week:	
			Officers Rank & File. 1. O. Cols.	
			146. 40 22	
			4627 40 22	

K A Anderson O/c H.Q.
Lo & F.Re

Army Form C. 2118.

WAR DIARY
or
INTELLIGENCE SUMMARY
(Erase heading not required.)

Instructions regarding War Diaries and Intelligence Summaries are contained in F. S. Regs., Part II. and the Staff Manual respectively. Title Pages will be prepared in manuscript.

Place	Date	Hour	Summary of Events and Information	Remarks and references to Appendices
In the Field	8.5/16	8 A.M.	Refer 8 A.M. over. 8.45. Arrangements made as to the postal of Regt guard on 675th Suppy details dispatched to the Field in question, and he superintend the loading of the correct amount in G.S. Wagons. Units wagon	
	9.5/16	8 A.M.	Refer 8 A.M. over. 8.40 A.M. Report received from the 7th Kings Shropshire L.I. stating received 140 lbs of decomposed meat. Kept out and investigate the matter and found their report is correct, and issue presented meat in lieu. This is the first time about a report of this kind as been received by me.	
	10.5/16	8 A.M.	Refer 8 A.M. over. 8.40 A.M. Routine as usual	
	11.5/16	8 A.M.	Refer 8 A.M. over. 8.45 A.M. all refilling Points visited & the D.A.G.M.G. of the Division	
	12.5/16	8 A.M.	Refer 8 A.M. over. 8.40 A.M. weather changed.	

K. Arthur Colliffe
S.o. S/L R.E.

Army Form C. 2118.

WAR DIARY
or
INTELLIGENCE SUMMARY

(Erase heading not required.)

Instructions regarding War Diaries and Intelligence Summaries are contained in F. S. Regs., Part II. and the Staff Manual respectively. Title Pages will be prepared in manuscript.

Place	Date	Hour	Summary of Events and Information	Remarks and references to Appendices
In the Field	13/5/16	8 A.M.	Refee over 8.45 A.M. Tobacco issue visited and everything correct.	S. Applees
	14/5/16	8 A.M.	Refee over 8.40 A.M. Arrangements made that green Fodder shd. be sent each day to Refeeling Post, and be distributed with other forage each morning, and sent up to the units with their supplies.	
	15/5/16	8 A.M.	Refee over 8.40 A.M. Potatoes on hand re-sacked and re-stacked, all the loose sacks being rotten owing to heavy rain.	
	16/5/16	8 A.M.	Refee over 8.40 A.M. Lime juice can not be issued three times weekly, on half demand. Fuel for incinerators cut down to 3 cwt per week per 1000 men.	
	17/5/16	8 A.M.	Refee over 8.40 A.M. Potatoes received from Divisional Park train.	

F. Andrews Capt. ASC.
3rd Army Rfs.

Army Form C. 2118.

WAR DIARY
or
INTELLIGENCE SUMMARY

Supply Coys.

(Erase heading not required.)

Instructions regarding War Diaries and Intelligence Summaries are contained in F. S. Regs., Part II. and the Staff Manual respectively. Title Pages will be prepared in manuscript.

Place	Date	Hour	Summary of Events and Information	Remarks and references to Appendices
In the Field	18/5/16		Refee 8 A.M. over 8.45 A.M. weather very hot and dry. 1000 kilos onions purchased to own in trenches, the allowance to 4.3 per man. As remarks of the vegetable ration the issue of potatoes. Eight thousand kilos potatoes purchased by Q.O. and placed in store.	
	19/5/16		Refee as usual 8. A.M. over 8.45. weather fine visit all unit and find everything correct.	
	20/5/16		Refee 8 A.M. over 8.40 Rations as usual Tobacco issue to troops	
	21/5/16		Refee 8 A.M. over 8.45 Rations as usual Brought strength to end of the week light draught cattle. All ranks Shires. 40. 22	
			5093. 149.	

Lt. Andrews Capt A.S.C.

Army Form C. 2118.

WAR DIARY
or
INTELLIGENCE SUMMARY

(Erase heading not required.)

Instructions regarding War Diaries and Intelligence Summaries are contained in F.S. Regs., Part II. and the Staff Manual respectively. Title Pages will be prepared in manuscript.

Place	Date	Hour	Summary of Events and Information	Remarks and references to Appendices
In the Field	22/5/16	8. AM	Rfee over 8.20. Last day of horse Transport from Rfee to Mechanical Transport Column to resume their work on 23rd inst.	
	23/5/16	6.30 AM	Rfee horse arrive 6.30 AM. Rfee 7.15 PM over 8 PM. Lorry Transport issued put in to work attached to Rfee. Which is doing its work on 24th inst.	
	24/5/16	6.30 AM	Lorries arrive 6.30 AM. Rfee 7.15 AM over 8 AM. Visited all units and found everything correct.	
	25/5/16	6.45 AM	Lorries arrive 6.45 AM. Rfee 7.15 over 8 AM. In addition to usual units the following units were attached at Rfilley Point R.E. 136th Army Troops company R.E. 242 Div Amm Column. S V Cable sectn. 27 Kite Balloon Sectn. 3rd Divisional Salvage Compy. 141 Fuel Ambulance H.Q. T M Batty.	

Arthurs C.H.Age
R. A.
Go. 14th

Army Form C. 2118.

WAR DIARY
or
INTELLIGENCE SUMMARY

(Erase heading not required.)

Instructions regarding War Diaries and Intelligence Summaries are contained in F.S. Regs., Part II. and the Staff Manual respectively. Title Pages will be prepared in manuscript.

Place	Date	Hour	Summary of Events and Information	Remarks and references to Appendices
In the Field	26/5/16		Lorries arrive 6.45. Refilled 7.15 ove 7.55 AM. First units of the 53rd Bde proceed to test area. Five hundred kilos over received. Weather rainy & cold	
	27/5/16		Lorries arrive 6.45. Refilled 7.15. ove 8AM. All units proceed with rations on 24/5 & first line, handed over to the 53rd Division together with the 1st Entrenching Bttn and 11th Labour Coy R.E. The 88 Field Ambulance to be returned by the 9th Bde. " 141st " 76th Bde The Third Div. Salvage Coy 7th Bde weather fine. gulfeta Syrup used at Rafeeh Post, also pickles.	
	28/5/16		Lorries arrive 6.45. Refill 7.15. ove 8.4M. host Dump in present position. Convoy moves to new area. Brigade strength at end of the week all ranks Officers Light Draught Coft 4524 1289 33	

K.T. Andrews Capt. RFC
2o. JMRC

WAR DIARY or INTELLIGENCE SUMMARY

Army Form C. 2118.

Place	Date	Hour	Summary of Events and Information	Remarks and references to Appendices
In the Field	29/5/16	6.30	Battn. arrived new area. Kit inspection. Pipes sounded fall in lengths. Coord.	
	30/5/16	6.20	Battn. arrived. Pipes 8.20 a.m. over 9 a.m. received as confirmed sick. Also received Band.	
	31/5/16	6.20	Battn. arrived. Pipes 8.20 a.m. over 9 a.m. Fruit complaints inspected, and fruit (strong) sent for confirm. Ten unit strength confirmed. The complaint was fraudent. Angus slaughtered to end of Str. outs. to return as proper.	
			All ranks. Shine. Light Draught CoH.	
			2607. III. 262. 19.	

M Andrews C/Lt/Hff
S.o./A.P.A.

S.O.g.I.f.13a.

M/16 S.O. 9th I.Bde.

Army Form C. 2118

WAR DIARY
or
INTELLIGENCE SUMMARY.
(Erase heading not required.)

Instructions regarding War Diaries and Intelligence Summaries are contained in F.S. Regs., Part II. and the Staff Manual respectively. Title pages will be prepared in manuscript.

Place	Date	Hour	Summary of Events and Information	Remarks and references to Appendices
BAILLEUL	30-4-16		Lorries arrives 8.30 a.m. Offloaded & clearing 8.45 a.m. Rapidly commences 8.55 a.m. Lorries move off with great dispatch. Rapidly finish 9.50 a.m. 3 hrs on retail.	
"	1-5-16.		Sunday - no alarm	
"	2-5-16.		Lorries arrives 8.15 a.m. Rapidly commences 8.50 a.m. Finish 7.45 a.m. Others routine.	
"	3-5-16.		Routine as normal.	
"	4-5-16.		Captain arrives direct from stables. Time waggons at 8.35 a.m. about 3 hours later than usual. Waggons offloaded by 9.5 a.m. Rapidly commences at late finishes 10 a.m.	
"	5-5-16.		An Sgn yesterday but waggons arrives between 7.30 a.m. 8.0 a.m. Rapidly commences 8.45 a.m. Finishes 9.10 a.m. Others routine as usual.	

E.M. Nead
Capt. A.S.C.

Army Form C. 2118.

WAR DIARY
or
INTELLIGENCE SUMMARY.
(Erase heading not required.)

Instructions regarding War Diaries and Intelligence Summaries are contained in F. S. Regs., Part II. and the Staff Manual respectively. Title pages will be prepared in manuscript.

S.O. 9th Inf. Bde.

Place	Date	Hour	Summary of Events and Information	Remarks and references to Appendices
BAILLEUL	6-5-16		Wagons arrives at Refilling Point from mules between 7.30 a.m. & 8.0 a.m. Refilled ammunition 8.35 a.m. do several including tea & vegetables. Rifles, picks. 9.35 a.m. Others moved on as usual.	
"	7-5-16		Routine as for 6/5/16	
"	8-5-16		Routine as usual	
"	9-5-16		Wagons arrives from mules as above. Load includes tank myrrh, leave as (100 lbs) & ambulances diurnally ourselves for issue to ammunition company	
"	10-5-16		Leave as usual also grenades & other matters as usual except for yesterday	
"	11-5-16		Routine as usual	
"	12-5-16		Routine as above	
"	13-5-16		Routine as above	

EW Ned M.
Capt. & Adjt.

Army Form C. 2118.

S.O.9. 7th Inf. Bde.

WAR DIARY
or
INTELLIGENCE SUMMARY.
(Erase heading not required.)

Instructions regarding War Diaries and Intelligence Summaries are contained in F. S. Regs., Part II. and the Staff Manual respectively. Title pages will be prepared in manuscript.

Place	Date	Hour	Summary of Events and Information	Remarks and references to Appendices
BAILLEUL	15-5-14		Magneto opened fire - nodes 5 between 7.15 am & 7.30 am. Reply commences 8.30 am all rounds no rounds judging pieces for the & great vegetables. Rapidly fired by 9.30 am Others rounds as usual.	
"	15-5-14		Routine as above. No green fodder available.	
"	16-5-14		Routine as usual. Green fodder rounds as usual	
"	17-5-14		Routine as usual.	
"	18-5-14		Magneto rounds fire - nodes 5 between 7.30 am - 8.0 am. Reply commences 8.30 am. Same as usual evaluation. Give green fodder & carrying troops in the area. Rapidly finished 9.15 am. Other rounds as usual	
"	19-5-14		Routine as usual. Rapidly 8.0 am.	
"	20-5-14		Routine as usual	
"	21-5-14		Routine as usual	
"	22-5-14		Magneto opened 6.30. Officials delay 7. Same Reply commences 8.0 am. Evened 8.50 am. Others rounds as usual ending greenfodder	A. M. Neal Captain

T.134. Wt. W708-776. 500000. 4/15. Sir J.C. & S.

Army Form C. 2118.

S.O. 9th Inf. Bde.

WAR DIARY
or
INTELLIGENCE SUMMARY.
(Erase heading not required.)

Place	Date	Hour	Summary of Events and Information	Remarks and references to Appendices
BAILLEUL.	23-5-16	P.M.	Lorries arrives 6.45 am. Offloaded & leave by 7.15 am. Refilling commences 8.10 am. Square an issue of Lemons, Oranges & potatoes. Refilling finishes 9.0 am. & fell lorries as usual.	
METEREN.	24-5-16		Lorries arrive 6.30 am. Offloaded & leave 7.0 am. Refilling commences 8.5 am. Same no meat issued. Issued per supply of fresh vegetables. Supplies for units already at their new billets or moving to their new billets supplied extra 1/5 rations there. 9 units Gun 20 & R.F.A. R & F & met moving out. Relieved there.	
"	25-5-16		Lorries arrive 8.7.35 am. Offloaded by 8.0 am. Refilling commences 8.35 am. Leave as usual.	
"	26-5-16		Routine as normal. Lorries arrive 6.30 am.	
"	27-5-16		Routine as normal.	
"	28-5-16		Divisional & Brigade lorries arrives 6.30 am. Offloaded by 7.0 am. Refilling commences 8.30 am. Units previously notified of issue of hop 50 to Divison were notified & issue as usual.	

E.M.West
Captain.

Army Form C. 2118.

S.O. 9th Bgde

WAR DIARY
or
INTELLIGENCE SUMMARY.
(Erase heading not required.)

Instructions regarding War Diaries and Intelligence Summaries are contained in F. S. Regs., Part II. and the Staff Manual respectively. Title pages will be prepared in manuscript.

Place	Date	Hour	Summary of Events and Information	Remarks and references to Appendices
METEREN	29-5-16		Lorries arrives 6.30am. offloaded below by 7.0 am so Refilling 8.30 am. Lorries arrived including Grenades & S.A.A. Refilling finishes 9.30am. Staff route as channel.	CW/at Cyst All
"	30-5-16		Routine as above.	

S.D. 76th Inf Bde

Army Form C. 2118.

My 16.

WAR DIARY
or
INTELLIGENCE SUMMARY.
(Erase heading not required.)

Instructions regarding War Diaries and Intelligence Summaries are contained in F. S. Regs., Part II. and the Staff Manual respectively. Title pages will be prepared in manuscript.

Place	Date	Hour	Summary of Events and Information	Remarks and references to Appendices
Sheet 28 M. 32 & 53	1.5.16		Routine as usual.	
"	2.5.16		2nd Lieut H.J. Hirst proceeded to England on leave. Lieut A.C. Robinson acting as S.D. during his absence. Had a rifling point shot in weight.	
"	3.5.16		Visited units as usual. All satisfactory.	
"	4.5.16		Horse transport commenced drawing from R.R. Head. Wagons arrived at rifling point at 8.45 a.m. Reffilling 10.30 a.m.	
"	5.5.16		Wagons arrived at rifling point from 7 a.m. to 8.15 a.m. Reffilling 9.30 a.m. B. Col. on O.C. 7th Field Ambulance & 11 East Riding R.E.	
"	6.5.16		Reffilling 9.30 a.m. Some of the times - North Irish Horse, Divisional Cyclists, Motor Machine Gun Co., Reffilled with no operations for 1st Div from Divisional Corps today. 200th Machine Gun Coy, & Corps Road Staff & R.E. Rope Battery from 8th Brigade, Reffilled with no today for 1st time. Visited units this afternoon. All satisfactory.	
"	7.5.16		Reffilling 8.45 a.m.	
"	8.5.16		Routine as usual.	

A.C. Robinson
2/Lt 76 ? Head ?

Army Form C. 2118.

WAR DIARY
or
INTELLIGENCE SUMMARY.
(Erase heading not required.)

Instructions regarding War Diaries and Intelligence Summaries are contained in F. S. Regs., Part II. and the Staff Manual respectively. Title pages will be prepared in manuscript.

Place	Date	Hour	Summary of Events and Information	Remarks and references to Appendices
Sheet 28				
Mar b.s.3	9.5.16		Refilling 8.45am Lieut Robinson proceeded on leave & was relieved by Lieut Rogers. Complaint from 7th Field Ambulance that meat issued on 8th inst was not fit for consumption. I visited this unit & examined meat which was seen in places and stank. The meat was destroyed	
	10.5.16		Refilling 8.45am. Feeding strength men. 4723. H.D.141. LD 362 Cobn 23 mules 5 9. Routine as usual	Rogers Lt
	11.5.16		Refilling 8.35 am. 2/Lieut H L Hurst returned from leave & took over from Lt A E D Rogers 10.0 a.m.. Visited 8th Kings own - yeomanry 10th R Welsh Fus, 1st Gordon Hdrs, 7th Buff. Fus. - Gnarlie J bay sent to weld known unfit for consumption - this I ordered to be destroyed. Complaint from officer i/c S.10 III D.C. - 21700 Pte new returning from Hospital	
	12/5/16		Routine as usual. Refill at 8.45 am.	
	13/5/16		Complaint sent to D.D.A. regarding shortages in Oats received for Brigade. Scale 3 plus for marauders charged & some for invalids	HHKeus (?) Lt R.A.S.C. C.O. 7th Bde f.S.

T2134. Wt. W708-776. 500000. 4/15. Sir J. C. & S.

Army Form C. 2118.

WAR DIARY
or
INTELLIGENCE SUMMARY.
(Erase heading not required.)

Instructions regarding War Diaries and Intelligence Summaries are contained in F.S. Regs., Part II. and the Staff Manual respectively. Title pages will be prepared in manuscript.

Place	Date	Hour	Summary of Events and Information	Remarks and references to Appendices
Sheet 28.				
M 32 b 5 3				
	Sunday 14/5/16		Various Units of Brigade – Divl Supplies, 1st Gordon Hrs, 10th Rwbl Horn, 76th Bde F. Amb. & 76th Field Ambulance & 76th Bde Machine Gun Coy – The latter Unit retained 30 cts. & 7th L.H. Ambulance & 76th Bde Machine Gun Coy – The latter Unit retained 30 cts. – Bacon except for consumption – Aeroplane fumigated & F.S.O. –	
	Monday 15/5/16		Routine as usual.	
	Tuesday 16/5/16		Various 8th Kings Own Royce, Rwbl, O.M. Elsing R.E. Replace been issued except for consumption in 14th. –	
	Wednesday 17/5/16		Routine as usual –	
	Thursday 18/5/16		Various various Branches. Thanks for not taking vegetables. – Routine as usual. –	
	Friday 19/5/16		Various 8 Kings Own, 10th Rwbl, 1st Gordons, 2 Supplies & 76th Bde M. Gun Sectn. –	
	Saturday 20/5/16		Lorries No. 331.66 on Lipton's Column returns on 22nd, railhead being rail G.S. Wagon came to-day – Shortage of E. Meat & Bread very stresoever. –	
	Sunday 21/5/16		2 G S Wagons loading 1 Railhead being issued by Lipton's Clean a/commencer Bulger Camp. –	
	Monday 22/5/16		Routine as usual. New Price for to-Lot Rations received –	

W. H. Moore Field A.S.C.
To 76th Inf. Bde.

T2134. Wt. W708—776. 500000. 4/15. Sir J. C. & S.

Army Form C. 2118.

WAR DIARY
or
INTELLIGENCE SUMMARY.
(Erase heading not required.)

CO. 1/6th South Staffs
Instructions regarding War Diaries and Intelligence
Summaries are contained in F. S. Regs., Part II.
and the Staff Manual respectively. Title pages
will be prepared in manuscript.

Place	Date	Hour	Summary of Events and Information	Remarks and references to Appendices
Sheet 28 M.32.b.5.b.				
	Tuesday 23/5/16		Routine as usual — Visited Co. 1/6th Bele SDR SDS as following relief —	
	Wednesday 24/5/16		Visited all Infantry Units of Bde Group & 1/6 Bele. Machine Gun Coy. —	
	Thursday 25/5/16		Routine as usual — Demands for lantern slides for 253 Tunnelling Coy RE, 82 Sup Battery RSA, YMCA & V Corps Rear School Staff — Forwarding 274 for all Units as usual. Indented for "Supply Bde" complete less 2 Coys own Planes — In addition indented for 3rd SH Qrs., 3rd Salvage Coy, HQ Pks 3 Signal Coy, Sub Ordnance, ♢142 Field Ambulance for feeding 2087 in new area. —	
	Friday 26/5/16			
	Saturday 27/5/16		as above. Red Units demanded 25/5/16 for last time these units having been handed to 50th Division — Demands for Brigade complete & rations demanded yesterday. — Leave Gros Peperinghe at 10.30 for new Camp at FLETRE (W.S.d.7.8) Sheet 27. Ripling Camp W.S.d.5.2. (Damaged) Visits O.C. Supply Column arranges for lorry for straw left behind at old Camp to be brought to new Camp — Exchanges with Co. 1/5th Brigade 2 two potales. —	

H.H. Spling Lieut RC
D. 1/6 S. Staff Regt

Army Form C. 2118.

S.9. 76th Infantry
Instructions regarding War Diaries and Intelligence
Summaries are contained in F. S. Regs., Part II.
and the Staff Manual respectively. Title pages
will be prepared in manuscript.

WAR DIARY
or
INTELLIGENCE SUMMARY.
(Erase heading not required.)

Place	Date	Hour	Summary of Events and Information	Remarks and references to Appendices
FLETRE				
W. S. d. J. 8. (Camp)				
W. S. d. J. 2. (R.P.)				
	Sunday 28/5/16		Fed all units. Looking over ranges - in addition to units first troop landed on 25/5/16. Lines 6.45 am Rifles 9 am. Sent to Stanmore for Green Forage - (2 Waggons). Visited all units of Brigade in own area - also the 142 Field Ambce.	
	Monday 29/5/16		Complaint re Manuals being received in Wm - countersigned. 6 S.S.O. Rifle sling straps Mark II for last supplied as before. 8 King Aeroplanes.	
	Tuesday 30/5/16		Camp moved from W. S. d. J. 8. to new camp at Q. 27. 6. 29. (EECKE) occupied in April. - Rifles shirt drops units for last time. - Visited DOC 76th Inf. Bde re companies of the clergy of Bread coming to Infantry as company with that service of RSC. units re Influenza that small funds somme could not be raised with Aurene & also Field Ambulance notifications & further that the 10 SC Coy feeding the Brigade has brewed ovens.	
				[signed] LO 76th Inf. Bde.

Army Form C. 2118.

S.D. 76U Infty. Bde.

WAR DIARY
or
INTELLIGENCE SUMMARY.
(Erase heading not required.)

Instructions regarding War Diaries and Intelligence Summaries are contained in F. S. Regs., Part II. and the Staff Manual respectively. Title pages will be prepared in manuscript.

Place	Date	Hour	Summary of Events and Information	Remarks and references to Appendices
EECKE (Rybrug Road)	Q 27 b.2.9 Q.21.d.5.2			
Wednesday	31/5/6		Practice shoots of Regt. Snipers. Explanations from Officers on plans regarding battle orders of preed being issued to keep the aeroplane 9 forwarded to S.O. 3 Divn. Company on the town guard night for consumption — these incurred the aeroplane —	Appendices Issued N.S.L. S.O. 76 U Infty Bde
	31/5/6			

T2134. Wt. W708—778. 500000. 4/15. Sir J. C. & S.

S.S.O 3RD DIV.

S.S.O. 3rd Division.
Vol 6

Army Form C. 2118.

WAR DIARY
or
INTELLIGENCE SUMMARY.
(Erase heading not required.)

Instructions regarding War Diaries and Intelligence Summaries are contained in F. S. Regs., Part II. and the Staff Manual respectively. Title pages will be prepared in manuscript.

Place	Date	Hour	Summary of Events and Information	Remarks and references to Appendices
# PIETRE	1/9/16		Detailed that the Division is expected to meet the Army about 9th inst. —	
	2/9/16		4 hr. pictures arriving at various dumps from today. Hd. qr. Bty 177A left for 6th Div totay. —	
	3/9/16		Divn. to attack last night — Campaign forms orders issued to us all the R.T.M. of A that unit — Lieut 107th Batty + 22nd Bgde Hdqrs. Wipping out Canvastown —	
			Rogue went with OC Divn. to see BGQMG 2nd Divn. Cameron reference repairing Prins which was found in Cmillow — Burrotown Rd. — Capt Stokes left today for Camp D in Curredon. Liaising with him a supply station from I Co. — arranged with Gurkha M. orffs of troops for the Gunners.	
	4/9/16		9th In Bgde. under orders [illegible]. Gurkha Cdrs. began left for new Camp after repairing this morning. Went to Dulgines (leaving area) with OC Divn. Vehr. O.C. 1/16. Rind train to [illegible] moves.	
			9th Inf Bgde. also advanced flights known from the 6th 7 Hussars. left there afternoon for Cumnner Cmls morning. — 76 In. Bgdr. [signature] Occupy Camp vacated by 9th Inf Bgde. Raining during [illegible] this morning.	GOC 3rd Divn.

Army Form C. 2118.

WAR DIARY
or
INTELLIGENCE SUMMARY.
(Erase heading not required.)

Instructions regarding War Diaries and Intelligence Summaries are contained in F.S. Regs., Part II. and the Staff Manual respectively. Title pages will be prepared in manuscript.

Place	Date	Hour	Summary of Events and Information	Remarks and references to Appendices
FLETRE	5/6/16		4 Coy EC moved to G 31 D church - refilling point at G 3 D - Divisional Supply moved back from Camp D opposite up with 4 Co - refilling point G 3 on Shanken-Poperinghe road. 2 Bn EC moved from BECKE into 4 Co Camp at FORTEN HOEK. O1 & 4 C.3 B Church) arranged with D.E. 2nd Can. Divnl. Train refilling supply of fuel to our troops while in his area has breakdown of Co Camp.	
	6/6/16		Potatoes continue to come in abad condition. Cases are much torn. Complaints to the R.S.O. request D.D.T.S.T. both further potato supply for this division as we always had over 30 tons in store - Conference from Q.M. South K. R.F.O. re supply of rations received a letter repeating reports up unions not it considered that their officers were making harmony trouble.	
	7/6/16		Went oudson in from? Left - Overhauled and as units to not of Coy Camps for use of 9 th Se Byte while in Trenches at St Eloi,	Arthur, Capt SC

T2134. Wt. W708-776. 500000. 4/15. Sir J. C. & S.

WAR DIARY or INTELLIGENCE SUMMARY

Army Form C. 2118.

Place	Date	Hour	Summary of Events and Information	Remarks and references to Appendices
FLETRE.	8/6/16		Stn. Staff under orders for Canadian sector on — then recd. Cancel Bulldust head.	
	9/6/16		orders received at 11pm from G that the 76th Inf Bgde was to entrain tomorrow for 2nd Army. Trains are tomorrow by road and the morning 9 Rations issued on 13th twice. 20th K.R.R.S. 2 S.B Field Co.R.E Transport for entrain from 9th R Reds. Inf. Bgde from Appilly on 12 trained.	
	10/6/16		Brigade transport at 7:30am entraining entrainisation of Inf Bgde's Looking for 7th Div Inf Bgde. 7th Inf Bgde including Helpra 1st Yorkshire, 10th R.W.Fus. Transport battery 71 to Smiths, 1/7 R. Amsters v 2 R.AMC left by road at 11 am (Ruff) Transport touched with ration for 12 + 13 th road. Looking for night at Wennon Cabell. 8th Inf Bgde from Hulhmessen moved 9th Inf Bgde into Locre in Below circle touched 9th Inf Bgde Nature to Hulhmessen moving billets of 8 R Noble PR Bowen. No 3 Co M.C moved up to battle camp vacated by 14 Co as G.3.1 D 6.4 Sheet 28$ + New Co to be occupied Itres Camp on Sheerkim Corner. d.53	

Army Form C. 2118.

WAR DIARY
or
INTELLIGENCE SUMMARY.
(Erase heading not required.)

Instructions regarding War Diaries and Intelligence Summaries are contained in F. S. Regs., Part II. and the Staff Manual respectively. Title pages will be prepared in manuscript.

Place	Date	Hour	Summary of Events and Information	Remarks and references to Appendices
FLETRE	13/9/16		Supplies conv: 13th inst for 76th Bgde leaving Proven dumps at Proven depot this morning — No 2 Ammunition Column 76th Subgde. Etc known 2 sub sappers 8th Bullock tender for training area + Supply wagons 76 D Trunk Company return for train 13th inst. All attached units transferred to 9th D. Bgde for rations. Weather very hot mild	
	13/9/16		Amn ration indent for 314 In Bgde + RFA Lispon Singdy trades # for 76th Subgde drawing from St Omer Railhead from this morning. C 2 Amn Comps to B HOUSE - Rations but drawn on our 41350 rec'd on Ay W	
	14/9/16.		3317. Stores being a detail were (illegible) wh L + C – Raining all day. Reqts (illegible) for forage Opn. Also prated 2 to 21 HOUSE. Also L.O. 76th Subgde. – Orders received that remainder of fel Division move to training area from 17 Kinst. Sound sufficient letter/clothing to 30. 36. 9th & 5th Iv Kgte to lift in SSO Rec	

T2134. Wt. W708—776. 500000. 4/15. Sir J. C. & S.

Army Form C. 2118.

WAR DIARY
or
INTELLIGENCE SUMMARY.
(Erase heading not required.)

Instructions regarding War Diaries and Intelligence Summaries are contained in F. S. Regs., Part II. and the Staff Manual respectively. Title pages will be prepared in manuscript.

Place	Date	Hour	Summary of Events and Information	Remarks and references to Appendices
FLEURE	15/1/16		Arrangements made with DD of S & T 2nd Army that reinforcements for 9th & 16th Brigades Ammunition Columns WATTEN from reinforcing the 17th and that the 8th & 9th Suff's People at Caestre from 17th to 20th incl. Should DD of S/S & T. These fuel not written than on 17th. but to be issued on left in Drawing area by 15th Division - at 2:15pm. Arrived all Supply Officers & arrangements made for work. Arranged with Sub Director to return Chaliene ABC and with Sub Direct Sewin Station 1/ Gas Riving ABC to Buringham 17th inst. Staffed Supplymaker to our note on our system of Statistics - Heavy Rain during Morning ?	Khimire SSO

Army Form C. 2118.

WAR DIARY
or
INTELLIGENCE SUMMARY.
(Erase heading not required.)

Place	Date	Hour	Summary of Events and Information	Remarks and references to Appendices
FLETRE	16/5/16		Handed over Materiel for C&R. 8th K.R. Div. reports 5 th Corps. Minimum of Stock to next Indts handed over to SSO 24th Divn. Sent yrd at Bailleul containing 125 T.15 coal. 24 hrs. corke 33½ hrs wood, also Show Coal at Escelle handed over to SSO 24th Divn. — Coal General Williams Divn S & G rtd travel visit to be thorough. Coal issued at Escelle Indts ETO 1 G. Orders received from 8th Corps 20th K.R.R. 7 th Queen Batt. & Divnl Mortar School. 8th Divn from Infantry on 18th inst. Necessary arrangements made with SSO 50th Divn & Trawps Co. to draw temporary rations for 8th Corps for interval between 17/4/16 & 18/4/16. Trawps reporting at 2 pm for 9 th Ln. Bgds. —	
	17/5/16		8 th Ln. Rgds & 3 GASC Coys marches from Co. left by train this morning from Bailleul for training area. Train Hd. gro. left for training area at St. Martin. 3rd Echn RTM returned in line last night. Left for Staffing area which thorough from 8/10 to HSC. 3rd Echn. at Pickem. Weather fine, somewhat cold.	[signature]

T2184. Wt. W708–776. 500000. 4/15. Sir J. C. & S.

WAR DIARY
or
INTELLIGENCE SUMMARY
(Erase heading not required.)

Army Form C. 2118

Place	Date	Hour	Summary of Events and Information	Remarks and references to Appendices
ST Martin (Rimeux)	19/6/16		Lorries for divl. troops dumped at Staples this morning & Lorries packed up return for Lorries: 19th coming further. C.R.A. relief Lieutenants in bed over for tyrant chaip & Relieved by Cannonatem Brun stay. 1st W.Y. & 8th F. Hulme, Saturday Sec. 9th B. M. Curl's Strews Charlie c/i Col. Redvers G.R.E. Left Capts. My move in intercom Cobell. Capt Veal & Capt Ifrey to Captf Louvries under Taxfurl S. return this morn for Cowa, 19th dumped at Louvries. Cobell to duty. Return for Cowa, 19th was for 9th divn. Appx dumped at J 36 C.S.1. about 27 M.N.E. & training area. Nov to Counts in o MONNEOVE about 27 M.N.E.	
	M/M/16		tractors trans. Lorries returns for 28th dumped as ESQUERDES, details N.O.1G' Camp in training area. Lorries for Front D under Captl Veal dumped at WULVERDINGHE. aoua D.D.V.S.T. to inspected Comel W Capts from 10th & 50T for next three days. Weather cold, showery.	J Mt Cuncem Capt 550

WAR DIARY
INTELLIGENCE SUMMARY

Army Form C. 2118

Place	Date	Hour	Summary of Events and Information	Remarks and references to Appendices
St Martin	20/8/16		Group D made their return for Corps: 21Ch on arrival in training area, apart from Brigades Co' MC moved their billets. 8th Ln Regt, refitted in Details for our time today, after refitting at 8th Regt today. Pony transports left behind by 17th Divn, are not in very good condition. Horst CRA headquarters in refitting of forage. Weather fine warm.	
	21/8/16		8th Suff Regt'n continued in training area today - No 3 Co' Camp at HOULLE, owing at Q.18.a.3., Sheet 27A SE, returns for reinforcements 7th K.S.L.I. and BOISDINGHEM by 3 to this evening - Plenty of excellent Green forage still at present obtainable in this area. Weather fine cold	[signature] Capt SO

WAR DIARY
or
INTELLIGENCE SUMMARY

(Erase heading not required.)

Army Form C. 2118

Place	Date	Hour	Summary of Events and Information	Remarks and references to Appendices
ST MARTIN	22/4/16		Enemy have arrived that he received during last 3 days supply for the Brigades particularly noticeable — Telephoned Offices J.D.D. & J.J.J. 9nd Army men instructed to send D'Cault. this afternoon return 1st line. no travel after 10 hours — they came westwards from N.C.O. 91 yards.	
	23/4/16		20 hrs. Col. arrived 1 pm, clouds interviewed to discuss this afternoon. General visits has been unable to obtain and arrangements this morning. orders received to supply return. sound tests for 116 movements amount from Brine or S.R. int. tops of 50 men in. Offrs. Reclouded from D.A.O. accompanied to exhibits dump on roads with returns. He arranged for by the C.R.A. with Offrs. Inclusive Comm. J. Part, Capt Anderson O.O. 8th Infantry regt. today. Offrs inclups Comm. J. Part, R. Robinson R.O. 3rd Regt. Duel on S.O. Lt. Peirce R.O. 9th to Pte on R.O. 6th in Bgde. — Capt Hawkins from 33rd Divnl S. Col. the R.O. 9th in Bgde. to take effect from 24th inst., all abbreviations (except Col Anderson) taking heavy not during afternoon morning with low clouds & opticing.	J. Hawkins O.C.

WAR DIARY
or
INTELLIGENCE SUMMARY
(Erase heading not required.)

Army Form C. 2118

Place	Date	Hour	Summary of Events and Information	Remarks and references to Appendices
SWARTKOP	22/8/14		Letters for NCO Recruits drawn with 3.B. Weather fine.	
	23/8/14		Attended meeting in orderly room of O.C. Train Companies re move. Hopes now returned to proceed. Weather fine.	
	24/8/14		30 years men returned to civilians. Raining part of day.	

WAR DIARY
or
INTELLIGENCE SUMMARY

Army Form C. 2118

Place	Date	Hour	Summary of Events and Information	Remarks and references to Appendices
St Martin 27.6.16			Meeting of all train officers in orderly room at 10.30 am to discuss work. — Individuals at 5.30 to listen to an lecture on 1192.50 Iron & steel Notional fuze by M. Van den Bernatt. Cable laid on 31/3/16 for 5 cable pits found rough ground. R.O.E. auth. — ord. Wealth. Delivered 3110 K from forge (S.F. & 2nd Army) 8 S.F. ref. primers amm... Estimate delivered 3110 K from forge 5.F/r a conference of S & F.50 Main E. front after at 5pm = 1192. 50 Fr. Weather real with fine rain	
28/6/16			The Germans from today in reply known notice known rumour, denote repelling known for all posts today in anticipation of known. St Pierre R.O. quiet the returned from leave. weather was between 7am & 10 am afternoon fine. 6 known Provisions under rifle known from 17/16	
29/6/16			6 oz. potatoes & .075 pounds onions issued in addition to ordinary from today also Ports. theor. 3 known (B) known, 3 in. battalion opening divers suffer from 21 Army auxiliary artillery training continuing.	

Army Form C. 2118

WAR DIARY
or
INTELLIGENCE SUMMARY
(Erase heading not required.)

Instructions regarding War Diaries and Intelligence Summaries are contained in F. S. Regs., Part II. and the Staff Manual respectively. Title Pages will be prepared in manuscript.

Place	Date	Hour	Summary of Events and Information	Remarks and references to Appendices
St Martin	30/8/16		Instructed Coy to settle in the evening to farmers for forage & potatoes — also Officers in reserve (weather good)	[initials]

WAR DIARY
or
INTELLIGENCE SUMMARY.
(Erase heading not required.)

Army Form C. 2118.

S.O. 3rd Div¹ Troops

Place	Date	Hour	Summary of Events and Information	Remarks and references to Appendices
Flêtre	June 1		Lorries arrive 8.30 a.m. refilling 9 a.m. & finished 10.15 a.m. Thirty one units are now being fed.	
"	" 2		Routine as usual. Sian waggons go to Steenvoorde for 5000 Kilos green forage.	
"	" 3		Routine as usual.	
"	" 4		Routine as usual. After dump the suffy section is split into two, Capt. Stokes going to OUDERDOM with one half its portion, the gunners. I am remaining at FLETRE refreshing the remaining ten units of Sin. Suffy.	
"	" 5		Sin refilling, on FLETRE & on OUDERDOM. The 107 Batt. again after being two nights at STEENVOORDE on a firing school, & are returned by Capt. Stokes. Forty men left behind by the Zeppelin are returned at FLETRE.	
"	" 6		Routine as usual.	
"	" 7		Routine as usual.	
"	" 8		Routine as usual. The forty men taken flight by us leave.	
"	" 9		Routine as usual. Capt. Stokes changed his billet on the 6th & camp near RENINGHELST, on ABEELE St Julien road, refilling joint POPERINGE WESTOUTRE road.	

WAR DIARY or INTELLIGENCE SUMMARY

Army Form C. 2118.

Place	Date	Hour	Summary of Events and Information	Remarks and references to Appendices
Stka.	June 10		Routine as usual. Lies waggons go to BAILLEUL. 9 R. platoon, one of STEENVOORDE. 9 gun groups. Lieut. Stobo is now drawing water from spring for day. First he is purchasing 9 R. gate of OUDERDOM.	
	" 11		Routine as usual.	
	" 12		Routine as usual. 23rd Regt H.Q. return came to FLETRE & one sent on to Cfr. Stobo	
	" 13		Routine as usual.	
	" 14		Routine as usual.	
	" 15		Routine as usual. A/G Refilling 9 Tpk came from Cpr. Stobo, & Lieut. Parker who came from me at FLETRE.	
	" 16		Refilling for last time at FLETRE & RENINGHELST, both sections march out in afternoon & night at STAPLE where they billet for the night.	
Staple	" 17		Horses bonded down & stay one night at STAPLE unloading 6.30am, refilling 23 unds 8am. Finish at 10am & re-eqt R.O. & 23rd Regt H.Q. two men left behind with three others who report they arrived 7.30pm & were returned. The Coy moved out 10.30am & marched to ESQUELBECQ.	S.O. & Anct July 88

Army Form C. 2118.

WAR DIARY
or
INTELLIGENCE SUMMARY.
(Erase heading not required.)

Instructions regarding War Diaries and Intelligence Summaries are contained in F. S. Regs., Part II. and the Staff Manual respectively. Title pages will be prepared in manuscript.

Place	Date	Hour	Summary of Events and Information	Remarks and references to Appendices
Esquerdes	18th		Refilling ESQUERDES, lorries arrived 7.15 am, refilling 8.30 am, back from unit returned.	
"	19		Lorries arrived 8 am refilling 8.30 am.	
"	20		Routine as usual. Chester R.E. returned for four km.	
"	21		Routine as usual. Truck for unit returned.	
"	22		Routine as usual.	
"	23		Routine as usual.	
"	24		Routine as usual.	
"	25		Routine as usual.	
"	26		Routine as usual.	
"	27		Routine as usual.	
"	28		Routine as usual as runway. A second refilling in afternoon lorries arrived 2.25 pm, refilling 3.15 pm. 2 motion jacked on waggon & night.	
"	29		Oxygen delivery return, refilling taken place 3.30 pm.	
"	30		Routine as yesterday.	

WAR DIARY or INTELLIGENCE SUMMARY

Army Form C. 2118.

S.O. 8TH INF BDE

S.O. 8th [signature] Lloyd Bell

Place	Date	Hour	Summary of Events and Information	Remarks and references to Appendices
In the Field	1.6.16.		1 omi arrived 8.15. Rifles 9 A.M. Over 9.35 A.M. Visit with and field everything correct. Some complaints received from units regarding had condition of issued milk, that in any case in Potatoes unfit for consumption. New Zealand Bread.	
	2.6.16		1 omi arrived 8.15. Rifles 9 A.M. Over 9.40 A.M. Ten thousand Kilos Potatoes received. Cheshire Field Coy/pay. R.E. returned for rest time.	
	3.6.16		1 omi arrived 8.15. Rifles 9 A.M. Over 9.15. Green Fodder, ordered to staff reserve HQs Ration, Cut 30m to 800 kilos per diem.	
	4.6.16		1 omi arrived 8.15. Rifles 8.45. Over 9.30. Tobacco 155 ore. Issued for Engr oil received. Brigade strength at the end of the week All Ranks 3660 Strs 140 L.D. 277 Obs 19 / 122	

Rgt. A. Lieut. Capt. RR
S.O. 8 Inf Bde

Army Form C. 2118.

WAR DIARY
or
INTELLIGENCE SUMMARY
(Erase heading not required.)

Place	Date	Hour	Summary of Events and Information	Remarks and references to Appendices
In the Field	5/6/16		Lorries arrived 8.15. Rifles 8.45. Other 9.20. Weather cold and showery. Visit all units and find everything correct.	
	6/6/16	8.15	Lorries arrived 8.15. Rifles 8.45. Other 9.20. Weather 500 Kilos straw drawn from Store and issued as usual at the rate of	
	7/6/16		Lorries arrived 8.15 am. Rifles 8.45. Other 9.25. From Hospital Kilos Potatoes received from Railhead. Company standing by in rear of a Coy.	
	8/6/16		Lorries arrived 8.15am. Rifles 8.45. Other 9.20. 2nd Batn. The 18th of K.R.R. and 5th Corps Q.S astroid by the Ungle. No truth of New Zealand Corpuel Week received. Take anem a that cost the several pounds cost to each & Suck my Bread Lateral being used for Sacks.	

for Robert Cutt III
Q Offg Lt. Col.

Army Form C. 2118.

WAR DIARY
or
INTELLIGENCE SUMMARY
(Erase heading not required.)

Instructions regarding War Diaries and Intelligence Summaries are contained in F. S. Regs., Part II. and the Staff Manual respectively. Title Pages will be prepared in manuscript.

Place	Date	Hour	Summary of Events and Information	Remarks and references to Appendices
In the Field	9/6/16		Lorries arrive 8.15 Rafa 8.45 over 9.15am Kat sweres unld and find everything correct. Weather still changeable.	
	10/6/16		Lorries arrive 8.15 Rafa 8.45 over 9.20 Rodhe & unl	
	11/6/16		Lorries arrive 8.15 Rafa 8.45 over 9.30am Totams 234	
			Reports Strength to El Shiria HQ 114 / All Ranks 3807 / K.O. 289 / NR 19 / Road Mem 12	
			The company occupied over 2pm men oft Refilly	
	12/6/16		Lorries arrive 7.45 Rafa 8.25 over 9.10 am Refilly Coke & Charcoal arrived. Health very bad, rain all day. Arrangement made for the supply of pine-folds with local contracts	

K.M. Ashcroft Capt RE
OC 248 RE Co

Army Form C. 2118.

WAR DIARY
or
INTELLIGENCE SUMMARY
(Erase heading not required.)

Place	Date	Hour	Summary of Events and Information	Remarks and references to Appendices
In the Field	13/6/16		Lonui arrive 7.45 AM Refer 8.25 ore 9.10. Patrols sent to the old camp. The K.R.R. again attacked & rather two 12½" but into the 61st Corps R.E. tents. Not changed Anaysteh and will Camden Dinner Pa Corl	
	14/6/16		Lonui arrive 7.45 AM Refer 8.25 ore 9.10. Attacked, by a hvy 45+ of Runn, gave. This + according used from Reserve left to hand. Some 5.Six Gallery Run with 2 D. Heavy gun again fell during the night Rained with old fort weight count.	
	15/6/16		Lonui arrive. 7.45. AM Refer 10.30 AM ore 11g.15 AM ace Offic weight out checked. The Hay orter was good + the considerably indirect. The fuel dent order was for the display	KAlubery Capt. ?th g.o.?/?

2449 Wt. W14957/M90 750,000 1/16 J.B.C. & A. Forms/C.2118/12.

WAR DIARY
or
INTELLIGENCE SUMMARY

(Erase heading not required.)

Army Form C. 2118.

Place	Date	Hour	Summary of Events and Information	Remarks and references to Appendices
In the Field	16/6/16		Lewis arrive 7.15 AM. Rifles 8.25 over 9.15 AM. The 56th Corps R.E. returned by me on that last time they 451 of Rum give triple milk to the Bryan beatles gun. Three thousand fit fingered Kilos potatoes drawn per store.	
	17/6/16		Lewis arrive 7.45 AM. Rifles 8.25 over 9.15 AM. The 20th Bn Kings Royal Rifle Corps without by me filled out one Lewis Range H.G. beatle gun.	
	18/6/16		Lewis arrive 7.45 AM. Rifles 8.25 over 9.15 AM. Routine as usual.	
	19/6/16		Lewis arrive 7.45 AM. Rifles 8.25 over 9.15 AM. Arranged light to have two Dumps on the 2nd B Inst.	# 18th Inst
			Brigade Strength at the end of the week *	

Officers 40 Rank and file 2724 Animals L.D. 284 R.H. 30 R.B. 30 In all Allan G. Stephens Capt/Att 2-0 2nd B.Co

2449 Wt. W14957/M90 750,000 1/16 J.B.C. & A. Form/C.2118/12.

Army Form C. 2118.

WAR DIARY
or
INTELLIGENCE SUMMARY
(Erase heading not required.)

Instructions regarding War Diaries and Intelligence Summaries are contained in F. S. Regs, Part II and the Staff Manual respectively. Title Pages will be prepared in manuscript.

Place	Date	Hour	Summary of Events and Information	Remarks and references to Appendices
In the Field	20.6.16		Lorries arrived 7.45. Rifles 8.245 AM. Rifles sent time in old area. Two Rifles Forage which Lts. to water the Batts. to leave at were held on the early hrs.	
	21.6.16		Lorries arrived 2 P.M. Rifles 2.20. over 1 P.M. over arrangement Regt. to hand over supplies stores. The 24th Rn Canadian taking over, all Cooks and Clerical not always drawn. The 24th Division taking over Potatoes. So Dinnt took place on the date. The Company over etc in area. Arrangement made re. supplies of coal, Green Forage and Potatoes. less. Site of Rifles cleaned.	
	22.6.16		Lorries arrived 8 A.M. Rifles 8.30. All the Units Stffs wagon had not arrived Rifles delayed Stffs to est as each Stffs wagon arrived. Lieut A.C. ROBINSON takes over duties of Stffs Officer. C.H.B. W. Johnson 2nd Lt. R.A.	

WAR DIARY
or
INTELLIGENCE SUMMARY

(Erase heading not required.)

Army Form C. 2118.

Place	Date	Hour	Summary of Events and Information	Remarks and references to Appendices
In the field	23/6/16		Lorries arrived 8 a.m. Weather warm.	
	24/6/16		Lorries arrived 8 a.m. Capt. A.C. Pearce took over duties of Require Camp Officer.	
	25/6/16		Lt. Col. 3rd Bn., Lt. Col. 3rd Jn. R.E., 3rd Signal Co., Advanced M.T. Workshop, M Cable Section, 51 Mobile Vet. Section, & Field Ambulance ACG'd by on today for first time. Jemadar Singh - All Ranks Strn. 1190 L.D. Pts. Small Mnls. #603 145 608 20 12	
	26/6/16		Routine as usual.	
	27/6/16		Attended meeting at Rlwy. Bazar 4 p.m. with regard to evening wear.	
	28/6/16		Attended meeting of Br. Mnltn. at Pete. Hsp.	
	29/6/16		War dumps today - 8 a.m. & 3 p.m. Lorries arrived 3 p.m. Postal arriv.	
	30/6/16		Lorries arrived 3 p.m. Potatoes delivered to lorries as ordinary commodity. Ret. Stay/k. All Ranks Strn. 1190 L.D. L/D Sml. Mnls. 168 578 20 17 POST	

A.W. Clinton Lieut.
S.O. 82 Bgd. Inf. Aud.

So.92ⁿᵈ Inf Bde

Army Form C. 2118.

S.O. 9th L.F. Bde

WAR DIARY
or
INTELLIGENCE SUMMARY

(Erase heading not required.)

Instructions regarding War Diaries and Intelligence Summaries are contained in F.S. Regs., Part II. and the Staff Manual respectively. Title pages will be prepared in manuscript.

Place	Date	Hour	Summary of Events and Information	Remarks and references to Appendices
METEREN	31-5-16		Training resumes 6.30 am. Offended to leave by J.O. Refill commences 8.30 am. All nerves on prepfl including free coffee gelsh speak rage allee. Repeh furtes 7.30 Other ranks to Genoual	
"	1-6-16		Training resumes 8.10 am. Offended to leave by 8.35 Refill commences 9.10 am. Routine as usual	
"	2-6-16		Routine of normal as usual	
"	3-6-16		Routine as usual	
"	4-6-16		Routine as usual. The Res. relive to move at 4 hours notice.	
WESTOUTRE	5-6-16		Training resumes at working parties. OS were at 8.30 am. Offended to leave by P.S.B. Refill commences 9.0 am. Lunaris unusual actively field eng table + specfuly attached with supplies to waffen. No 3 & 4 Coy releaving supplies. Little moving of the normal shft will be no move to Condh cattle. Coy. Mess at M. and all met is located anua. RENINGHELST	

T2134. Wt. W708-776. 500/000. 4/15. Sir J.C. & S.

Army Form C. 2118.

WAR DIARY
or
INTELLIGENCE SUMMARY.
(Erase heading not required.)

S.O. 9th Bde.

Instructions regarding War Diaries and Intelligence Summaries are contained in F. S. Regs., Part II. and the Staff Manual respectively. Title pages will be prepared in manuscript.

Place	Date	Hour	Summary of Events and Information	Remarks and references to Appendices
WESTOUTRE	6-6-16		Lamies opens 5 p.m. Commences 8.35 am. Offloaded Calais 8.30pm. Troughs as usual. Relieving parties of 7.30 pm.	
"	7-6-16		Lorries arrives 7.45 am. Route as usual	
"	8-6-16		Route as usual	
"	9-6-16		Route as usual	
"	10-6-16		Route as usual	
SPAEXEN	11-6-16		Lorries arrives at usual time. Marched from Westoutre all roads as usual, halted. Relay finished 9 am. Supplies (officers to work in Chateau Camp) moved to CHAEXEN 8.6 pm.	
"	12-6-16		Lorries arrives 8.10 am. Offloaded Calais by 8.35 am. Lorries away 8.45 am. Lorries arrived with guns from Kittstown. Retour finished 9.30 am. Retour amplies (A/A to 10th E.) takes two Battrs. to Ray'd Carvalier amplies. Afterwards supplies a/a of Left Batts. in KEMMEL Sector. Other system as usual.	

M Wilstone
Captain

WAR DIARY
or
INTELLIGENCE SUMMARY.
(Erase heading not required.)

Army Form C. 2118.

Remarks and references to Appendices: S.O.9 & Appx

Place	Date	Hour	Summary of Events and Information	Remarks
SHAEXEM	13-6-16		Aeroplanes arrives 8.15 a.m. Offloaded order by 8.45 a.m. Petrolling commenced 8.50. All lines as usual/probably one-fold attack negotiable. Caplin a/c reported Ceaseing firing 9.35 m J. Otter + orderlies as usual	
"	14-6-16		Routine normal. All commands, tanks & wing regts as above as aspect demands from base. All ought to first to be attempted at present	
"	15-6-16		Routine as usual	
"	16-6-16		Aeroplane arrives 8.15 a.m. Petrol filled, repeating 2.6 finished 9.30 a.m. Aeroplane offloaded by 9.30. Refuelling commenced 9.45. All wanes a usual. Including piece/parts of any wires pocketage fitting. All complete. Supply Sergeant reported to Comd off Inf B.M.R.	
"	17-6-16		Company proceeded to II Army lorry arrives by train	2nd Lieut Capt R.E.

Army Form C. 2118.

S.O. 9th [?]

WAR DIARY
or
INTELLIGENCE SUMMARY.
(Erase heading not required.)

Instructions regarding War Diaries and Intelligence
Summaries are contained in F. S. Regs., Part II.
and the Staff Manual respectively. Title pages
will be prepared in manuscript.

Place	Date	Hour	Summary of Events and Information	Remarks and references to Appendices
MONTRÉCOURT (MORDAUQUES)	18-6-16		Bombing commences 8.15 a.m. Shrapnel taken by 8.45 a.m. Artillery commences 9.0 a.m. All again no rifle sights reported. Rifles: Rifle fires 9.40 a.m. Otherwise nothing exceptional	
"	19-6-16		Routine as above also group folder issued.	
"	20-6-16		Routine as usual.	
"	21-6-16		Routine as usual.	
"	22-6-16		Lewis gunners' course 7.45 a.m. Rifle drill at 8.30 a.m. all ranks on usual club drill group meetings.	
"	23-6-16		Routine as usual excepting absences.	
"	24-6-16		Routine as before.	
"	25-6-16		Bombing commences 8.15 a.m. Routine as usual	
"	26-6-16		Routine as usual.	O W Kerl Capt H.C.

WAR DIARY
or
INTELLIGENCE SUMMARY.
(Erase heading not required.)

Army Form C. 2118.

S.O. 9th Inf Bde.

Place	Date	Hour	Summary of Events and Information	Remarks and references to Appendices
MONNECOVE (NORDAUSQUES)	27-6-16		Lorries arrives 8.0am. Offloaded Jelem by 8.30am. Relief commences 8.35am. All lines to move including potatoes & green fodder. Refilling finishes 9.15am.	
"	28-6-16		1st refilling no moved horses arrives at 2nd refilling at 2.45 pm. Refilling finishes 3.45pm. Supply vehicles to company lines.	
"	29-6-16		Supplies to coy at 30 am. R. Lilly commences 3.30pm. moved arrives 3.0pm. R. Lilly commences 3.30pm. moved away. Jelem to company lines. Covered	

E M Loul
Capt att
CO 9th Inf Bde

S.O. 76TH INF. BDE

Army Form C. 2118.

WAR DIARY
or
INTELLIGENCE SUMMARY.
(Erase heading not required.)

Instructions regarding War Diaries and Intelligence Summaries are contained in F.S. Regs., Part II. and the Staff Manual respectively. Title pages will be prepared in manuscript.

Place	Date	Hour	Summary of Events and Information	Remarks and references to Appendices
EECKE	Q27b 2.9 R.P. Q21b 5.2			
	Thursday 1/6/16		Lorries arrive 8am – Refilling 8.45am – Visited Bullring 1st Gordons Then, 76 Bde Machine Gun Coy & 1/1 E Riding R.E. – 100% Place received for destruction –	
	Friday 2/6/16		Routine as usual.	
	Saturday 3/6/16		Visited Units of Brigade Group – 7 Field Ambulance, 8 Kings Own Pioneers & Coy Supplies – Shrinkage of Day's issues of 1st Royal Scots kept for consumption	
	Sunday 4/6/16		Orders received of Brigade to move forward this am at present occupied by 9th Brigade – The Brigade as a whole moving tomorrow 5/6/16 with the exception of 2nd Suffolks who are moving tonight – Bns 3rd Bn Royal Scots moved tonight & billeted in "Ango" Jolin 51 – Trans Battery moves to LOCRE tonight – Orders rec'd from Train Hqrs for supplying on 5th to Coy marked by A Coy III D.T. at X 4 C (cross roads) on METEREN — SCHAEKKEN road (Anat 27) Refilling Pourdrock X 4 C.2 — (Sheet 27)	
	Monday 5/6/16		See on	

J.M. Plunkett, Lieut. O.S.
to 76th Supplies

T2131. Wt. W708—776. 500000. 4/15. Sir J. C. & S.

Army Form C. 2118.

WAR DIARY
or
INTELLIGENCE SUMMARY.
(Erase heading not required.)

Army reg. 76 W. Diaries and Intelligence
Summaries are contained in F.S. Regs., Part II
and the Staff Manual respectively. Title pages
will be prepared in manuscript.

Place	Date	Hour	Summary of Events and Information	Remarks and references to Appendices
	Monday 5/6/16		After refilling dump — moved from camp in orchard above Sw Toppen (the 3rd Battn) and to LOCRE — the remaining dump refilled up & gun moved with Bry from area — Location found in new area 76. Bde MGs Sheet 27 X.17 c.4.4. 8 Bty Gun. X.10.c.24. 102 Rawelsd. X.17.a.31. 76 Bde MGun. 7.M Battery X.1.d.32. 1st Gordons Sheet 28.S.76.6.4. 2 Suffolk Regt LOCRE. —	
	Tuesday 6/6/16		From 8.10 am Repld gun — All Ambulances yesterday on 34 mm (water) & Suffolks fed by Sw trop at FLETRE. — Refill T.M. K Guns (19 VDR) for bad time this time having been Hauptmann & Sine troop at FLETRE — 7th Field Ambulances (CHEEKS) & 142 Field Ambulance (1603 WAS RAIDED) returned returning from new area — Indeed that the Suffolks Gun nearly power on our our whole G.S. wallies as I came from locre rain which fell during yesterday evening — It was walking my front hippo that Brae Greaney & new Bde all day — there two permanent Shelter in new Refilling Point	

[signature]
76 Bde Mar

Army Form C. 2118.

WAR DIARY
or
INTELLIGENCE SUMMARY.
(Erase heading not required.)

Instructions regarding War Diaries and Intelligence
Summaries are contained in F. S. Regs., Part II.
and the Staff Manual respectively. Title pages
will be prepared in manuscript.

Place	Date	Hour	Summary of Events and Information	Remarks and references to Appendices
(M) FONTAINE HOUCK + H.C. (from Rouen) Rifling Point X 4 c 2 -	Wednesday 7/6/16		4 horse fatalities received from outlying Hrs arrived with us today. Coy about 130 per cent to war. Visited 1st Gordons Hrs 10th R Welsh Fusrs & 8 Kings Own Regt. Lorries & 13 am right 9 am. Routine as usual. Visited Gardens. Ordered fresh four for forage received during period.	
	Thursday 8/6/16		Lee in addition General Units. Siv Grande School, Labour Coy, Kr. Routine as usual.	
	Friday 9/6/16		I am received a rifling front out wardrobe. She a Stafford wearing four enemy wounds. Visited 7th Rd. Machine Gun Coy. The details (34 men) from Last Suffolks I heard required their third car wife. I therefore paid them from various in the morning.	
	Saturday 10/6/16		Lorries farm (arr at 8.30) Rifle at 9. Pt Whitley having been invalided yesterday was sick & Pt Starr issued meal in his place. Report re Sacks car & SSD, & re Stockyard & Forage & Adjutant. Manor Routine.	

Withhurst L.M.C.
Do 176th Sept ree

Army Form C. 2118.

WAR DIARY
or
INTELLIGENCE SUMMARY.
(Erase heading not required.)

S.O. 76th Inf Bde

Place	Date	Hour	Summary of Events and Information	Remarks and references to Appendices
X 4 C 4.4 FONTAINE HOUCK Sunday	11/6/16		Order received from S.O. that Brigade were not today to leaving area. N. 7. St Omer - All Units of Bge move up 8 Rags Ammn Places & Dentifripes leave at 11 am tomorrow. - Other units leaving at 1 pm and in rear - 76 Bde H.Q. 10 R. Welsh. Leave + 1 pm, Green HR, 76 Bde M. Gun Coy + T.M. Bty, + 2 Coy 15th mens & Warners. Copper Staling fromight - 4th Rance sent in charge of trunks + g. greed. I have detailed by 9 Wars for duty with the 3 Bns left behind. Arrangements made with S.O. for supplies on their march. He sent out to Warners Copper for refilling on morning of 12th. Supplies (for enough?) arrive together tonight. 14 6. am + 19 7 West's 1/Col. 11th - Lt Colman reland. 14 6. am + 19 7 West's 1/Col. as Sanitary Lectr. Jas from Coy R.S. for to Sanitary Beat. transferred to g. R. Self repelling from 15th ind. - Lt SL Field Ambee transferred from 8th Bde - Attached	

M Major CGS
76 Inf Bde

WAR DIARY
or
INTELLIGENCE SUMMARY.
(Erase heading not required.)

Army Form C. 2118

Instructions regarding War Diaries and Intelligence Summaries are contained in F. S. Regs., Part II. and the Staff Manual respectively. Title pages will be prepared in manuscript.

Place	Date	Hour	Summary of Events and Information	Remarks and references to Appendices
	Sunday 13/6/16		Men after filling up & getting their own rations & slopps in old arm- drew over stores & supply wagons by rail. Supply wagons arrived by rail at the hut lines. Checked 86 slopps to C. Keep. Own contingent of supplies to be delivered to the respective companies in lieu of travelling loaded on then - theory supply wagons will be enabled to proceed immediately after drawing stores & filling lists & free of waiting for consumption 14th.	
	Monday 14/6/16		Supply leeks (less 4 men supply tender) X' Pearce - right Unit - of Bde less staff officer & Reap Coy at Watheres opened - after departure of keep proceed to Merlancourt near Wateth where bag station at 2 P.M. + got rations. Leave at 11.45 having entrained supplies & slopps for I. Lot Officer at 5.30 p.m. Then left for 50 & would supply. W.M. Loek Lt. Col.

T2131. Wt. W708—776. 500000. 4/15.   Sir J. C. & S.

WAR DIARY
or
INTELLIGENCE SUMMARY
(Erase heading not required.)

Army Form C. 2118.

Place	Date	Hour	Summary of Events and Information	Remarks and references to Appendices
	Monday 12/6/16 Tues. 13/6/16		Wagons of R.E. & Cav. Inf. arrived at R.H.S. Lumbres at 11am and 13th & after drawing stores supply to HOULLE, the latter being the camp of M. Roy. Rifle Brigade in Square at Houlle opposite Church, where Hauts Som. Transport was 6 H.S. away. R.E. Co., Anderson acting as Supply Officer return myself R. Co. St Omer — Servants & for supplies each night in billets for the Signallers on R.B.'s & Han. rest & H.Anderson etc. & Ken de etoune & turn to R.S.O. St Omer.	
HOULLE	Wed. 14/6/16		R.S.O. St Omer closed. No wire June & Front Wg &c. down. No Candle, Sharp, &c, &c (Cats vacation) & no despatch clerks without M.O. Artifice Rations as usual — Apr. 33/3 forwarded by message from H.Anderson & Co. via Supp'y Chain. World by S.Co. III Divn.	
	Thurs 15/6/16		Expected all amounts arriving & anything front forwarded round to O.C. 171 Divn Train by D.R.L.S. — Startys gone in following order Maj. 1st Meat & Potatoes	

H.H.Hawkes Lt RASC

WAR DIARY
or
INTELLIGENCE SUMMARY.
(Erase heading not required.)

Army Form C. 2118.

Place	Date	Hour	Summary of Events and Information	Remarks and references to Appendices
HOULLE	Friday 16/6/16		Routine as usual — No issue of Lime Tins made with L/Wgs —	
	Sat'y 17/6/16		Semame forwarded to S.T.Co. for replying water station in 17a. Last day of receiving supplies from S.T.Co. — Two Lacks of Sugar which appeared Short were being weighed were found to weigh Short by 13 lbs total loss one — Complaint forwarded to D.S.O.	
	Sunday 18/6/16		Supplies received from Watten railhead. In addition to ordinary kits signed every H.Q. 3 Sn. 2 Advance M.P. Winter, 3 Sn Ordnance 3 Signed Coy. R.E. & Sir J. French School	
	Monday 19/6/16		Routine as usual	
	Tuesd 20/6/16		Chicks & Units of Adv. Remp Steel at Str Store as laid out. No supp's issued.	
	Wed 21/6/16		No further issue — Routine as usual — Baths on 7 Bn. & 81/8/...	
	Thursd 22/6/16		Issue received (Colony)	
	Friday 23/6/16		Units Indents for Stores (7 Sn: Bottles intoxicating bills for Sm) forage	
	Saturday 24/6/16		Routine as usual — Attended as member of Court of Enquiry re: chalk of No. 3rd ... P.S.C. at Eggerden	

J.P. Murray Major
OC 76th Engineers

WAR DIARY
or
INTELLIGENCE SUMMARY.
(Erase heading not required.)

Army Form C. 2118.

Instructions regarding War Diaries and Intelligence Summaries are contained in F. S. Regs., Part II. and the Staff Manual respectively. Title pages will be prepared in manuscript.

Place	Date	Hour	Summary of Events and Information	Remarks and references to Appendices
HOULLE	Sunday 25/6/16		Divine Service G Res Corps — Australian Tom arrived — arms along the Coutts received in Evan G.and when 3 P.M. — Australian gun gun	
	Monday 26/6/16		for review — These units G.Res. F.M. who are very anxious the when the stood review G Brit F.M. rode the lines G.am —	
	Tuesday 27/6/16		Attended H.Qn. 11" D & I the letter regarding forthcoming move by O.C. Train — & later as Brigade H.Qrs. discussed D. Mvr. G. Brigade to O.C. Train made suggestions to facilitate supply work when on the move — It suggested that in lieu G rations being carried for midnight — midnight the D.m should hold up a portion G cover the following days breakfast then in future making supplies last from midday Tuesday —	
	Wednesday 28/6/16		Refill as usual at 8.45 & Train start from present time 3 p.m. refilling 3.45 Leave G. Port G. Benne (3 men & 1 off.) arrive at the refilling —	
	Thursday 29/6/16		Levin 3 pm refilling 3.45 Leave G. Benne (lays) recovered from Leave 3 pm refilling leave (whitson week)	
	Friday 30/6/16		Levin 3 pm — Totals received for Rations to hand G. arrive G3 daily Brnnes (supplemented by Local Purchase) an extra G4 days with who coming — One sergt & 2 recruits as reserve Inspected	

W.1131. W.1708—276. 500,000. 7/15. Sir J.C. & S.

3rd Division
War Diaries
Divisional Train
S. S. O.

July to 31st December
1916

WAR DIARY or INTELLIGENCE SUMMARY

Army Form C. 2118

SSO W Division
SSO 3rd Division

Place	Date	Hour	Summary of Events and Information	Remarks and references to Appendices
St Omer	1/7/16		Orders received at 2.20 a.m. that the Divn was to proceed by train to 4th Army area. First train leaving at 10.17 a.m. Horses were up captains for Divn. Breakfast for the 3 Brigades warning both left this morning for Divn. Sandwich supplied in friends of moves per Canteen. Sandwiths supplied to all the RE's & the Field Ambulance trains & full advance party to went with an advance party and M.T.B.'s the units and returned with unopened rations. Brigades returned & field day in S. wagons. Hd Tps returns & field out repelling points & blue Capt Peck left at 11.10 a.m. that units in morning in various were informed at detraining stations i.e. Candas & Doullens, 3.S.W. Kemps want & Platoon & arrived at Doullens with 3.S.W. Kemps and S.Col. afternoon inspected repelling points informing O.C. Col. 2nd S.O. Ret In Ridge on Reserve. Initiative for officer at Huescourt. (Col Cameron John Silverton)	VII

Army Form C 2118

WAR DIARY
or
INTELLIGENCE SUMMARY
(Erase heading not required.)

Instructions regarding War Diaries and Intelligence Summaries are contained in F.S. Regs., Part II. and the Staff Manual respectively. Title Pages will be prepared in manuscript.

Place	Date	Hour	Summary of Events and Information	Remarks and references to Appendices
HEUDECOURT	27/7/16		Informed Office Relations Officer ceased in his area & refused from to keep news & Copies to Divisions of troops available. Divisions troops located at Cauves. Visited all Divisions - Supply Officers - all under fresh orders before coming to report Officers for fuel indicated by D. Col where in charge to divisions. No Petrol. It was necessary for D. Col Supply personnel on Vignacourt advance refilling was made at 7.30pm. Divn HQrs moved to BOISBERGUES - heavy fire occurred.	
BOISBERGUES	27/7/16		Ordered refill at 6.30 am that Divn wanted. Moved to Vignacourt area - 9 waggon workshop personnel work train &c. @ 7 pm Petrol filled at MAHOURS, 8th Regt at FLESSELLS, 9th Regt at CHARLES T VIGNACOURT. RA at FINCOURT- Capt Hodges absent all day & two workshop at Boisbergues 19th H.T. RES Capt Hodges failed to pick up their lorries & bring this lorries chain Division - ineluded awaiting orders to advance - refilling at 7.30pm lost at FLESSELLS	Fletcher Mention five.

1875 Wt. W593/826 1,000,000 4/15 J.B.C. & A. A.D.S.S./Forms/C. 2118.

WAR DIARY
or
INTELLIGENCE SUMMARY

(Erase heading not required.)

Army Form C. 2118

Place	Date	Hour	Summary of Events and Information	Remarks and references to Appendices
FLESSELLES	4/7/16		Orders received at 10.15am that the Division will move at 5.30pm to Amiens area - Group system to be temporary. Enemy aeroplanes over during the afternoon - fired on by 50p's return. TMAC will rejoin 16th Division - XXIIth Bde. Rifles to COISY, 8th Bde. Rifles to FLIXECOURT, & 9th Bde. Rifles & 19th Bde. to HALLOY & CORBIE. Ammunition Column to DOMART S. POULAINVILLE – Bund situated Hdqrs. refitting. Rifled at 3 pm n heavy rain (and malaprete) in front of 5 Col. Horse artillery trenches by O.C. T 30 Battery KROO (revers), on the Somme day then dropped also with K.R.Roc (revers), attached to Heavy Group dropping near Querieu from A.E Battery (see past)	
CORBIE	5/7/16		Supplies dumped at 3 am Enemy motor transport moving this morning will worth of 4pm bought captured. 8th Bde Rifles, him R.F.A to To Toe Thunder Section to CORNET. VAUX - 9th Bde. him R.F.A & Section D.M.C. to Dedion FRANVILLERS LAHOUSSAYE. 76th Bde. Rifles lines R.F.A moved to CORBIE this afternoon. 500 men of Ireland batn went to Corbie this evening with rations for this unit refilled at Corbie this evening wounded men to Tomorrow by horse transport at 3 am. Tomorrow morning at L.C.3.8 (Gravelines) train to Etrevinnes Brigadier (?) weather fine	

WAR DIARY
or
INTELLIGENCE SUMMARY
(Erase heading not required.)

Army Form C. 2118

Place	Date	Hour	Summary of Events and Information	Remarks and references to Appendices
CORBIE	6/7/16		Lt. Col. Berry left for England today. Major Traill from [illegible] Division taking his command of this train. Transport from Front Trenches supplies were brought by horse transport & dumped on a siding near 3 [illegible] dump. Capt. Miller in charge — Brown flour over its dump at front. Went round the changed bivouacs for preparedness of burial.	
	7/7/16		To the strand changes this morning — leaving horse during daylight. 7th D. Reps. relieve 33rd Reps. in upper section. Refilling or rushes to [illegible] horse transport. Supplies are [illegible] changed in [illegible] by S. Col when cleaned in detail by [illegible], all [illegible] found & [illegible] renew before [illegible]. 5&7 Co R.E. Complained they were short of train & carry on investigation. The complaints found the stating [illegible] incorrect. The O.C. R.E. Co. apologized for having been misled by his O.M. Sgt.	[signature]

WAR DIARY
or
INTELLIGENCE SUMMARY
(Erase heading not required.)

Army Form C. 2118

Place	Date	Hour	Summary of Events and Information	Remarks and references to Appendices
CORBIE	9/7/16		8th and 9th Supplies left tonight. 9th Company left tonight - Went Corbie to transfer 17 4 Bar iron rations to forward dump in MONTAUBON about A.D. at Carnoy. Orders received to return 255 A.R. Cavalry working party, attached 8th Q. type for rations from 10 a.m.	
	9/7/16		Convoy drawing this morning in Briquete ground sheets from units, as system Tarpaulin supplies from 1st Army found unsatisfactory, leaving to Considerable delay. Placed in charge of supply dump of Army RO 360 at Carnoy. Mudguards moved today to GROVETOWN L.T.C. Train BOODST strong pack train to strength & firmness was brought up to ordered to 50 & 75% respectively, as present proportion of light & heavy totals considerably excellent.	
GROVETOWN	10/7/16		XIII th Corps to draw from railhead at Midnight but owing to total arrival to supplies caused 4 H.Q. army in consequence. Some trains have been ordered, owing to damp weather unable to dump owing to wet state of ground between dump & motor lorries water pine.	[signature]

WAR DIARY
or
INTELLIGENCE SUMMARY
(Erase heading not required.)

Army Form C. 2118

Place	Date	Hour	Summary of Events and Information	Remarks and references to Appendices
GROVETOWN	14/7/16		Returns drawn for P. Briquet R.E. attached to 101st Div. Sig. Coml. one cart from Rear dump. Arranged with R.T.O. that transport unused drew provisions at 6am but if train arrived earlier than this supplies would be off loaded dumped by fatigue party — this arrangement necessary owing to uncertain time of arrival of train.	
			3 SC ORE attached for rations.	
			Lieut. S. Cal re delivery of 1000 field tins for Division 7 & 10 for train Cos.	
			7 cft of Cavalry fatigue party transported to 104 Division. Remainder went to HAPPY VALLEY.	
	17/7/16		3 Co. unable to find Cavalry party until this morning owing to their failing to leave out a guide on the road.	
			O.O. 84 received re disposition of train dewainow in attack on Trônes.	
			Orders received placed up Supply transport of 76th I. Bg with Rations for Cois. 13Kns. Comhlerance of RSO re shortage of vehicles the fuel train & diesel support of J.M. Hospital available — to forward BDO of C.T. reporting no increase	J. Lucien Capt. I.S.O.

1875 Wt. W593/826 1,000,000 4/15 J.B.C. & A. A.D.S.S./Forms/C. 2118.

WAR DIARY or INTELLIGENCE SUMMARY

Army Form C. 2118

Place	Date	Hour	Summary of Events and Information	Remarks and references to Appendices
GROTE NOVA	11/7/16		Attack started at 3.30 a.m. — Outposts withdrawn by 7.18 in daylight and taken over at 10 a.m. Pack train advanced to follow on tracks made from Corps blocd at H.70 by development with H.70 it was settled down at train as usual. This was done in view of conventional time of trial. Post on the line slowly without unnecessary heavy rain during morning.	
	11/7/16		Pack train shelled upon getting into position until 7.40 then moving. Orders received offenses were brought held up to retain for all water and S. Col to ease up balance at sundown. Wounded carried with 2nd Queens because the advance had cut to memory. Unable to ascertain how we conventional as yet.	Johnson alst S.C.O

Army Form C. 2118

WAR DIARY
or
INTELLIGENCE SUMMARY
(Erase heading not required.)

Instructions regarding War Diaries and Intelligence Summaries are contained in F.S. Regs., Part II. and the Staff Manual respectively. Title Pages will be prepared in manuscript.

Place	Date	Hour	Summary of Events and Information	Remarks and references to Appendices
GROVETOWN	16/7/16		Went S/Col re petrol limber (broken) Pack Train arrived at 6 a.m. for use of the Train to ration firm base up by S. wagons also a supply of rations. Strength increased to about 70% Serving lorries arriving — Fighting strength 16.5.91 — Casualties about 20 ors.	
	17/7/16		Pack Train this morning taken to 7 wards the front line. 16 ors to the brecuits wagon & 8 of S.A.T. from 2 dumps each supplied. Lanced over beacon in rations dump. Strength 16.5.92 O.R.	
	18/7/16		Train report 6 a.m. — 7 ors to meet 2 wagons of breads. Wrs. & officer, — Mens were employed for all units. Sent up this afternoon by 4th army waggons the consumption of 3 days (afterwards altered to 2 days) C.I. rations arrangements made to commence to-morrow to thin out ors bring these down from Grovetown dump — other wounded from 6 & 4th army. That the C.I. ration be not to be commenced until further orders. All arrangements made to commence Strength 17.067 O.R.	Kearney oct. no

1875 Wt. W593/826 1,000,000 4/15 J.B.C. & A. A.D.S.S./Forms/C. 2118.

WAR DIARY or INTELLIGENCE SUMMARY

Army Form C. 2118

Place	Date	Hour	Summary of Events and Information	Remarks and references to Appendices
GROVETOWN	19/7/16		Positions did not arrive until 8.30 am today - [Meat?] ration to [Bread?] 50%. Orders received that 3rd Divn would move to the right & relieve the 9th Divn in the line. Went with O.C. Trains & OC 9th Divn Train re taking over 7 transport waggons in forward position - On this [unit?] be arranged by Supply Co. Strength 166 gh & ar - coal cut today. Weather fine.	50%
	20/7/16		Arranged with S.S.O & Senior Police Officer & refitting & renewals. Wdgrs R.B.Co Capt G.E. XII th Corps. HS AR. 151 Divn [Cavalry?] attack 157 AR. [Ruislarry?] Transport South Co 57 AR 9th 40 horses. 33rd Bgde 15th Divn the attached train for relieve from tomorrow (repelling) Necessary arrangements made. Strength [Detail?] (am not Mule) 1659 1 ar. Coal cut today. Thunder & rain.	

WAR DIARY or INTELLIGENCE SUMMARY

Army Form C. 2118

Place	Date	Hour	Summary of Events and Information	Remarks and references to Appendices
GROVETOWN	21/7/16		Following units trooping attached from 9th Divn from relieving tomorrow C. Coy 9th Corps Cyclists B1aR, det N Hussars 30aR, Ditchean Butts, (Wiltshire Regt) 73BaR 19th-13th 39th Co Rifles. 26th N Hussars 77aR 63 LD. No 1 Troop 4th Fd Survey 17eo F.L.D. Ditcheans 8mth D.A.C. 94aR 49th Siu Rifle. 53M Si Rifle 18th Division leaves tonight. Some strict W feeling through 14 this Division. Strength of Divn abt 16,917aR. I think Monettes Enemy 10 wounded brought fine review. – Cauled. abt 1,500. Total Casualties abt 3,400aR. Forpe 76th SiRifle about 1,400.	
	22/7/16		Irwin arrived 8.45 this morning. 296 hundred very Httry heavy shared in difficult weights in ground toward its wounding at reinforcements was concluded. – This breaks but it difficult for the Stal officer to make a comprehensive talk is back billed to be fastened. Avenues 7 Companies.	
	23/7/16		wand abaor O.I. natives take Division, necessary destructions wounds from 337 slim and. Further down on to October moving to Common Church 71800 authur king hen blown tools by shell fire. Metropolis: making fund	A.K. Leary SSO

WAR DIARY
or
INTELLIGENCE SUMMARY

(Erase heading not required.)

Army Form C. 2118

Place	Date	Hour	Summary of Events and Information	Remarks and references to Appendices
GROVETOWN	24/7/16		Lieut J new relieved Battery today. C.O's Charcoal out until further orders meantime.	
	25/7/16		Instructions recd at 5pm to move into new rations - issue number 154 ment Hdqrs 4th Army (Investigation Depot) 2 Detachments with 3rd Div Cavalry to retain their own supply Fridge.	
	26/7/16		8th Inf'y Regt'l team this trial today for MENUITE with R.C.G. & Wellton transp Reserves of Ambulance Wagon in when nearest Station - Instruction from Q. When no est established train to 2nd Division for rations at Railway transports tough - broadcasting.	
TREUX	27/7/16		9th In Regt'l left for VILLE SUR ANCRE, 36 train to MEMMITS - Direct T train transportation to TREUX. meantime.	
	28/7/16		70th In Regt'l to MERRICOURT, an ambulance will remain at Grovetown for several days Longs. No 1. 2. 9. & 60 serviced in Garrison Camps.	[signature] Col S.a.

Army Form C. 2118

WAR DIARY
or
INTELLIGENCE SUMMARY
(Erase heading not required.)

Instructions regarding War Diaries and Intelligence Summaries are contained in F.S. Regs., Part II. and the Staff Manual respectively. Title Pages will be prepared in manuscript.

Place	Date	Hour	Summary of Events and Information	Remarks and references to Appendices
TREUX	29/7/16		Marched from BUSSY and via EDGEHILL, DERNACOURT over as GROVETOWN from movement. Our R.S.O. at Edgehill managed to arrive at 6.05 a.m. visited S.S.O. 2nd Divn firing batteries Francis Kingman's attached to 3rd Bron which on his return by later Brown from 3rd Ct. Some of these units did not clear their positions today, - they afterwards however these firing batteries (OBUS) managed with O.C. Supply Col Stacks for not in country at various various Division in country. weather fine & very warm.	Anderson CAS. S.O. 3rd Divn
B	30/7/16		Good day of loading at Grovetown. Some C. left for Ville sur Ancre, and 2 C. for Treux. S. Col Poffyn beavy fire every warm.	
	31/7/16		Loaded as Edge Hill by time transport this morning & have refilling points as follows, 1 Co. E15 D 22 - 2 C. D 59 D 4. 3 Co. E16 C 29 1st C. E 25 O.8.4. Chief C. D. weather fine very warm. Shortyn 1605O a.R.	

SO,3 P? Div Troops

Army Form C. 2118.

S.O. 3 Div¹ Troops

WAR DIARY
or
INTELLIGENCE SUMMARY.
(Erase heading not required.)

Instructions regarding War Diaries and Intelligence Summaries are contained in F. S. Regs., Part II. and the Staff Manual respectively. Title pages will be prepared in manuscript.

Place	Date	Hour	Summary of Events and Information	Remarks and references to Appendices
ESGUERDES.	1/2/.	1.00 am.	Ration delivered 1.00am. Refilling starts 2pm as soon as waggon return from units, & waggon wait if necessary & necessary. Coy march out 7pm. & entrain WISERNS, train leaves 10.52pm.	
"	2"		Travel all night, between CANDAS 9am & march to BOISBERGUES. Train arrived 7.30pm. Ration dumped & general unloaded for night.	
BOISBERGUES	"		Refilling 7.30am. 15 waggons drawn as they return from units, the last units did not draw until 1pm. D.A.C. fail to draw on this march, have been allowed their 1st ech taken of F.A. units to length & kept on same to govern next from units.	
			At 4.30pm march to FLIXCOURT. horse lines 7.30pm & bivvy in FLIXCOURT BETHENCOURT road. Guard mounted 8.45pm for night.	
FLIXCOURT.	3".		Refilling from 8am. & finished 1pm. March of 15.0X when no expected to stay the night, but received orders to load up filling in noon as possible, horses arrived 3.30pm & refilling finished 6pm refilling from 1st ech were out & BOURDON, at cross roads near B.O.O.YARD. March out 9pm, 1st unlay all night arrive DOORS 8.30pm, AFK c 27 mid. march uit coy.	

Army Form C. 2118.

WAR DIARY
or
INTELLIGENCE SUMMARY.
(Erase heading not required.)

Instructions regarding War Diaries and Intelligence Summaries are contained in F. S. Regs., Part II. and the Staff Manual respectively. Title pages will be prepared in manuscript.

Place	Date	Hour	Summary of Events and Information	Remarks and references to Appendices
DOURS.	5 July		Arrive DOURS 8:30am, horses watered 3/or refilling finished 5:20pm	
"	6"		As refilling but with Coy H BROVE TOWN nr BRAY.	
BRAY.	7"		Ration drawn from railhead BROVE TOWN 6am & refilling taken place at same place.	
"	8"		The first train expected at midnight 7-8" did not arrive until 5am. Refilling 8:30am	
"	9"		Ration drawn in bulk 6am from railhead. Refilling 7:30am finished 8:25pm	
"	"		Refilling joint one mile north of BROVE TOWN railhead. 24 units drawn	
"	10"		Routine as usual.	
"	11"		Routine as usual.	
"	12"		Routine as usual. Refill 25 units.	
"	13"		Routine as usual. Potatoes received from Jackson exchanged for cheese held in reserve or reserve dump	
"	14"		Routine as usual.	
"	15"		Routine as usual. Refilling 25 units.	
"	16"		Routine as usual.	

Army Form C. 2118.

Instructions regarding War Diaries and Intelligence
Summaries are contained in F. S. Regs., Part II.
and the Staff Manual respectively. Title pages
will be prepared in manuscript.

WAR DIARY
or
INTELLIGENCE SUMMARY.
(Erase heading not required.)

Place	Date	Hour	Summary of Events and Information	Remarks and references to Appendices
BRAY	17 July		Routine as usual. Refilling 2 units.	
"	18 "		Routine as usual. A full issue of rum sent to units in Flanders. Two	
			waggons were sent out one delivering to all R.F.A. to others to D.A.C. at	
			their lines.	
"	19 "		Routine as usual.	
"	20 "		Routine as usual.	
"	21 "		Routine as usual.	
"	22 "		Routine as usual.	
"	23 "		Routine as usual. Full issue of rum sent to R.F.A. D.A.C. & R.C. at	
			"	
"	24 "		Routine as usual. Full issue of rum to all units.	
"	25 "		Routine as usual. Full issue of rum to all units.	
"	26 "		Routine as usual.	
"	27 "		Routine as usual.	
"	28 "		Routine as usual.	
"	29 "		Routine as usual.	

Army Form C. 2118.

WAR DIARY
or
INTELLIGENCE SUMMARY.
(Erase heading not required.)

Instructions regarding War Diaries and Intelligence Summaries are contained in F. S. Regs., Part II. and the Staff Manual respectively. Title pages will be prepared in manuscript.

Place	Date	Hour	Summary of Events and Information	Remarks and references to Appendices
BRAY	30 Jly		Routine in camp. Refilling 26 units.	
TREUX	31"		Marched 1.30pm to TREUX. Rations drawn from railhead 6.45am at DERNANCOURT. Refilling 7.45 at DERNANCOURT. MEAULTE road, one mile from DERNANCOURT. 26 units drew rations.	

WAR DIARY
or
INTELLIGENCE SUMMARY

(Erase heading not required.)

Army Form C. 2118.

S.O. 8th A. Bde

A.A. 8 A. Bde

Place	Date	Hour	Summary of Events and Information	Remarks and references to Appendices
In the Field	1-7-'16		Entrained at 11.02 a.m. at WIZERNES with 4 men of Reputating party & 1 Bdkshop R.E.O. Arrived at CANDAS at 7.30 p.m. & proceeded to billet at GORGES. Billeting party at GORGES on arr. BERNAVILLE - CANAPLES Rd.	
	2-7-'16		Lorries arrived at 8.10 a.m. Refilled during the day. Lorries started again at 7.30 p.m. No coal.	
	3-7-'16		Refilled at 7 a.m. Marched off at 8.30 a.m. Battalion HQ & Bde. HqRs. billeted at FRESSELLES. Reg. at MOLICOURT. Refilling point at cross roads North of "T" in CLINCOURT. Lorries started at 4 to 5 p.m. for Al Bde v at 7 p.m. to M.W. Bl. R.F.A. Refilled M.W. Bl. R.F.A. HqRs, 129 Bty H, 43 letter D.A.C., a second time v finishing at midnight. Also refilled H.Q group country Bn.HQ, R.A.H. R.E. H.Q, Bn. H.Q, Siglnl Coy R.E., A.O.C. YM Coffee tester. 3 Tons of Coal arrived at 2 p.m.	
	4-7-'16		3½ Tons of Coal arrived at 7 a.m. Refilled 3.4 a.m. Heavy rain. R.F.A. with us for Cal firel. H.Q group afield with us. Bde. marched out at 8 p.m. for ALLONVILLE. Lorry wagon marching with A.S.C. By Arthurton Lieut S.O. 8th A. Bde	

Army Form C. 2118.

WAR DIARY
or
INTELLIGENCE SUMMARY
(Erase heading not required.)

Instructions regarding War Diaries and Intelligence Summaries are contained in F.S. Regs., Part II. and the Staff Manual respectively. Title Pages will be prepared in manuscript.

Place	Date	Hour	Summary of Events and Information	Remarks and references to Appendices
Little Bethel	5-7-16		Column arrived at 3.15 p.m. Ran on refilling point. Halfpenny carried a supply lorgers. Remainder left with Cap. Pol. Refilling point at Church at Allonville.	
	6-7-16		Bde. marched out at 9.30 p.m. for CORBIE. Sent truck at 9 a.m. Marched at 10.30 a.m. arrived at 3 p.m. at 4.7.a.2.0. Shot 6&7 Helped to retard R.E. Park Pan and ay supplies at this point	
	7-7-16		Bde began Refilled from point at 4.7.a.3.8 that 6-7 at 11 a.m. finished to units in afternoon Bde h trucks arfd at 7/8-7-16.	
	8-7-16		VI Mn Mr taken A.O.C. Sanitary section Bde Retainers bn loose refilled by us Bde Staff Office unit 14 D.KCOR 4.D. Coy 18 Bowl mats 217/16 134 365 12 4619 Loading 1st Cav Div working party at CHERNY filled unit.	
	9-7-16		Saw Bde Supplies from railhead starting at 6.50 a.m returned at our camp Refilling 7.30 a.m A.O.C left m	
	10-7-16		Refilled at Millencourt 5.30 a.m Started at 9.30 a.m	
	11-7-16		Refilled at Millencourt 6.30 p.m Sanitary section left m	
	12-7-16		Posted Bde H.Q. beyond CARNOY	

2449 Wt. W14957/M90 750,000 1/16 J.B.C. & A. Forms/C.2118/12

Army Form C. 2118.

WAR DIARY
or
INTELLIGENCE SUMMARY

(Erase heading not required.)

Instructions regarding War Diaries and Intelligence Summaries are contained in F. S. Regs., Part II. and the Staff Manual respectively. Title Pages will be prepared in manuscript.

Place	Date	Hour	Summary of Events and Information	Remarks and references to Appendices
In the Field	12-7-16		Drew 1000 ft. Equipment tent. New potatoes.	
	13-7-16		228 Coy. R.E. Shelled with no ill effect. Visited unit in HAPPY VALLEY.	All correct.
	14-7-16		Routine as usual. Brigade strength :— M.D. + Sick 251 / All ranks 5097	E.D. 417 / C45 18 / Batt Mules 12
	16-7-16		Visited units — all satisfactory.	
	16-7-16		Visited units. Run wire to Def. Bns R.E. Coys. Sect Arb., H.Q. Gun Coy.	
	17-7-16		Routine as usual. Run wire.	
	18-7-16		Visited units. Run wire.	
	19-7-16		Routine as usual.	
	20-7-16		7th K.S.L.I. received 129 reinforcements. Brigade strength :— M.D.+Sick 146 / All ranks 3975	H.D. 436 / C45 18 / Batt Mules 12
	21-7-16		Routine as usual.	
	22-7-16		7th K.S.L.I. received 122 reinforcements. 12th S. W. Bor. D.C.L.I. No.1 Group 4" Hill Survey & Rifled Grens 12th + 96 from 111 Northumberland Fusiliers ordered by the Bde. from the account. Visited Bn. Helium in trenches.	A.W. Rifles ind A.W. Rifles ind S.O. 8ᵗʰ K.R. Rif

2449 Wt. W14957/M90 750,000 1/16 J.B.C. & A. Forms/C.2118/12.

WAR DIARY or INTELLIGENCE SUMMARY

Army Form C. 2118.

Place	Date	Hour	Summary of Events and Information	Remarks and references to Appendices
In the Field	23-7-16		Visited units. 8th East Yorks received 342 Reinforcement	
	24-7-16		Routine as usual.	
	25-7-16		Brigade commanding to come out of trenches tonight.	
	26-7-16		Visited units. Brigade out of trenches. Units move to MÉAULTE.	
	27-7-16		Rationed 12th Station M.F.E.L. No 1 Group 9th Field Survey Coy of 1st Anti Aircraft Northumberland Hussars & 3rd Brit Redoubt Coy for last time — Ree 62.D. E 16 f Cent.	
	28-7-16		Company marched out at 10 a.m. to MÉAULTE. Visited all units. Refilling in camp. a delivered rations on arrival loading at railhead as usual. 8th Field Ambulance still at BRAY. COR 13.15 and in MÉAULTE.	
			Rationing XI Mobile Vet Section only in addition to Bde units.	
	29-7-16		6 tons of coal dumped in camp.	
	30-7-16		Routine as usual.	
	31-7-16		Railhead trading at FERNANCOURT at 7.0 a.m. Cheshire Field Coy. R.E. at VAUX.	
			Bde. Strength: All ranks H.A. Mules R.D P.Or Pack Mules
			3598 134 21 16 11

A.W. Robinson, Major
S.O. 8th Inf. Bde.

WAR DIARY
INTELLIGENCE SUMMARY.
(Erase heading not required.)

Army Form C. 2118.

S.O. 9th Div? DAC

Place	Date	Hour	Summary of Events and Information	Remarks and references to Appendices
MONNECOVE (NORDAUSQUES)	30-6-16		Supplies loaded yesterday afternoon at refilling point. Lorries arrived from Rte 28 & refilling commenced 3.30 pm. Lorries re-manned with Engl. Off. + one Driver. Refilling finished 4.30 p.m. Empties + Rations in Ongoing lorries.	
MONNECOVE (NORDAUSQUES)	1-7-16		Only engines sent to units to enable them to refill.	
DOMÉMONT (DOULLENS)	2-7-16		Lorries dumped at BERNAVILLE. Units refilled as usual in ammunition & supply. Wagons returned to Company dispersed.	
VIGNACOURT	3-7-16		Supply wagons unloaded & filled to truck at once & marched to VIGNACOURT and delivered in turn to Companies. Lorries arrived 9.30 pm. with Ra units + Sable Rte + 2dn Sable R/F.A + No 1 Sect. DAC. All units more refilled & except companies in firing line. These wagons at 5.30 pm, assembled + left with R/F.A + DAC reply refilled at that hour.	
VIGNACOURT	4-7-16 7.0 pm		All supplies delivered to units & they have returned to our billets. Lorries arrived 2.30 pm. Refilled by 4.10 pm. 9 mans of ALS4 in Company lines, under escorts of 5.30 pm that all empties + 23 m. Empty R/FA + No 1 Sect. DAC move to rejoin their units, which from 9th Rifle reserves to rejoin at P.& D. to POULAINVILLE. Supply wagons unloaded with Company.	

E W Head
Capt
9th Div

Army Form C. 2118.

WAR DIARY
OR
INTELLIGENCE SUMMARY.
(Erase heading not required.)

S.O. 9th [?]

Place	Date	Hour	Summary of Events and Information	Remarks and references to Appendices
POULAINVILLE (AMIENS)	5/7/16	7.30 a.m.	Company with Supply wagons moved to Lt [?] proceeded at [?] to railhead point. All down on arrival (also [?]). Rations all. Received supplies. S.H.S [?] then returned to company. Wagons returned to company. Arrived at 10.45 a.m. to LAHOUSSOYE via ALLONVILLE and QUERRIEU. *23 Bde R.F.A. + 1 Sect DAC reached units D.A.C. group, *112 MB Tet Cost + Landset + Colny's attached from D.H.Q. group to this (B) group. *this group by motor lorries proceeded this afternoon.	
GROVETOWN RAILHEAD BRAY	6/7/16	10.0 a.m.	Supply wagons arrived LAHOUSSOYE 2.30 am & immediately proceeded to [?] supplies. Mines it again empty at 6am to GROVETOWN. No weighing.	
"	7/7/16	10.0 p.m.	Supplies loaded by train transport at railhead at 10 am. Supplies delivered to units at MORLANCOURT. The routine unused. Conl was as given previously during.	

[signature] Captain

Army Form C. 2118.

S.O. 9th Inf. Bde.

WAR DIARY
or
INTELLIGENCE SUMMARY.
(Erase heading not required.)

Instructions regarding War Diaries and Intelligence Summaries are contained in F.S. Regs., Part II. and the Staff Manual respectively. Title pages will be prepared in manuscript.

Place	Date	Hour	Summary of Events and Information	Remarks and references to Appendices
GRAVETOWN RAILHEAD	8/9/16	9.0 p.m	Supply wagons loaded direct from barge at railhead. Bde. returned to CARNOY. all nums as usual to Bray	
BRAY	9/9/16	7.0 p.m	Entire wagons loaded as yesterday. barnes & coke returned to Trunks Depôt as to be wound	
"	10/9/16	7.0 p.m	Supplies loaded direct to horse transport wagons at railhead. Coke brought to company lines & unloaded. wagons returning empty. Rations, coke & several nums to Bde. Other nums as usual	
"	11/9/16	10 p.m	Supplies loaded in bulk to horse transport wagons at railhead 5 at Buffalo in empty lines at 9:30 a.m. all nums as usual. Coke & coal loaded & transferred in trucks	
"	12/9/16	10 p.m	Loaded at railhead 5. 7.30 am. Railhead at 8.30 am later. rations & all nums as usual	
"	13/9/16	10 p.m	As for 12th	
"	14/9/16	10 p.m	As for 13th	

[signature]

Army Form C. 2118.

S.O.9 Intelligible

WAR DIARY
or
INTELLIGENCE SUMMARY.
(Erase heading not required.)

Instructions regarding War Diaries and Intelligence Summaries are contained in F.S. Regs., Part II. and the Staff Manual respectively. Title pages will be prepared in manuscript.

Place	Date	Hour	Summary of Events and Information	Remarks and references to Appendices
GROVE TOWN RAILHEAD BRAY.	15/7/16	9.30 am	Regtl Supplies loaded direct to Stores Lpk wagons at railhead, which Railway Co (TrypLine) all viewed as usual including fruit vegetables, coke & charcoal. Refilling finishes 10.30 am. totter returns as usual.	
"	16/7/16	9pm	All went to refuge 15th inst	
"	17/7/16	9pm	Routine as usual	
"	18/7/16	9pm	Routine as usual	
"	19/7/16	9pm	Supply wagons went late at unit's request for forward troops refilling unto 10/30 am. Routine as usual of present.	
"	20/7/16	10pm	As above refilling at 9.0 am all issues as usual	
"	21/7/16	9pm	Routine as usual	
"	22/7/16	9pm	Routine as usual	
"	23/7/16	9pm	Routine as usual	
"	24/7/16	10pm	Routine as usual	

CMWhitehead
Capt ASC

WAR DIARY
INTELLIGENCE SUMMARY
(Erase heading not required.)

Army Form C. 2118.

S.O. 9th Inf. Bde.

Instructions regarding War Diaries and Intelligence Summaries are contained in F.S. Regs., Part II. and the Staff Manual respectively. Title pages will be prepared in manuscript.

Place	Date	Hour	Summary of Events and Information	Remarks and references to Appendices
GROVETOWN BRAY.	28/7/16	10 pm	Landed in bulk at 6.50 am from wells. Coy have transport. Rifles in Company lines at 9 am all ranks in want.	
" "	26/7/16	10 pm	Routine as above.	
" "	27/7/16	9 pm	Routine as above. Orders to Amiens to TREUX	
" "	28/7/16	9 pm	Routine as above	
" "	29/7/16	10 pm	Routine as above	
VILLE SOUS CORBIE	30/7/16	9 pm	Landed in bulk at 7.10 am at miles. Refill supply Company lines to men over & supplies delivered.	

Signed W. Ward
Capt. a/c

S.O. 76 ℨ Inf. Bde.

Army Form C. 2118.

WAR DIARY
or
INTELLIGENCE SUMMARY
(Erase heading not required.)

Instructions regarding War Diaries and Intelligence Summaries are contained in F.S. Regs., Part II. and the Staff Manual respectively. Title Pages will be prepared in manuscript.

Place	Date	Hour	Summary of Events and Information	Remarks and references to Appendices
Morlle	July 1st 1916		Orders received over turn — the fully refitting — Lieut Engineer Joss hitherto 2nd Lieut Wilson leave with Walker the entire Stones? Leave for Entraining Station @ 11 pm.	AR 4697 HD 144 357 56 9 Enclosed Cabbarl
	July 2nd 16		Arrive at DOULLENS Jon Troops Staining Train & MACEER (know x 1 Ry Mgt) night ahead as Train @ 8pm. No Losing moved previous evening with advance party refilled in morning at 6am — thereafter in camp for crew? We must	
	July 3rd 16		Train Loaded to WAGNIES — moved thence remaining at ADVARDS NAOURS. Rgt at 8pm — in Forres village Fed at 4 OSK Ogre & 40800 Ogre & 6 (est AMC)	
	July 4th 16		Refitting — Worked all through Bde lines 76 Bde MG Bry & TM Battery — Lovero-dinner show while terrible rain was falling — Bread ration under new forward & Brigade turned out Recrent orders issued to IDs of ISO also to all WB 11 B and dir. camped — Remainder to return all Artillery vagons after refilling — Villers & Coisy arriving at 2 am turn straight to Ilts Lytt Ja Falmar Villers & Coisy in Brigade ordered repeated morning refilling at 5pm at north side J Coisy. Orders received to move at 9pm — (made arranged at Rybling & met at stream with Bodin Lorries) — move to at 930pm new Ranneville, Querrieu Lahoussoye & FRANVILLERS awaiting arr. about 3 am on	
	July 5th		Having received orders to send ration immediately Klink Rahin off proceeded to Brigade with collected supplies. As I am not continue licence our Nelly, Reine Molen got to Bray there troop showers A → Refilling Pont at Ralled B. → Ration demanded sthff 7K a days at Rellebeau	
	July 6th		(4) on 5th stamped at point C in reserve	Alfredy Sanborn Lt Col 76th Iny Bde.

WAR DIARY or INTELLIGENCE SUMMARY

Army Form C. 2118.

Place	Date	Hour	Summary of Events and Information	Remarks and references to Appendices
Grove Town L7a.	July 7th 1916		Zeppelin anchored & dropped 2 bombs - shrapnel on Transport Group. to consolidate orders the bivouac - Reveille at 10 a.m. - Kemp. taken a big. with living sufficient to suffice during this trip to [?] (Brigade arriving at a time -) the supplies ready to go to go to Point C & after refitting the return of P.M. Transport & ammun. was taken unchanged for FM Bund & dumped at the evening before - Supplies were sent on this advance to Bois les CELESTINS then returning where rations were sent on to CARNOY. Reserve Transport rations for Bde to 7 Bgde - Reserve at L7a?	
	July 8th 1916		Summary for 33/31st consisted for 1st line Stores. Refill as yesterday. Dump extended from 10 am till 1pm owing transportation Staffs [?] all kinds of Brigade except 2 Company, also Field Ambulance - at Bois des CELESTINS. Front was made & Platoon Supply & Trench was redeployed - Dump to the men Routine as usual - Staff Capton 76th Bde issued instructns. were to be formed two wire they all being furnished on all packed IF, CL - 200 Bell Petrol issued under SMC 9	AR 30/30
	July 9th 1916		Trench mortars & Bde Section. Supplies. Experimentat for all Infantry Units - IF, 7Bde or 72nd RA. Supplies loaded direct from Rail Head Carnoy, 76th Railhead dump to write back opposite the junction of Bgde Dump - Carnoy Town - Rifling 8. 18am & wagons all Ideas Johnny 5 a.m. - 9 10 am - 600 at Carnoy town - Rifling 8. 18am & wagons all Ideas Johnny 5 Field Ambulances drawn Trepots Partial two wanted (150 per Infantry Unit) also 7 Field Ambulances drawn 500 below Phot our return this morning supply - Demand for all infantry. Candles in no appear about 5 33.6 a.m. no undercurrents evils to outposts on 33.6 Orl.	
	July 10th 1916			
	July 11th 1916		Visited units 7Bde - Iran a 5 am refile at over at 6.00 am - (Octant orders stores at Railways at 11.30 am but men afterwards dropped 8. 3.30 pm yesterday as above -) Routine as usual -	
	July 12th 1916		Routine as usual -	

H.Hinrey Lieut A.S.C.
O. 96th Inf Bde -

Army Form C. 2118.

WAR DIARY
or
INTELLIGENCE SUMMARY
(Erase heading not required.)

Instructions regarding War Diaries and Intelligence Summaries are contained in F.S. Regs., Part II. and the Staff Manual respectively. Title Pages will be prepared in manuscript.

Place	Date	Hour	Summary of Events and Information	Remarks and references to Appendices
Eversholt (Army)	Thursday July 13th 1916		Visits to Kings Own, 2 Suffolks, 10th Rifles, 78th Brigadier (all of 4th) except Y.M. Beds'r who are in the woods and E & Brigdy gunner. Reports on moved at 8.0 am. — (Coming limited 6.30 am at Railhead.) —	
	July 14th 1916		Routine as usual. — Rain in trenches.	
	July 15th 1916		Train arrives 1½ hours late at Railhead. Refill at Eusan. — Routine as usual. Three waggons &c. waiting till evening to follow up train to trenches of Bols in trenches. — (16 visions.) — Rain in trenches.	
	Sunday July 16th 1916		Leave at Railhead 6.30 am. refill 8 am — Tea Balk Sector who served for distribution. — A further horses g. train arrives at Boutheau Railway Depot g. distribution. — A further horses g. train arrives at Boutheau Railway Depot, 2 Suffs. 4 R.S., 4 Indian ration — A further horses g. train arrives at Boutheau Railway Depot, 2 Suffs. King's Own, 1 Royal, P.S., 4 Indian were sent to Hdqr. Royal Fields & relief, aux Relief aux. Adv. L.D. St. 2 Ambulances — Royal Field went in exactly reverse so. 3 Div D. — Mounted Routine eclaitat (?) me than be sent without another g Brg D. — Mounted Routine sent to checkset.	AR 4958 FAD 170 St. 2 D 30 S.A.A. 4
	July 17th 1916		Weedon H.Q. 3 Div (Maj. Mtaleey) 7 Field Ambulance. — Usual routine — went to Amiens to purchase Lords & Dr. & petral stings the week for water. To waive supplies to the rest of pit the Red Cross g Divisional Depots.	
	Tuesday July 18th 1916		Routine as usual. Rain moved & reserve indents for purchase	
	Wednesday July 19th 1916		Supply train did not arrive till 8.30 the morning. Loss of Railhead 9.45 - 10.1 gasoline indent their dawn &c. supplying firm dump at 9.45 - 10.1 gasoline indent their dawn &c. 8,450 v 87 lings m 133. — Suffks Widst skin as change. —	
	Thurs. 20/7/16		Routine as usual.	

H.H. Hickey Lt ASC
O. 70th Bge. Bde.

Army Form C. 2118.

WAR DIARY
or
INTELLIGENCE SUMMARY
(Erase heading not required.)

Instructions regarding War Diaries and Intelligence Summaries are contained in F. S. Regs., Part II. and the Staff Manual respectively. Title Pages will be prepared in manuscript.

Place	Date	Hour	Summary of Events and Information	Remarks and references to Appendices
Grovetown (Bray)	Friday July 21st 1916		Received other messages of 20th & later intent to things from further instruction to 150. — Visited 7th Bn. M. Gun. C. & 76th Bde HQrs. between Bécordel Montauban. Had narrow escape whilst leaving — shell falling within 10 yards but failed to explode. — Routine as usual. —	
	Saturday 22/7/16		(15) AR Left 101 bombing Sch & Batln Scout bomb (not in camp now Carnoy) & 3 Bn. Sgt. Reserve N.T. Bay. 57 AR & 9x Horses. — Routine as usual. —	
	Sunday 23/7/16		Rejoining at 5am. Fresh troop No of 101 Gordon Htrs — Somme Irene went up during afternoon to fighting areas — Supplying ants, Gum reprints sent by orderly who came from Staff Regt. Includes for men, duplicate quantity ammun. but came from Staff Regt.	
	Monday 24/7/16		Routine as usual — Julienne went Bernard & returned. Gen J. Frost Veys. — Run sent up to all units in forward trenches.	
	Tuesday 25/7/16		Sir S. Veys afghan received Len. J. Frost. — Bde advised from Travalés Forcesdi from by N.17 (Reference map) Coin du Taille — Sims by placed in stores change as not to Ribehers. Rail totals to.	
	Wednesday 26/7/16		Lack Garments of Divn returned to Ribehers. Routine as Usual.	
	Thursday 27/7/16		Visited all units & Gen. Evans (U.O. 18 of 8th. & M.Gunner.) — Returned. 3 Lack Israel issued & 1st Garments of Dvsn to Ribehers — No Veys drawn during Somme in last Dansen were brown EMERICOURT — L'ABBE after opening — Orders cancelled.	

A.P. Reeves Lieut. Col.
C.O. 75th Inf Bde.

WAR DIARY
or
INTELLIGENCE SUMMARY

(Erase heading not required.)

Army Form C. 2118.

Instructions regarding War Diaries and Intelligence Summaries are contained in F.S. Regs., Part II. and the Staff Manual respectively. Title Pages will be prepared in manuscript.

Place	Date	Hour	Summary of Events and Information	Remarks and references to Appendices
GRAVETOWN (RAY)	Friday 28/7/16		Units of Brigade move to MERICOURT. — Train leaving at railhead bay and get two charged — Brades 18. W. Riding Regt. at MERICOURT. this Unit will be arrived to MERICOURT. —	
	Saturday 29/7/16		1 g.w. M Coy. Can. Coy. started above No 1 Group & Lunny Coy. 2 hrs. 30m. late by 147. Coys. X X Cable Section. — The three last named did not arrive for this return. — Routine as usual. —	Stationery 3 Forage M.D. 154 L.D. 643 C6 22 3 Mule, 9 A.R. 4146
	Sunday 30/7/16		Move after refitting to TREUX (M RANCH) about 2 K. from Bryant Over. — Camp with field train. Nos. 1 — Refilling from 50 yards N. J. Railway crossing TREUX — BURE Road on left hand side. — Attached units directed arrive to 2 Workstation as usual from No Supply Column Figures. —	
	Monday 31/7/16		Lines & Railhead commencing at 8.45 am. Been drawn from Resume supply with Supply Column — Refilling 9 am. — 20 R.R.R. Join in after upholding & Ray. — All Infantry units 9 Brigade visited Went to Amiens & purchase ordnance supplies for 2 Coy 111 & Services authority from Train O. —	

H. Holmes
Lieut Col
to 46th Inf Bde

S.S.O, III Div

S.S.O. 3rd Division

Vol 8

Army Form C. 2118

WAR DIARY
or
INTELLIGENCE SUMMARY
(Erase heading not required.)

Instructions regarding War Diaries and Intelligence Summaries are contained in F.S. Regs., Part II. and the Staff Manual respectively. Title Pages will be prepared in manuscript.

Place	Date	Hour	Summary of Events and Information	Remarks and references to Appendices
TREUX	1/5/16	—	Routine as usual. Weather fine & very warm	
	2/5/16		R77 left the line for rest. 25 R77 reinforcements billeted in train camp. Poss train arrived 7.45am - turned over between Boscon in reserve store. Weather fine, very warm	
	3/5/16		Supply train arrived at 4.45pm. (due at 2am) - repairing at 6.30pm from strained syphilis when used to finishing 300 ounce dogs. business to be made up with train up & dead functions of train replace weather fine, warm. Supply train in position 10.30 am.	
	4/5/16		Weather fine, warm. while in rest area men in the usual horse meetup on Wednesday & Saturday	
	5/5/16		Supply train in position 2.30am. 5 battn 20th K.R.R. E/batty XXC Co. 1500 men from 76th 2 Bngde to procure men of F 16. (Wor Carry). Arrangements made by O.C. 3 Co & Transport Supplying 10 time coal obtained from bivouacs.	McLennan Capt S.O.

Army Form C. 2118

WAR DIARY
or
INTELLIGENCE SUMMARY
(Erase heading not required.)

Instructions regarding War Diaries and Intelligence Summaries are contained in F. S. Regs., Part II. and the Staff Manual respectively. Title Pages will be prepared in manuscript.

Place	Date	Hour	Summary of Events and Information	Remarks and references to Appendices
TREUX	6/9/16		Supply train in position at 7.45 am today. 20 tons coal received from Wimereux today. Arranged with O.C. P. Col. Steurs Lorries to draw coal tomorrow to clear coal weather fine.	
	7/8/16		Train in position at 6 am. Lieut Ansion. Nevil left for Laundry. weather fine warm.	
	8/9/16		Train in position at 6 am. Lieut R.S.B. at Wimereux weather fine warm.	
	9/9/16		Train in as 6 am. morning Nevil from Boulogne to Treux today by Lorries. day warm.	
	10/9/16		Completed move. Narrow thing to Treux Orders received that Divn. is tomorrow took into line at once, relieving 53rd Divn. train to take over Canteen? and Divn. train. Raining during afternoon.	[illegible signature] Col SC

WAR DIARY or INTELLIGENCE SUMMARY

Army Form C. 2118

Place	Date	Hour	Summary of Events and Information	Remarks and references to Appendices
TREUX	11/8/16		Saw SSO 2nd Division at Frouchtown re taking over - Took up to Saus Pits today. No 2 who tried couple at Frouchtown Service at Railhead 9am. Issued one outfit bag, Sugar, cheese, bacon, from reserve. Ongoing to want of provision arranged with S.O. Indian to take over stores. The divisional reserve ought to be kept must increase.	
	12/8/16		Went down T.I.T with O.E. Train Rampaged Sarrians. 1 foot must stream to take effect on quality to forestall — no information attainable re change of railhead. 6th Suffolks B. and Pats Relay, 36 Train arriving in old camp for forward. Hand Hut go to 73. AVB at Forkestrue. weather quite warm. Strength Pubs.	
Frouchtown	13/8/16		Train Hut grs to Frouchtown — toothmen fall drunk from 2 subdion at Frouchtown railhead.	J Alexander SSO

Army Form C. 2118

WAR DIARY
or
INTELLIGENCE SUMMARY
(Erase heading not required.)

Place	Date	Hour	Summary of Events and Information	Remarks and references to Appendices
Smootown	14/8/16		To train Smootown. R7A morning up blue prop, musketry, 4 Lee SAE + CRA who were tomorrow. 6 have can't find it by lorry from Trans - Orders from Du[?]s Col to leave at 11am for two hours train to Smootown. Other regt confused with Co, word that these lines went where before Smootown. unable to ascertain until late evening which in any case must from tomorrow — eventually informed by 13th Corps that it must be Edge Hill tomorrow — from 10th at Smootown. Instr from ant Brin by wire ? Corps for return from tomorrow 13th Corps Trette, 238 AM Co PS, 87 Canvas trestle P.T. North Answers - all 626. from 13th Corps. C. Co Cyclists & 4 Co. Total Strength about 1400 AR. 100 horses. 3 Brigades into line tonight. Raining during the afternoon & night. Strength 1900 & AR.	

Army Form C. 2118

WAR DIARY
or
INTELLIGENCE SUMMARY
(Erase heading not required.)

Instructions regarding War Diaries and Intelligence Summaries are contained in F.S. Regs., Part II. and the Staff Manual respectively. Title Pages will be prepared in manuscript.

Place	Date	Hour	Summary of Events and Information	Remarks and references to Appendices
Graffham	15/3/16		Pack train up to 60% 7 meal, 25% Pom, 15% Pork&beans & hay 17.5% bread. When Coal arrived, drawn 1 lb/gun to Pot/Sat Tor at L 249.8 Issues from reserve >>> MT GHQ. 14 >>d AT GHQ. 183rd Tunnelling 15th Kite Bath Sec all but Co from 131th Corps MG cyclists B&Co. Truck of steam 105 DAM >>>o Rams. Rations from Boinneu. Hauled one 67 t/un coal & 2 3/4 t/un coal to be cleared from any lump. Any overseen oppr&tion having dropping afternoon. Remaining — I.C. & Gordons strength >>>4 all	
Forward True Gracftham	16/3/16		Forward striking Point 1 Co. at 7, a > 9, > Co K12 & S.1 3 Co L78 > 7 4 Co L7 a & 2 q. 776 t 22 t th A2 th >>>2 t >>o into line 8th Suffolk in support.	
-,-	17/3/16		Nunineous today. Friday Strength >>>3 all. Weather fine.	
-,-	18/3/16		Nun ivars today. Pack train increased to >>>o - but train amount without Sugar Jam or milk this caused continual inconvenience as RSO could not refuse to reposition but the issues to Crobie reported it B S F C T. water not during but day. Fight Strength 19,869	[signature] Capt & O

1875 Wt. W593/826 1,000,000 4/15 J.B.C. & A. A.D.S.S./Forms/C. 2118.

Army Form C. 2118

WAR DIARY
or
INTELLIGENCE SUMMARY
(Erase heading not required.)

Instructions regarding War Diaries and Intelligence Summaries are contained in F. S. Regs., Part II. and the Staff Manual respectively. Title Pages will be prepared in manuscript.

Place	Date	Hour	Summary of Events and Information	Remarks and references to Appendices
FORT HERTZ Frontier	18/9/16		Rear guard orders issued to transfer all attached units to 35th Division. The rear guard previous plan moving to rest area 76th Field to Happy Valley, 9th & Sand Pits and 9th to Citadel Tonight. 35th Division likewise going on leave. R74 Remain in until further orders. Cavalry appear to have moved somewhat. Rand Guinea is used for Remedy, which now remains.	
—	20/9/16		Transport following units to 35th Division for transport load was 232, 742. M.T. Co. R.E. 183rd Inneelling Co, 13th Rly Pln Co. -B Co 14th Torpa Cyclists, 238 M.T. Co R.C. escort pig & railhead. Northward Numan to 35th Division on 17th inst, 37th Column Baln absorbed into units on 18th inst. Friday 0.5 1800's a.R.	
—	24/9/16		Orders received at 7 p.m. That Supply Column will return tomorrow between the Blood at escort returns tonight. Well necessary arrangements has Q movement all units is notifying tomorrow at 6.30 am. Friday strength 15,096. Ammn are to transfer Jericho Chandetin	

1875 Wt. W593/826 1,000,000 4/15 J.B.C. & A. A.D.S.S./Forms/C. 2118.

WAR DIARY or INTELLIGENCE SUMMARY

Army Form C. 2118

Place	Date	Hour	Summary of Events and Information	Remarks and references to Appendices
FLESSELLES	27/9/16		S. Glenn dumped transport lines for 76th Bgde & Mercourt, 80th Bgde at Havents, 79th Bgde at Vielle Surplise at 6/Gun Bvd Sho Donally Bon transport the morning but afternoon by S. Glenn from HEILLY ad the Divnl transport moved the Division Ground by road today to FLESSELLES area. Ammunition trucks by Louis Tournon. S. Col. (sen. 150 Monition) Journeyed to service 67FLESSELLS. These three have received at ROUGUE MAISON arranged refilling points for tomorrow. Divnl R.B. & Col. J.Q. Divn Hd Qrs at FLESSELLS. Thundershine.	
BERNAVILLE	28/9/16		Ammunition Trucks left Truen by train, returning as Ordn Dept. refilling at 7 am/ by 76th Bgde, 8/9th Bgdes on HAVENAS - FLESSELLES road. Road marched in Bow QUEMAISON. Columns there at 10.30 am, went to ST RIQUIER, our railhead arrived at ST RIQUIER, our railhead. Divnl Hd Qr for tomorrow, saw R.S.O. there. Half Bgde Train marches in afternoon, 76th Bgde to HALLST BONSERIOS area, 9th Bgde to FIENVILLERS, Brand Hd Qrs Hdqr Brand to BERNAVILLE area, 9th Bgde to FIENVILLERS, located refilling point for tomorrow. Van arrived at ST RIQUIER necessary arrangements made that 2 Co of water, 3 Co at Bernaville HCo at Frèvilliers weather fine.	

1875 Wt. W593/826 1,000,000 4/15 J.B.C. & A. A.D.S.S./Forms/C. 2118.

Place	Date	Hour	Summary of Events and Information	Remarks and references to Appendices
BERNAVILLE	24/9/16		Refilling this morning at 8th Bde. H.Qrs. on Bernaville. Abbeville troops lead of T.B. 9th Subgps on main road 4 miles west of Fienvillers. 7621. Pofgs on Hem - Fienvillers road opposite master. Went forward. Divisions moving in & near area Bray. Saw R.S.O. at Fresnes retaining on 26th. also new Q offrs Supply Column. Inspection fine.	
FRECHEN LE GRAND	28/9/16		Refilling at 7 am. Saw R.Paco yesterday. Divisions moving northwards. Yesterday to Bondes-Fiquy, Forth, Vregnies. Once H.Qrs. Forth. 8th rd.gp. Bottles, Frohen-le-Grand, Marans area. H.Qrs. Warans. 9th Subgp. - Sorrurus - Barly, Mezerolles, Remaisnil. H.Qrs. Remaisnil - Sent H.Qrs to Frohen-le-Grand. Train H.Qrs in field. War log. H.Qrs. Frohen confirms. 20th K.R.Rs rail H.Qrs units. Capt. Anderson acts as S.O. to this group. Tried with O.C. Train to find lorry returns to 1st Corps, inform there that 16th S. Staffm wanted Load up from Aylesby 28th. Wire Brethaw 7 New R.S.O. that 7 O.C. 16th S. bat travels western Supply arrangements. Also saw O.C. 16th Land Down at Vaun arrange. Raining during four of afternoon	Acknowledge

Army Form C. 2118

WAR DIARY
or
INTELLIGENCE SUMMARY
(Erase heading not required.)

Place	Date	Hour	Summary of Events and Information	Remarks and references to Appendices
FLERS.	26/9/16		Unit finished at Trévent. M.T. returns issued there by order ? D.D.T. 5rd Army. When D3 trains although has been 7 men per train, including repliables. Sent O. Cdr. loads of without delay for the last train was after dumping tomorrow dawn before 18th Division as Refilling Points today. - Motorcycle on main road N & T Vaequerie, 3 Co. and Gr. group FROHEN LE GRAND - WAVANS Rd. 4 Co. Frohen le Grand Thiepval Rd. Divisions upper northwards of Albert & R. Peple Hill's group to Guinecourt Mericourt - Ecrivere, Fleury, Flormumont - Blanqueval area HQ's Blangerval, 9th Inf Bgde. Mainil, St Pol - Terras Ivergi - en - Terras, Monchaux, Sarisours, Haravers, HQ Beauvilles. Direct Heavy Artillery, Croix, Servieur, Erricort, Beauvois. HQ. L Capiose Hornville. Burial HQ FLERS. Divan HQ in field nearby went with O.C. train to 3rd Army, also 104 Corps, T.D.O.T.P.S.T. front Army. Notify arrangements informed. Thus 3 and S. Col. moved some in place of 4 th. S. Col. for scheduled days. Saw O.C. 3rd and S. Col. re location. Phenomenon. Considerable rain during the day, bring Heavy transports no fuel could be carried on the roads. P.O. by order ? O.C. instruction S.O.'s to keep certain amount of wood necessary for carrying transport trailer from Corps (164) that we are driven up the reserve rations (2000 men × 5 (10 train) offer Islanded by 7th M.G. H	J.A. Drummond Cass Lt Col

1875. Wt. W593/826 1,000,000 4/15 J.B.C. & A. A.D.S.S./Forms/C. 2118.

WAR DIARY
or
INTELLIGENCE SUMMARY

(Erase heading not required.)

Army Form C. 2118

Place	Date	Hour	Summary of Events and Information	Remarks and references to Appendices
MOUCHY-CAYEUX	27/8/16		3rd S. Bat. Moved Early from Mouex held by 16th S. Bat. now Bethune. Entrained now fraind dets on train during Morning. Nfilling at 7 am on entraining. 8th Rifle & Negro Bngde 2.10 go N by same route. N[?] S on Ecoire S. 9th Rifle St. Pol. Humieres Rd. 76th Rgde St. Pol. Humieres Rd. Krovers were northwards to: 8th Rgde Sachin, Prevoy, Marest, Troiggy, Savin, Heyns Troigny, 9th Rgde Bryard, Heoting, Contiville, Wavans, Fleury, Auvin, Bergueneuse, Heyns Heatrie, 76th Rgde, Siraceg, Predifin, Fiefs, Heuchin, Eguine, Caffrey, Heyns Eguine. Divisional Hdqrs from at Mouchy - Cayeux. Three Heyns in fields nearby. As the ROK KRRs were with 76th Rifle Brigde loading groups - 76th Photograph, "Wings Co" & "Similarly" left for Nouex to mines both units to rations under arrangements to be made by Camp Commdt. in Cn tn. Considerable rain at Anrovers during day. Strength 12,500 aP 2 Co at Henichin, 3 Co at Warest. 4 Co at EPS.	
Vaudricourt	28/8/16		Units 4.60 Nfilling front N Trumpet pt. T. RRs ration to Vaudryle. Wind reached N Bethune. 3rd S. Bat. Throws through 10th General Mill. Nfilling finished (7am) 8th Rfle at Marest. 9th Rgde & Harer. Front on ANV/N-Bergunernafl. Vaudryle in square at Heuchin. Servicecar Mores established as follows reft qk Rfles which Nurses in forward area Fosting. 9k Suffolk to Heuchin area. 76th Rgde to Troigny, Pioneers to Mouex. Ber mines Train Negro & 3 Cos to Chateau at Vaudricourt. Wires D.D. & S.T. first Army to send cars to Morest refused to venture by 30th inst. Raining during Nfilling 1 & m Fregment victories during the day.	Melwvenler SSO

War Diary / Intelligence Summary

Army Form C. 2118

Place	Date	Hour	Summary of Events and Information	Remarks and references to Appendices
Vaudricourt	29/8/16		Went with Col. Bethune, 3rd S. Col. looking there for last time, also from reserve trench held by 16th Divn. Artillery fires. 9th Bgde H'qrs. 8:30am at E.2.c.0.7 (Vaudricourt). 9th Inf. Bgde. H'qrs. an yesterday. 76th In. Bgde. relieves 9th Inf. Bgde. Divisions have exchanges as follows: 9th In. Bgde. to hover to mines. 9th In. Bgde. to Tangry, then 76th In. Bgde. & Army & Brucq & Houchin & to arrive at Vaudricourt and & Pernincourt Camps. The 3rd Divn will relieve the 16th Divn on the H & I & K trs L.14 trs. See. 9th In. Bgde. relieving the 97th Bgde on Aug 31. Sept 1st and 76th In. Bgde. the 11oth Bgde. on Sept 1st, 2nd. Trench Marguerite road left by 16th Divn for this Divn. Swo Devon Major extremely heavy rainstorm this afternoon lasting for 3 or 4 hours, roads becoming flooded in some cases to a depth of 1 foot. Saw O.C. 16th S. Col. re loading tomorrow.	
—	30/8/16		16th S. Col. load at rail-head today in place of 3rd S. Col. Train was first left for us by 16th Division — Coal 16 (?) tons came up two ordered, 15ton Left-Sgt. Runaway, never found block of his yard. — do enquired at Vaudricourt T.own. Artillery fired (8:30am) 8th. Bgde. E>E. 0. g. 9th B'gde E>S. 29, 76th Bgde. E>E, 3, E. Train H'qrs. E>E Central 76th Bgde Houchin. 9th In. Bgde marks to mines. This H'qrs. moved back by Motor transport from H'qrs to Sand pits on 3rd line & free train ___ Art 5500 lbs. (I went via roads) Mining report attached.	J.Munro Capt. S.S.O.

WAR DIARY
or
INTELLIGENCE SUMMARY

Army Form C. 2118

Place	Date	Hour	Summary of Events and Information	Remarks and references to Appendices
Vaudricourt	31/8/16		Nothing 8.30am. Arms on Today. Went ourselves [illegible] refitting horses on Brittons - have to have Rd - Two horses from 2SO+D.th Brian Comprest Regt R7A 573aR HDQ LDS18 13=Tm 23aR, 17Rnt Tunnelling Co 810aR HDQLD2 from from 3rd Septr RCo toPrs from train wounded to 15 OVD up to 2SD hours. 4 7kn surage to receive two horses. Strength 14SSOap Jules known trenches free	[signature] Capt SB Inspector

S.R.E. DIV TROOPS.

Army Form C. 2118.

S.O. 3rd Divl Troops.

WAR DIARY
or
INTELLIGENCE SUMMARY.
(Erase heading not required.)

Place	Date	Hour	Summary of Events and Information	Remarks and references to Appendices
TREUX	1st May		Railhead DERNANCOURT. Rations drawn from railhead 6.45 am. Refilling 7.45 am. on TREUX VILLE road. 25 units down.	
"	2"		Routine as yesterday.	
"	3"		Routine as usual. Sgt. Cratell & L/c. Cunliffe were wounded by bomb in fire & an Officer & hospital. Sgt. Hardey attached to supply detail.	
"	4"		Routine as usual.	
"	5"		Routine as usual. L/c. Adams came from base as clerk.	
"	6"		Routine as usual.	
"	7"		Routine as usual. Two women came. O.C. Young & O.C. Weaver.	
"	8"		} Routine as usual.	
"	9"			
"	10"			
"	11"			
"	12"			
"	13"			
"	14"		Routine as usual in morning, move took to GROVETOWN in afternoon.	

Army Form C. 2118.

WAR DIARY
or
INTELLIGENCE SUMMARY.
(Erase heading not required.)

Instructions regarding War Diaries and Intelligence Summaries are contained in F.S. Regs., Part II. and the Staff Manual respectively. Title pages will be prepared in manuscript.

Place	Date	Hour	Summary of Events and Information	Remarks and references to Appendices
GROVETOWN	15th Aug		Pushed out to but line DERNANCOURT. Ration wagon by waggon & refilling	
"	16"		GROVETOWN 10 a.m.	
"	17"		Pulled GROVETOWN. Ration drawn midday 8 a.m refilling 9 a.m.	
"	18"		Routine as usual. Rum issue.	
"	19"		Routine as usual.	
"	20"		}	
"	21"			
"	22"		Refilling as usual, no accounts, no second refilling 4 p.m. The other boys went out with their Bdes.	
"	23"		Ration drawn from HEILLY by Supply Col. Refilling 4 p.m.	
"	24"		Routine as usual.	
"	25"		Routine as usual.	
"	26"		Routine as usual.	
"	27"		Refilling 11.30 a.m.	
"	28"		Routine as yesterday.	

Army Form C. 2118.

WAR DIARY
or
INTELLIGENCE SUMMARY.
(Erase heading not required.)

Instructions regarding War Diaries and Intelligence Summaries are contained in F. S. Regs., Part II. and the Staff Manual respectively. Title pages will be prepared in manuscript.

Place	Date	Hour	Summary of Events and Information	Remarks and references to Appendices
GROVETOWN	29 Aug		Lorries do not arrive until 11:30 owing to difficulty of driving at night. Shortage of meat & bread this is to be made of tomorrow.	
"	30 "		Lorries arrive late again 11:30 for Groveries have to be bought from B.O.R.D.E.	
"	31 "		Routine as usual.	

S.O. 8 Inf Bde

Army Form C. 2118.

WAR DIARY
or
INTELLIGENCE SUMMARY
(Erase heading not required.)

S.O. 8" Inf Bde

Place	Date	Hour	Summary of Events and Information	Remarks and references to Appendices
In the field	1/8/16		3rd Quil. Manages Coy attached for rations — Strength 35 attached. Lieut Demaakk took over duties of P.O. 8" Inf Bde pro Col. A.C. Perrine	
"	2-8-16		Visited Bde Hd Qr. roll call units. All satisfactory. Rum issue today	
"	3-8-16		Railhead loading 5.45 p.m. Rifles at Railhead	
"	4-8-16		Railhead loading 10.30 a.m.	
"	5-8-16		Rum issue today	
"	6-8-16		Routine as usual.	
"	7-8-16		Visited Bde Hd Qrs. all battalions & 8th MG Coy. 8th Mle Green Coy. Bde. Strength — Attached — H.R. Plums L.D. Offrs O.Ranks 3655 — 1443 — 411 — 18 11	
"	8-8-16		Routine as usual.	
"	9-8-16		Rum issue today.	
"	10-8-16		H.M. the King, H.R.H. the Prince of Wales & the C in C. General Munro were here this morning.	Col Plumpton Visit P.O. 8" Inf Bde

Army Form C. 2118.

WAR DIARY
or
INTELLIGENCE SUMMARY

(Erase heading not required.)

Instructions regarding War Diaries and Intelligence Summaries are contained in F. S. Regs., Part II. and the Staff Manual respectively. Title Pages will be prepared in manuscript.

Place	Date	Hour	Summary of Events and Information	Remarks and references to Appendices
In the field	11-8-16		Aeroline fell on R.E. dump in THE CITADEL. Sheet 62J. F.15.	
"	12-8-16		Bde moved to HAPPY VALLEY. Sheet 62J. A.3.	
"	13-8-16		Orders from Division to be ready to leave Bde moved to Sheet 62J. F28 at short notice. d5.x9.	
"	14-8-16		Visited all units.	
"			Routine as usual. Bde Strength:-	
"			All ranks H.D. Rhine 4 D. Oth. 3rd Ranks	
"			4148 140 401 18 11	
"	15-8-16		Company moved in the evening to Sheet 62J. L.7a.	
"	16-8-16		Railhead loading at BECOURTOWN at 9 a.m. Billing in cars.	
"			Visited units. Bde moved in to billets Fonchelles in afternoon.	
"	17-8-16		Run issue sent up to be left by D.M.'s until called for by O.C. Coys.	
"			Visited units. Inf Bns, R.E. Coy & Fd. Amb. Lecture Given.	
"	18-8-16		Same ration of Rum issued to above units.	
"	19-8-16		Same ratio of Rum as yesterday +	

A.C. Robinson Maur
S.O. 5th Inf. Bde.

WAR DIARY
or
INTELLIGENCE SUMMARY

(Erase heading not required.)

Army Form C. 2118.

Place	Date	Hour	Summary of Events and Information	Remarks and references to Appendices
In the field	20.8.16		Attack relief of men as yesterday. Brigade went to Rest Bn 3. E.18.r.E.2.4. Visited units.	
"	21.8.16		Complete send off men to Brigade. Brigade moved to MÉAULTE. Patrols 3rd Durh. Rangers Bn. for last time. Bn. Strength: - Attack H.Q. this L.D. Off. Rank & file 3839 168 422 15 11	
"	22.8.16		Refitting at MÉAULTE. Lorries arrived at 6.30 a.m. with supplies from reserve dump. Company moved off having starting point at MÉAULTE with Bde. transport at 10.30 a.m. Arrived at POULAINVILLE at 9.15 p.m.	
"	23.8.16		Refitting 2 kilometres from RESSELLES on road to CANAPLES at 7.30 a.m. Supply wagon marched on to billets. - 2 Royal Scots 7 K.S.L.I. & 9th M/G Gun Coy to PROUVILLE-BEAUMETZ, 8 Scot Yorks to EBERNAUVILLE, 8th Bde. H.Q. Coy. 41 Royal Scots Battalion to R. BEAUCOURT, Chorlier Field Co's. R.E. to EPECAMPS, 8th Field Ambulance to OMEQUERIE, 9th Company A.F.C. to JOMESMONT. Arrived 6 p.m. Units arrived by train today. 3rd Dur. Emm. M.Gs. 42 Kilometres from BERNAVILLE on road to BONSBERGUES near S.O. 8th Ack. Rde.	

Army Form C. 2118.

WAR DIARY
or
INTELLIGENCE SUMMARY
(Erase heading not required.)

Place	Date	Hour	Summary of Events and Information	Remarks and references to Appendices
In the field	24/8/16	8.30 a.m.	Convoy arrived 8.30 a.m. Visited all units.	
"	25/8/16	6.30 a.m.	Convoy arrived 6.30 a.m. 2nd Royal Scots - 89. 1st East Yorks - 116. Reinforcements arrived but kept entired to Company transferred to BEAUVOIR-RIVIERE - arrived 11 a.m. Bn. Hd.Qr. at FROHEN-LE-GRAND. 8th Bde. Hd.Qr. at WARNES. Capt. HAWKINS temp S. offr. L Coy. S.O. Hd.Qr. Group.	
"	26/8/16		Convoy arrived 6.45 a.m. at WARNES. Company marched to ECOIVRES - arrived at 1 p.m. Bn. Hd.Qr. at FLERS. 8th Bde Hd.Qr. at BLANGERMONT.	
"	27/8/16	6.30 a.m.	Convoy at 6.30 a.m. at ECOIVRES. Supplied to 3rd Del. Coy. Col. to last time. Coy. arrived to MARŒUIL arrived 5.15 p.m. Bn. Hd.Qr. MONCHY. Bde. Hd.Qr. TINCRY. Hd.Qr. group transferred to L.Bde.	
"	28/8/16		33rd Ral Sup. Col. Coun arrived at 7 a.m. on man and rest of MAROEUIL Coy. marched to VAUDRICOURT arrived 4.30 p.m. Bn. Hd.Qr. at THOREOURT. Bde Hd.Qr. at RUITZ. Q.M. Lieutn Road. S.O. 6 Inf. Bde.	

WAR DIARY
or
INTELLIGENCE SUMMARY

Army Form C. 2118.

Place	Date	Hour	Summary of Events and Information	Remarks and references to Appendices
Allonville	29/8/16		Ref Sheet VAUDRICOURT Ref 36A. E 28 c.o.9. Lorries arrived at 8.30 a.m. 9 tons of coal arrived. Bde H.Q. at NOEUX - let mines. Chalkie told Cg R.E. O 2th Royal Sea at MAZINGARBE. Remounts of Brigade at NOEUX - let mines. 9 tons of coal arrived. Visited units.	
"	30/8/16		Issue of ammn. Started new coal dump to division.	
"	31/8/16		16th Div. Sup. Col. Lorries arrived at 8 a.m. Visited all units. Strength of Brigade —	

All ranks   H.D. Horses   L.D. Horses   Pack mules   Draft mules
3729   133   370   12   11

A.E. Phenton
S.O. S.A. officer

S.O 9th Inf Bde

WAR DIARY
or
INTELLIGENCE SUMMARY.
(Erase heading not required.)

Army Form C. 2118.

Instructions regarding War Diaries and Intelligence Summaries are contained in F.S. Regs., Part II. and the Staff Manual respectively. Title pages will be prepared in manuscript.

Place	Date	Hour	Summary of Events and Information	Remarks and references to Appendices
VILLE-SOUS-CORBIE	3/1/7/16	9 p.m.	Landed in truck by horse transport at EDGE HILL (DERNANCOURT) unloads at 7.0 am. Refilled in Bde area at 8.0 am. All rains as usual other work to no avail	
"	1/8/16	10 p.m	Routine as for yesterday	
"	2/8/16	10 p.m	Routine as before	
"	3/8/16	9 p.m	Rain arrives very late at watches. Refilled 7.0 pm. All rains as usual	
"	4/8/16	9 p.m.	Train arrives 11.30 am. Truck containing 1 Bn. detricles of Reserve (except full) were missing from other trains and not available therefore no issue made.	
"	5/8/16	10 p.m	Train arrives 5.7.0 am. Refills at 10 a.m. Bde rains as usual. Other units as usual	
"	6/8/16	10 p.m	As for 5/8/16. Bde rains of 9 pm wrote to replace deficiency on trench mt (not available)	
"	7/8/16	9 p.m	Routine as usual	

E.M.W[signature]
Captain

Army Form C. 2118.

S.O. 9th Inf. Bde

WAR DIARY

INTELLIGENCE SUMMARY.
(Erase heading not required.)

Instructions regarding War Diaries and Intelligence Summaries are contained in F. S. Regs., Part II. and the Staff Manual respectively. Title pages will be prepared in manuscript.

Place	Date	Hour	Summary of Events and Information	Remarks and references to Appendices
VILLE SOUS CORBIE	8/8/16	9pm	Landed in truck by Bde at EDGEHILL (DERNANCOURT) unloaded @ 6.0 am Refilled at 9am in Bde area. All now as usual.	
"	9/8/16	10pm	Routine as above	
"	10/8/16	9pm	Routine as above	
GROVETOWN BRAY	11/8/16	10pm	Landed in truck for Bde by Divn transport at EDGEHILL (DERNANCOURT) unloaded. Refilled in VILLE two new trucks — company lines. Eighty wagons now — 16 little company of appl'd ul ??? in Railhead in new area	
"	12/8/16	9pm	Landed as above at 6.30 am. Refills down to billets of Bde near MÉAULTE at 9am. Otherwise as usual	
"	13/8/16	9pm	Routine now for western day	
"	14/8/16	9pm	Routine no ??? for 15th inst	
"	15/8/16	9.30pm	Landed as above at 8.0 am Refilled at 10 am Supplies to new Bde Hd Qtrs area near CARNOY. All ??? ??? — have ??? therefore.	

C W Clarke
Capt?

Army Form C. 2118.

WAR DIARY
or
INTELLIGENCE SUMMARY.
(Erase heading not required.)

S.O. 9th Inf Bde

Place	Date	Hour	Summary of Events and Information	Remarks and references to Appendices
GROVETOWN RAILHEAD B.H.Y.	16/8/16.		Landed in truck by Bde at 9am at GROVETOWN railhead. Rations at 10am. All ranks also greatful. Otherwise nout to record.	
"	17/8/16.		As for 16th. No rations much expected from railhead at pulled that convoys to move late started from CORBIE and delivers quickly to all units.	
"	18/8/16.		Loaded at 7.30am. Ordered at 9.30am motor to get up two to move transport lorries in time to be out to fill thro by midday. All the supply wagons cleared railhead front by 2 p.m. an other ration so received. Service of issue call up us after.	
"	19/8/16.		Loaded at railhead at 9a.m. Rations at 9.45 am all same as usual including fresh but also some to break stores to other units as ordered. Divisions vehicles in line at GUILLEMONT.	
"	20/8/16.		As for 19th. including ammunition. Supplies d/d to CITADEL area.	
"	21/8/16.		Routine as usual. Supplies d/d to new Bde area at VILLE SUR ANCRE.	

E.W. Leal
Capt. ASC

Army Form C. 2118.

S.O. 9th [Infantry?] Bde

WAR DIARY
or
INTELLIGENCE SUMMARY.
(Erase heading not required.)

Instructions regarding War Diaries and Intelligence Summaries are contained in F. S. Regs., Part II. and the Staff Manual respectively. Title pages will be prepared in manuscript.

Place	Date	Hour	Summary of Events and Information	Remarks and references to Appendices
MONTON VILLERS	20/8/16		Received from Supply Column at 6.30 at VILLE SUR ANCRE. Services of Pk. went & Materials. All supplies except forage delivered forthwith to units. Rations taken to report anywhere necessary to convey supply wagons to take advantage of by road. [?] nil. [?] forage delivered to units	
PIENVILLERS	20/8/16		Relieves at most part destination FLESSELLES & SYENACOURT at [?] from supply column. Wagons and vehicles booked to appear. Vehicles right down in various [?]	
"	20/8/16		Relieves on BERNAVILLE ROAD at 9 am from Supp Col. All rations as usual. Other rations to unusual.	
MEZEROLLES	20/8/16		Relieves as yesterday but at 6.30 am. Rations requires [?]. Supply wagons unable to sent units to their various billets after returning to company lines. Other units are sent.	
SERICOURT	26/8/16		Relieves from Supply Column at MEZEROLLES at 8.0 am [?] I have [?] all rations as usual. Supply wagon unable with company. Supplies [?] [?] returned in this order	

[signature]
[signature] Capt RE

Army Form C. 2118.

WAR DIARY
~~INTELLIGENCE~~ SUMMARY
(Erase heading not required.)

Instructions regarding War Diaries and Intelligence Summaries are contained in F.S. Regs., Part II. and the Staff Manual respectively. Title pages will be prepared in manuscript.

S.O. 9th Inf. Bde.

Place	Date	Hour	Summary of Events and Information	Remarks and references to Appendices
E.P.S.	27-8-16		Convoy arrives at SERICOURT at 6.30 a.m. Refills 7.0 a.m. Wagons marched with Company as usual via 8th Pol. Supplies 25/8/3. Other routine as usual.	Supplies 25/8/3
E.P.S.	28/8/16		Convoy to 3rd Div. Supply Columns 7.0 a.m. at point mentioned. Smile N. of ANVIN. Refilled (all wagons as usual) 9/8/16 unit. E.P.S.	E.P.S.
VAUDRICOURT	29/8/16		Convoy arrives as per S.S. & Supply 3/8/16 near Lappy. Wagons marched empty.	Lappy
" "	30/8/16		Convoy arrives at 8.30 a.m. Refilled at 9 a.m. Supply wagons in Company lines afterwards proceeding to new lines of unit. Other routine normal.	

D. McLeod Capt a/c
S.O. 9th Inf. Bde.

Army Form C. 2118.

S.O. 76 E Inf 1 Bn

WAR DIARY
or
INTELLIGENCE SUMMARY
(Erase heading not required.)

Instructions regarding War Diaries and Intelligence Summaries are contained in F.S. Regs., Part II. and the Staff Manual respectively. Title Pages will be prepared in manuscript.

Place	Date	Hour	Summary of Events and Information	Remarks and references to Appendices
TREUX	1st August 1916		Started all work of Res. Sy. Works, 2 Supply, 1 ofgroom, Stephens + Beatty Employed from groups how running ahead of Father - Emergens rolls LO. brings the mid supply list of week. Rations as usual. The supply train is arriving at my supplies time at EDGEHILL Siding.	
	2 August 1916		Received from the 2nd Maio - 4 LD raw rating a LO for men absence Supp's Eam not not arrive as Bulle till noon.	
	3rd August 1916		4 Races made all units of Brigade groups (as attached unit) Ration as usual.	
	4th August 1916			
	5th August 1916		Working parties 7 and Suff Regt & 5 being O.S. move up the line Other rations and supplies generally from the wagon being used - Q.M. often for supplies at F.16. -	
	7th August 1916		Supply train arrived at 4 am & refilling at 8 am - Shortt (2 hours) also supply S'Branch smoker Rations as usual - Pte Morris Reedect form is duty with supply flain - (Not being attached.)	
	8th August 1916		Refilling as yesterday.	

H.H. Hicks LMR
S.O. 76th Brigade

Army Form C. 2118.

WAR DIARY
or
INTELLIGENCE SUMMARY
(Erase heading not required.)

Instructions regarding War Diaries and Intelligence Summaries are contained in F.S. Regs., Part II. and the Staff Manual respectively. Title Pages will be prepared in manuscript.

Place	Date	Hour	Summary of Events and Information	Remarks and references to Appendices
TREUX	August 9th 1916	(Wed)	Visited all Coys M Units 9th R.C.M. Guards – Routine as usual.	
	Aug. 10th	Thursday	Units Established J Bergere at F.16 (The Citadel) or Bray. Attached Forward R. Bath? Stirling Rd + 2nd K.R.R. Coys. Old Egyptian Drain rested lower on 11th after yesterday's rifling to GROVETOWN (The Camp not occupied by the day.)	
	Aug. 11th	Friday	Rifled on usual – Issued about 14th a Diagram Rustic in a Diagrams ration. which are used from 1st Army Group to instructors the fire 3.3.6 Locker. Detachment of Units report.	
GROVETOWN	August 12th	Saty	Moved HQ & land & Coy Camp at Bray – Grovetown at K.12. – Rifling But 27.7.0. K.R.R. Coys moving to Craze (Bras Post Pursue Road)	(E.18.d)
			Supplies drawn from Edgehill Station as yesterday & arrived at Grovetown at 9 am. Rifling 11/10 am. All Units got arrived – Water & field green tents rectified units keens to supply Drums during afternoon. Two yellow gun horses at 80 gallons received at refilling point.	
	August 13th	Sunday	Rifling an yesterday. Megnetrinne H. Grand for tales K.12 & 53 these went to C. Res rested at Canoy Rd. Valley. Set New. may to FORKED TREE farm (F.1.a.b.)	
	August 14th		Visited all Coys Units – & Rlating RP. – Bets moves this afternoon of to the line – New location J Bets F.24 n & 7.23b. Bels HQ to Talus – Bosse S. Carnoy.	

F.A. Henrick Major
C.O. 96th Brigade

Army Form C. 2118.

WAR DIARY
or
INTELLIGENCE SUMMARY
(Erase heading not required.)

Place	Date	Hour	Summary of Events and Information	Remarks and references to Appendices
GROVETOWN	August 15th 16 (Monday Tuesday)		Drew supplies as usual from Railhead for five Units from 50th Div. (viz - B Cyclist Coy, XIII Corps did not arrive - 9.L.9., Labour Coy R. Lewis, 238 A.T. Coy & Northumberland Hussars Yeo. - After refilling moved camp about 500 yards main road tramp recipient division by start of Opn. - I have received orders refilling point to K.7.C.1.8. to supply point during July & for 35th Troops - Supplies drawn from Grovetown. - Issued all units as yesterday and new refilling point two cyclists when Divisions arrived. Starting at Suffolk M Gun Bn, Buckt Qn, T.M. Bty, Trench Mortars & Carriers; Rear and held Infy & Units & Bde Ptrl HQ & Chelsea inspected. - Ran out and had Infy Units Details J, then Bearers of T.M. also the two A.M.'s pending orders from R. - then Ran out supplies, 7th Bde HQ, & M.Gun Coy sent up catapults. The Divn J, then Waggon we sent by an Officer who stood all them an thin we would at about sending it up - (Supply recipient was all the time looking for "Q". Suffolk Regt (the new name) would not be moved without instruction from "Q".	
August 17th 16 (Wednesday Thursday)		Supplies for all units as same at 8.30 am but one 9.um, legun & mules arrived train, also 150th West Virg. & Paraffin & Bread did not arrive - Northumberland Hussars etate they do not receive rations from us as they are being fed by 35th Div HQrs. - Coal left by 2nd Div station are by now about Trin.	

Signed: A/Major
Lo 75th Bgde

Army Form C. 2118.

WAR DIARY
or
INTELLIGENCE SUMMARY
(Erase heading not required.)

Instructions regarding War Diaries and Intelligence Summaries are contained in F. S. Regs., Part II. and the Staff Manual respectively. Title Pages will be prepared in manuscript.

Place	Date	Hour	Summary of Events and Information	Remarks and references to Appendices
GROVETOWN	Friday 18 Aug/16		Supplies as usual. – Travel ration issued to all Supplies on Motor Transport. Violin at Merck of Bir. alongside. – Sup of 100 in ration issued of Suffolk Regt & Kings Own. – Routine as usual.	
	Saturday 19/8/16		The Sorme River bed buried in trenches. – Complaint re short weight of Hay sent. E.S. Mo average per bale = 64 lbs or 15.3 lbs short of specified weight. – Ration day. 300 in strength Kings Own. – 200 – Grenr. 200. – Suffolk 200. Bee moved to Happy Valley.	
	Sunday 20/8/16		Bee moves to MORLANCOURT. Also to RRPC. Some permanent bath units and water carts were used. Routine as usual.	
	Monday 21/8/16		Sup Bow fr MERICOURT. Rifled them Middle Station TREUX – MERICOURT. Road – formn Transport at 6.a.m. Rifles at 5am. Truffles & BERTANGLES aving 9 p.m.	
	Tuesday 22/8/16		Sup BERTANGLES & rifled to main road to HAVERNAS of FIEVILLERS - IGNACOURT Rame Supplies very miserable. – Shortage of bek vans, gave out 2 Bde transport past whole 10am & supply off joined with transport. Tpaad to MACHER wit detabd's on ord Bse Rakton at Le MEILLARD HQ Bk Stat Lordener. Tours axinced 1930. – 1030. Bread received.	
	Thursday 24/8/16		Routine as issued at 1930 a.m. rifles at 9.30. – 10.70. Bread received. – Routine as usual.	

Forms/C.2118/12.

Army Form C. 2118.

WAR DIARY
or
INTELLIGENCE SUMMARY
(Erase heading not required.)

Instructions regarding War Diaries and Intelligence Summaries are contained in F. S. Regs., Part II. and the Staff Manual respectively. Title Pages will be prepared in manuscript.

Place	Date	Hour	Summary of Events and Information	Remarks and references to Appendices
	Friday 25-8-16		Left Mesghen after griling at 7.30 — Led all units as house had himself sent troops huts attached into again. H.Q. Group 5 day. H.Q.R. do it same into FORTEL arriving about 4pm — Rendon Jones another evening & absolute necessity by Royster. — Griling of 266th Virginians & Pol man work	
	Saturday 26-8-16		Services. I went ourselves by air. — Trip to BEAUVOIS — Rifling and maintained St Pol. St Heuvin at barracks leaving from Beauvois. — Clouds & soft shade grass	
	Sunday 27/8/16		True after rifling to HEUCHIN — Routine as usual. — K.R.'s join from H.Q. group.	
	Monday 28/8/16		Rifles from Place Heuchin at 11am — all were satisfied as no first met on v. bent MOV when farm — Leeve after rifling field to Lain to Renou. — If Renou Rd. been brought & form 36aly join R.S.C. to Lain to Renou. — If Renou Rd. been brought from — Task Marot	
	Tuesday 29/8/-		Rifled in evan and Renou - U Pot — Afforts Mariot — Butters all agreed from Ulin rifling to MAILICOURT. — Saw Baffro. arranged from Supply Point; therefore though funny as no severe storm —	
	Wednesday 30/8		Rifled at VAUDRICOURT adv. road at Bethune — Borzymouth Catch to the village — Grant arrived from skings own F 162 voicing Congratulated on Lew's industrial return under note 31/8/ — vale Leo 157	
	Thursday 31/8		Loris of 1/16 stirr Supply Column drug supplies at same of field a front at yesterday at 9am. — Rifleing & 45. 2 Cavs & Pt Rom 6 Cents Catholics. to Unitimer — Complaining not to otherwise. —	

H.H. Hill J.W. W.R. Pt. 2449 Wt. W14957/M90 750,000 1/16 J.B.C. & A. Forms/C.2118/12

S.S.O. III DIVISION
Army Form C. 2118
V ol. S.S.O. 3rd DIVISION

WAR DIARY or INTELLIGENCE SUMMARY
(Erase heading not required.)

Place	Date	Hour	Summary of Events and Information	Remarks and references to Appendices
VAUDRI- COURT	1/9/16		Went railhead - Sent lorries to LABEUVRE for 40 men & horses (S.O. NUFORCE) & continue with fieldworks. Refilling at 9 a.m. railhead loading 10.30 at Bethune. 70th In Bgde with line tonight. Weather fine.	
	2/9/16		Went railheads - 9th Inf Bgde went to Nouex les mines. Marguinghe. Today. Sent out S.S. Lorries to troops. Arrived Chock at LABEUVRE. This unit attached 9th Bgde for rations. Weather fine.	
	3/9/16		Pack train (men & horses) taken for exercise near railway station. Place in Charge of G. Colman. Supply train bringing two horses. Lorries loading by hand transport tomorrow at Noeux les mines. 16th E. Col dumped supplies for Coal Trench today. Met R.S.O. at Nouex les mines re loading which necessary arrangements were made. Special orders issued re regulations of traffic in Returning road. Peter car was refilling forces on the R. les mines - Bethune Rd. 8th Rifle K.R.C. 9th Bgde K.1.A. 76th Brigade K.12.C. Weather fine.	Dinning Coss No.

1875 Wt. W593/826 1,000,000 4/15 J.B.C. & A. A.D.S.S./Forms/C. 2118.

WAR DIARY
or
INTELLIGENCE SUMMARY

(Erase heading not required.)

Army Form C. 2118

Place	Date	Hour	Summary of Events and Information	Remarks and references to Appendices
Van Dr???	4/9/16		Drawing supplies by horse transport from Nouex les mines from today at 9 am. Meeting point Sackapes K6.d, 7, anthgu K12a, 7647a9ze K1.2. Hewt Torquemie received supply for the Division - sawed for coal. Believed to been be been. Loading at railhead occupied up to midday weather fine. 4th Field Ambulance lorries on new repairing points by ?.Col. Hewt reached Q office. Paws etc further lorries reaching supplies for the supply. Travel 230 who stricken cattle & two chevrons & 60 louis wood. he wants. The cheval by horse transport. Running Cleaning of license.	
	5/9/16			
	6/9/16		Steam wood from Bruien. Fatigue party for coal to be supplied by train, thanks to cote lebewood by ?.Col. Transport conduct. Orders from Corps increase 100 g candles WhE 60 out of summaring OS allowance.	(February ???)

1875 Wt. W593/826 1,000,000 4/15 J.B.C. & A. A.D.S.S./Forms/C. 2118.

WAR DIARY
or
INTELLIGENCE SUMMARY
(Erase heading not required.)

Army Form C. 2118

Instructions regarding War Diaries and Intelligence Summaries are contained in F.S. Regs., Part II. and the Staff Manual respectively. Title Pages will be prepared in manuscript.

Place	Date	Hour	Summary of Events and Information	Remarks and references to Appendices
Vaudricourt	7/9/16		Went Coal dump & also to B.H.Q.S.T. Fleached Coal ready Supply.	
	8/9/16		Orders received that 117 Division on 14th/15th inst will be relieved by Canadian Corps, as this was probable, no trouble of course. OC Corps Supply Col. necessary arrangements made.	
	9/9/16		Went forward with OC Coin met 1 Co. on march up, would necessary Supply arrangements R.T.A. due in this area about 11 stories.	
	10/9/16		Searched for R.T.A. from tomorrow as these to receive on return to (Col f recapturing) R.T.A. no news left today begin between dumps we meet bat heart but for loading this Coy at Cawthrow tomorrow - have transport of Co. B/G for every to tyle in to this blood. as regret of A.D.S. station 12 am D.H.Q.S.T. asked to supply 1800 de pren (in lieu fettle) daily for me 2 premises - change of am ofpot Melvina in 3 days time in meantime up to 3000 a can be drawn from Cattle	

WAR DIARY
or
INTELLIGENCE SUMMARY

(Erase heading not required.)

Army Form C. 2118

Place	Date	Hour	Summary of Events and Information	Remarks and references to Appendices
Vaudricourt	11/9/16		RTA crews from town the train reached this morning by lorries. Supplies dumped at Marles - in times as 3.30 this after DSGS T train & 1 days supplies for D.T. & the 14th Div. on train reaches destin. killed by S. Element all over the chauves by S. element in future. Stores 6 humans one how P col. 170th Invintie? from Bethune drew rations from today from 8 9th unfolde daily issue ? Bear Candles. weatherfine.	
	12/9/16		S. column loading for RTA at Auchere this morning. Supplies future delivered tumores on train this evening. dumped at 3.30pm at K.12.C, ammunition home in this evening.	
	13/9/16		knd. Sto. loading at Wiffred (Whitehouse) by home transport this morning. Orders received from Corps Hours all filling points from main road. Selected new ones at K24A for 9th 18th Bdes. K23B for 76th Bgde. KK24C for Divisional (Permanent) obtained from HQ RA Ox. These return received Bt5.00 between from today. 2 op regTabtroplesmen Canlestonien puncture up deficiency. weatherfine. Capt	

WAR DIARY
or
INTELLIGENCE SUMMARY

Army Form C. 2118

Place	Date	Hour	Summary of Events and Information	Remarks and references to Appendices
Vaudricourt	14/11/15		Supply Col took Billing from troops, from 76th & 79th Bn Rifle Brigade (owing to troops not arriving) last 16 meat & biscuits. No bacon or cheese. 3 days supplies for the respective draws yesterday. No rations from Railhead. Forage dumped 2 p.m. refilling at 2.30 p.m. Composite Page R.T.A. from this division tomorrow. Strong rations drawn today. Hagn 18g1CRDM & 2 batteries to 3/51 Siege. C306,30 Batteries to 61 St Siege.	
	15 —		Supplies, & biscuits, (no bacon or cheese), drawn from troops today for the Division. Hand over to S.T & Wood drawn as S. of troops. Weather fine. —	
	16 —		Bns to supporting points at Les Brebis, Northern Cap. have two rations Ft only one carried by men. Rations now at 61 Relief (2 cap in 1st & two biscuits), Ammunition 680 O.T. rations (2 vo for each). 400 billets from R.B. Hagn 18g1o x 200 to	
	17 —		9 th Rgt to distribution Batteries on Line today. Nothing unusual.	
	18 —		Capt Veal left on leave. Capt Hawkins takes on 20 9th Rifles during his absence. Bns marginpaths leaving today.	J.Helmsdate[?] O.C.

1875 Wt. W593/826 1,000,000 4/15 J.B.C. & A. A.D.S.S./Forms/C. 2118.

WAR DIARY
or
INTELLIGENCE SUMMARY

Army Form C. 2118

Place	Date	Hour	Summary of Events and Information	Remarks and references to Appendices
Vendresse	19/9/16		Went Bethune re Supply of Stores required. Raining during day.	
	20/9/16		Replies received that the lorries will move BTCs Army Training Stuffy tomorrow. Necessary supply arrangements made.	
	21/9/16		8th Bgde left for Alouagne area today. Lorries met all just as at Wizernes/Gois to Town Major there. BSTs 5/7 overseen. 2nd Fd Amb Trio (1856) Lorried men to Town Major. Never to trains, as toStadfois. Motoring 8th Bgde as Alouagne. Supply stores as received from this morning. 9th Subgd here today for Burbure. 8th Fydd refill at Alovagne. Plans for training area. Went Lillers saw RSD. also went to Army Transport for Motor T. Stare Coal. Road Helps to Bonry.	[signature]

Army Form C. 2118

WAR DIARY
or
INTELLIGENCE SUMMARY
(Erase heading not required.)

Instructions regarding War Diaries and Intelligence Summaries are contained in F. S. Regs., Part II. and the Staff Manual respectively. Title Pages will be prepared in manuscript.

Place	Date	Hour	Summary of Events and Information	Remarks and references to Appendices
BONNY	23/4/16		76th Bgde one Coy for Albenque. 8th Sufffolk refilling at AUDINGTHUN in reserve. 9 do after at BURBURE. Machine Gunners to LILLERS from lorry. Oranges & prunes 4/6 from refashes day from one. Bonnel-Compt: Arton. The convoys busily found by 2. Col. Portion of brown troops refilling at Marles les mines. Remained at Bruveele mines & heutrofines.	
	24/4/16		76th Subgde refilling at Albenque as on THEROUANNE - DUNEBROUECQ REAR ROAD GLEM.. do do on CUTTEM - BEAUMETZ to AIRE Rd. 9th do Y in Berguynn. Portion brend troops at Marles les mines - Bruveeles at heuvreles heutrofines.	J Wilmington LtCol

1875 Wt. W593/826 1,000,000 4/15 J.B.C. & A. A.D.S.S./Forms/C. 2118.

WAR DIARY
or
INTELLIGENCE SUMMARY

(Erase heading not required.)

Army Form C. 2118

Place	Date	Hour	Summary of Events and Information	Remarks and references to Appendices
Boury.	29/9/16		76th In Bgde. Refilling new area at FLECHINELLE, all Divnl Troops (less 4 Divnl Rifle Bgde for detraining) at Hurionville.	
			10 Tons Coal to 2 Co. Westcappel	
		30/9/16	All unit refilling in known. Divnl Troops on RIVE.	
			THEROUANNE Rd Opposite 'Q' in St QUENTIN.	
			No 1 Co at St QUENTIN	
			2 Co at FLECHINELLE	
			3 Co " AUDINCTHUN	
			4 Co " BOMY-BOURT.	
			Arrangements made to get platoons from 6 GHQ Ammn Park at AIRE	J Murphy Lt Col

Army Form C. 2118

WAR DIARY
or
INTELLIGENCE SUMMARY
(Erase heading not required.)

Instructions regarding War Diaries and Intelligence Summaries are contained in F. S. Regs., Part II. and the Staff Manual respectively. Title Pages will be prepared in manuscript.

Place	Date	Hour	Summary of Events and Information	Remarks and references to Appendices
BOMY	27/9/16		Enemy shelled [illegible] cupps from town arrived & used a further 6·0·0 of [illegible], making 10 [illegible] in all, from M. Bernard. Ompost E. Libes; 28 Cars went & [illegible] from WARDRECOURS [illegible]. Slight rain.	
	28/9/16		Went A.I.R.C. [illegible]. Emptied with new Coming at [illegible]. Emptied curving a relaxation of 5 [illegible] cups from [illegible] [illegible].	
	29/9/16		Raining during morning. 7773's ble hundred in duplicate.	
	30/9/16		[illegible]	[signature] Capt. SSO [illegible]

1875 Wt. W593/826 1,000,000 4/15 J.B.C. & A. A.D.S.S./Forms/C. 2118.

S.O. 3RD DIV: TROOPS

Army Form C. 2118.

S.O. 3rd Divl Troops

WAR DIARY
or
INTELLIGENCE SUMMARY.
(Erase heading not required.)

Instructions regarding War Diaries and Intelligence Summaries are contained in F.S. Regs., Part II. and the Staff Manual respectively. Title pages will be prepared in manuscript.

Place	Date	Hour	Summary of Events and Information	Remarks and references to Appendices
GROVETOWN	1st Apr.		Lorries arrive 12.15 pm. Refilling 12.45 pm. Ration 31 Units. Supply waggons arrive before night.	
"	2 "		Ration as usual.	
"	3 "		Ration as usual.	
"	4 "		Ration as usual.	
"	5 "		Ration as usual.	
"	6 "		Ration as usual. Waggon men sell mill & serve mill then tomorrow. Iron	
"	7 "		rations MERICOURT of line line.	
"	8 "	4.30 pm	March from GROVETOWN to FRECHENCOURT. Refilling point at village. Lorries arrive 8.30 pm. Last units draw 8.30 pm.	
FRECHENCOURT	9 "		March to DOULLENS. Refilling point DOULLENS – ALBERT road, one mile from DOULLENS. Lorries arrive 4.30 pm. All units drawn by 10 pm.	
DOULLENS	9 "	4.30 pm	March to BOUBERS-SUR-CANCHE. Refilling point one mile west of village. Lorries arrive 4.30 pm. Last units draw 8.30 pm.	
BOUBERS	10 "	4.30 pm	March to BERGUENEUSE. Refilling point one mile south of village. Lorries arrive 4.30 pm. All units drawn by 8 pm.	
BERGUENEUSE	11 "		March to MARLES-LES-MINES. Refilling point on BRUAY road. Lorries arrive	

Army Form C. 2118.

WAR DIARY
or
INTELLIGENCE SUMMARY.
(Erase heading not required.)

Instructions regarding War Diaries and Intelligence Summaries are contained in F. S. Regs., Part II. and the Staff Manual respectively. Title pages will be prepared in manuscript.

Place	Date	Hour	Summary of Events and Information	Remarks and references to Appendices
BERGUENEUSE	11 Sept		4:30 p.m. all units finished draining 6:30 p.m.	
MINES-MARLES-LES-	12 Sept		March to VAUDRICOURT region, rest of Division. Refilling in afternoon sqn at shed 36"	
			H.L.D. 2.5.	
VAUDRICOURT	13 Sept		As refilling.	
"	14 "		Refilling 10 p. Rations are being drawn by Lorry transport from VAEUX-LES-MINES.	
"	15 "		Refilling 10 p.m. Refilling point K.17.D.1.	
"	16 "		Routine as yesterday.	
"	17 "		Routine as usual.	
"	18 "		Routine as usual.	
"	19 "		Routine as usual.	
"	20 "		Routine as usual.	
"	21 "		Routine as usual.	
"	22 "		Routine as usual.	
"	23 "		Routine as usual in morning. In afternoon the Centre forward A MARLES-LES-MINES Lorries arrived 7:30 p.m. Refilled 23rd d No Bde. artillery & D.A.C. The 42" Bde. relieved at MARLES-LES-MINES	
"	24 "		MARLES-LES-MINES. In afternoon march to MARLES-LES-MINES.	

Army Form C. 2118.

WAR DIARY
or
INTELLIGENCE SUMMARY.
(Erase heading not required.)

Instructions regarding War Diaries and Intelligence Summaries are contained in F.S. Regs., Part II. and the Staff Manual respectively. Title pages will be prepared in manuscript.

Place	Date	Hour	Summary of Events and Information	Remarks and references to Appendices
MARLESCES	26/7/16		Lorries arrived 7.30 am. Refilling found at CHOCQUES road near village. Refuel 40th Bde & 2nd Bde. artillery & D.A.C. 41st Bde artillery refill with 9th Infantry Bde. In afternoon went to St QUINTIN.	
St QUINTIN	26"		Lorries arrived 7.45 am. Refill all R.F.A. & mobile vet. Refilling point one and a half mile from AIRE or MAMETZ road	
"	27 "		Routine as usual.	
"	28 "		Routine as usual.	
"	29 "		Routine as usual.	
"	30 "		Routine as usual.	

Army Form C. 2118.

S.O. 8th Inf. Bde.

WAR DIARY
or
INTELLIGENCE SUMMARY
(Erase heading not required.)

S.O. 8th Inf Bde

Instructions regarding War Diaries and Intelligence Summaries are contained in F. S. Regs., Part II. and the Staff Manual respectively. Title Pages will be prepared in manuscript.

Place	Date	Hour	Summary of Events and Information	Remarks and references to Appendices
In the field	1-9-16		Hd. Qrs. group including 3rd Div. Hd Qrs., 3rd Div. R.E. Hd Qrs., 3rd Signal Coy., 3rd Div. Train Hd Qrs., 3rd Div. Salvage Coy., A.O.C., 5th Sanitary Section, III M.M. Vet. Section attached for rations	
"	2-9-16		Visited Hd Qrs. group units.	
"	3-9-16		No vegetables on pack train received	Cabbages, Carrots Turnips bought
"	4-9-16		Railhead loading by H.T. at NOEUX-LES-MINES or 9 a.m. Railhead on NOEUX-LES-MINES – BETHUNE road at K. 6.c Sheet 36 B. Visited Brigade units	
"	5-9-16		Hd Qrs. T.M. Batteries attached for rations.	
"	6-9-16		Visited units.	
"	7-9-16		Routine arrival Strength of Brigade Hd Qrs. group:-	

All ranks H.D. rations L.T. Cots. Small Arms
4277 — 162 — 18 — 11

A.E. Wовеnden Lieut.
I.O. 8th Inf. Bde.

Army Form C. 2118.

WAR DIARY
or
INTELLIGENCE SUMMARY
(Erase heading not required.)

Place	Date	Hour	Summary of Events and Information	Remarks and references to Appendices
In the field	8-9-16		Routine as usual	
"	9-9-16		Bn. vegs. on pack team. Cabbages, Carrots turnips bright received. Visited units.	
"	10-9-16		Routine as usual	
"	11-9-16		Routine as usual. Visited Bde. Hdqrs.	
"	12-9-16		Routine as usual	
"	13-9-16		Three days vegetable ration from Divisional Supply Column. Issued 1¼ ozs. per man to be made up by a further 2 ozs. of vegetables. Visited units	
"	14-9-16		Repairing Cart Staff 363. * 24 a.m. Lorries arrived 2.35 p.m. No fresh meat head have been reduced Bde. Slough	

Attack = H.Q. L.A. Bde. Pack Mule
4306 - 153 - 5765 - 18
11
S.O. [signature]

Army Form C. 2118.

WAR DIARY
or
INTELLIGENCE SUMMARY
(Erase heading not required.)

Instructions regarding War Diaries and Intelligence Summaries are contained in F. S. Regs., Part II. and the Staff Manual respectively. Title Pages will be prepared in manuscript.

Place	Date	Hour	Summary of Events and Information	Remarks and references to Appendices
In the field	15-9-16		No fresh meat, tried, have evidence at refilling point	
"	16-9-16		Rations brought by M.T. as before. Refilling point Sheet 36 B. K. 12.a.5.2. Fresh vegetable purchased locally	
"	17-9-16		Visited Bde. M.O. and units Help group units returned to last line transferred to Bde. Shops	
"	18-9-16		Routine as usual	
"	19-9-16		Routine as usual	
"	20-9-16		Routine as usual. Visited all units	
"	21-9-16		8th Fld Ambulance + Cheshire R.U. Eng. R.E. transferred. Belonging to 9th Bde. after refilling. 142nd Fld Ambulance & 56th Coy R.E. joined the Bde. after refilling. Bde. transport to ALLOUAGNE. Bde. H.Q. at ALLOUAGNE. Bde. Sheet -	

All ranks H.Q. Staff 63 Other ranks 11
                      118 - 593 - 18
                      4040
                                          S.O. 8th Inf By. B.C.

Army Form C. 2118.

WAR DIARY
or
INTELLIGENCE SUMMARY

(Erase heading not required.)

Instructions regarding War Diaries and Intelligence Summaries are contained in F. S. Regs., Part II and the Staff Manual respectively. Title Pages will be prepared in manuscript.

Place	Date	Hour	Summary of Events and Information	Remarks and references to Appendices
In field	22.9.16		Orders arrived at 7 a.m. Bde marched to ADINCTHUN. Bde HQrs at MEROUAMEZ. Train HQrs. Bomy.	
"	23.9.16		Reported 3rd Fd. HQrs. & 100 all ranks of 7 Div. 3rd Bn R.E. HQrs., 3rd Signal Coy. R.E., 3rd Divl. Train HQrs., 7 A.O.O. party of G Unit. Horses arrived at AUDINCTHUN at 7:45 a.m. 1 A.S.C. died. Ambulance & B-Coy R.E. returned to 9th Bde after refilling.	
"	24.9.16		Refilling point at BLEN on main road between COYECQUE & DENNEBROEUCQ. Lorries arrived 6.30 a.m. Bde the G.S. at OPEN D. Avion. Visited Bde H.M.	
"	25.9.16		Visited units.	
"	26.9.16		Visited units. Routine as usual. 108 conferences of F.A., K, S.L. recon. for East Yorks - 80.	
"	27.9.16		Routine as usual.	

A. C. Renton Lt.
B.O. 8th Inf. Bde.

Army Form C. 2118.

WAR DIARY
or
INTELLIGENCE SUMMARY
(Erase heading not required.)

Instructions regarding War Diaries and Intelligence Summaries are contained in F.S. Regs., Part II. and the Staff Manual respectively. Title Pages will be prepared in manuscript.

Place	Date	Hour	Summary of Events and Information	Remarks and references to Appendices
Rail head	28-9-16		Supply of vegetable at rate quoted. Potatoes being purchased locally by D.P.O.	
	29-9-16		Vintolie arrived.	
	30-9-16		Routine as usual. 1000 kilos of Straw for bedding arrived. Bin Straight —	
			All ranks HQ. L.B. Carts Riding Mules	
			4060 — 111 — 306 — 18 — 11	

A.E. Rhoding
Lieut.
S.O. i/c Sup. Dep. Rail head.

S.O. 9th Inf Brigade

Army Form C. 2118.

WAR DIARY
INTELLIGENCE SUMMARY
(Erase heading not required.)

S. O. 9th Inf. Bde.

Instructions regarding War Diaries and Intelligence Summaries are contained in F. S. Regs., Part II. and the Staff Manual respectively. Title pages will be prepared in manuscript.

Place	Date	Hour	Summary of Events and Information	Remarks and references to Appendices
VAUDRICOURT.	31/8/16		Lorries arrived 8.0 am. Offloaded ilker by 9.0 am. Refilles. All ranks as usual.	
"	1-9-16.		Lorries arrived 9.0 am. Refilles 9.30 am. Leave & other returns as usual	
"	2-9-16.		Lorries arrived 9.0 am. Refilles 9.30 am. Green fodder leaves as usual	
"	3-9-16.		Lorries as usual. Green fodder ⁊ should same fresh vegetables. Other returns as usual	
"	4-9-16.		Loaded up horse transport in back at NOEUX LES MINES. Refilled at usual between 9½ & 10½ of BETHUNE. All ranks as usual including green fodder. Grenades refilly 11.15 am	
"	5-9-16.		Routine as for H.Q.	
"	6-9-16.		Routine as usual	
"	7-9-16.		Routine as usual	
"	8-9-16.		Usual refitting. Attacked 3 tons clean from Purchase Repr. 3 Army at BETHUNE for issue for HD horses. Rode went to trenches.	

E M Wead
Capt a/c

Army Form C. 2118.

WAR DIARY
INTELLIGENCE SUMMARY.
(Erase heading not required.)

Instructions regarding War Diaries and Intelligence Summaries are contained in F. S. Regs., Part II. and the Staff Manual respectively. Title pages will be prepared in manuscript.

S.O. 9th Lifle

Place	Date	Hour	Summary of Events and Information	Remarks and references to Appendices
VAUDRICOURT.	9/9/16		Loaded in bulk by horse transport at NOEUX LES MINES, at 9.0a.m. Refilled in BETHUNE – NOEUX tons at 10 a.m. all issues as usual including green timber. Other rations as usual.	
"	10/9/16		As for 9th inst.	
"	11/9/16		As for 9th inst.	
"	12/9/16		Routine as usual	
"	13/9/16		Routine as above. Cheese ration reduced to 1½ ozs.	
"	14/9/16		Lorries arrives at refilling point in NOEUX – BARLIN road at 3o'clock pm. Refilled at 2.30 pm. Issues less tinned jam	
"	15/9/16		As for 14th inst.	
"	16/9/16		Loaded in bulk by horse transport at NOEUX at 9am. Refilled on NOEUX – VERQUIN road at 10am. all issues as usual also fresh vegetables locally purchased. Other rations as usual.	

EM Neal
Capt. ASC.

Army Form C. 2118.

WAR DIARY
INTELLIGENCE SUMMARY.
(Erase heading not required.)

S.O. 9th Inf. Bde.

Instructions regarding War Diaries and Intelligence Summaries are contained in F.S. Regs., Part II. and the Staff Manual respectively. Title pages will be prepared in manuscript.

Place	Date	Hour	Summary of Events and Information	Remarks and references to Appendices
VAUDRICOURT	17/9/16		Refilling point & times same as for 16/9/16. 500 kilos oat straw issued in all units for H.Ds horses (amended supply) also Green Fodder. (Above straw obtained from President Purchase Board 1st Army). Otherwise routine as usual.	
"	18/9/16		Refilling point & times same as for 17/9/16. All issues as usual including green fodder. Vegetable ration as usual (6ozs) plus 2 ozs onion for deficiency of 1½ozs cheese = 10 ozs altogether. Otherwise routine as usual. Rum issued at 5% to accord to strength in trenches only.	
"	19/9/16		As for 18/9/16.	
"	20/9/16		Refilling as for 19th inst. Sugar ration reduced to 2½ ozs on account of the milk being sweetened. (Milk rations 12 men to 1 tin).	
"	21/9/16		As for 20th inst.	
"	22/9/16		Refilled from 16th D.S.C. at 7.a.m on VAUDRICOURT - BETHUNE road. All P.MEAT & Biscuit. 56 Field Co RE & 142nd Fd Ambulance are retained by 8th Bde & Brigade Fd Br. RE & 3rd Fd Ambulance are retained by us. Also Div H.Qt Coy, Divisional H.Qrs, & H.Qrs RE draw form us that day. Cheese 3 oz ration. Fresh Vegetable issued also a light artillery waggon proceeded to heavy area & off-loaded in new trucks of units.	

C.Henderson Capt
A.L.C.

Army Form C. 2118.

WAR DIARY
or
INTELLIGENCE SUMMARY.
(Erase heading not required.)

S.O. 9th Inf. Bde.

Instructions regarding War Diaries and Intelligence Summaries are contained in F. S. Regs., Part II. and the Staff Manual respectively. Title pages will be prepared in manuscript.

Place	Date	Hour	Summary of Events and Information	Remarks and references to Appendices
BURBURE	23/9/16		Dump at 7 a.m. on BURBURE-LILLERS road ½ m. from 16th D.S.C. Units on 22/9/16 for Hdqrts. R.E. & 3rd Div. Grenade School. Routine as usual. Wagon proceeded after refilling to 2nd screen & off-loaded at new billets of units in rest area.	
BONCOURT	24/9/16		Dump at 8.30 a.m. on COHEM-BEAUMETZ-Enq-AIRE road from 16th D.S.C. Units as 23/9/16 plus Hdqrts R.E. 3rd Signal Co. A.O.C. Train Hdqrts. 56th Fld Bry RE & 142 2nd Fld Ambulance. 8th Field Ambulance & Plaston Fld Coy RE left on 23/9/16 for 8th Bde & were returned by the latter to-day. All return as usual. Fresh vegetables purchased locally issued to complete ration. Train headquarters moved to BOMY.	
"	25/9/16		Lorries arrive 8.20 a.m. Refilled as 24/9/16 plus 42nd Bde RFA and 129 Batty R.F.A. All return as usual.	
"	26/9/16		Lorries arrive as for 25th Inst. Refilled less 42nd Bde R.FA and 129 Batty R.F.A. Some fresh vegetables obtained from D.P.O. BETHUNE. Other routine as usual.	
"	27/9/16		As for 26th Inst. — units as 26th Inst. Some fresh vegetables issued to complete ration obtained from D.P.O. BETHUNE.	
"	28/9/16		As for 27 Inst. entirely.	
"	29/9/16		Units & refilling as for 27 inst. All vegetables issued were obtained from local purchase - none were obtained at railhead.	

G. Hawkins Capt
a/C.O. 9th Inf. Bde.

S.O. 96 Feb. Cusar

Army Form C. 2118.

WAR DIARY
or
INTELLIGENCE SUMMARY
(Erase heading not required.)

To Hell on Rete

Instructions regarding War Diaries and Intelligence Summaries are contained in F. S. Regs., Part II. and the Staff Manual respectively. Title Pages will be prepared in manuscript.

Place	Date	Hour	Summary of Events and Information	Remarks and references to Appendices
	Sept 1st 1916 (Friday)		Refilling on Railway Vanstreed road at 7.30 am - checks all suppliants - QM Stan S/Sgt at Noeux le Mines - Pte Wigman integrand there as unreliable Linguist - 11 m Jr Sun Vg - College Lewis's Stampers Tournaments - ten issue Sunday as arrangement have been made for no deep training on Park train that day -	
	Sept 2nd		Lorries arrive 4 am Refilling 9.30 am morton anuval Green Vegs Falutes from Béthune -	
	Sept 3rd (Sunday)		Freight Light J. Brigade - AR 50/67 WD 151 FD 444 Coto 20 Mules 26. Relieve as usual Refill for bathing from lorries - to show since gun railhead arrived - from Green Vegs -	
	Sept 4th		Shrap from Noeux le Mines Raidone at 9.40 Refilling at R 12.c (363) on main road from NCM & Bethune - Relieve all units - loth Division asked for reimbursement of receipt and payment during climb n 27 hulls - Authority given by Qt train for payment	
	Sept 5th Tues		Routine as usual -	
	Sept 6th Wed		" " "	
	Sept 7th Thurs		Authority for issue of ten rolls per man for his preparation	

H. Appleby, LMSC

Army Form C. 2118.

WAR DIARY
or
INTELLIGENCE SUMMARY

(Erase heading not required.)

Instructions regarding War Diaries and Intelligence Summaries are contained in F. S. Regs., Part II. and the Staff Manual respectively. Title Pages will be prepared in manuscript.

Place	Date	Hour	Summary of Events and Information	Remarks and references to Appendices
Sept	8th Fri		Routine as usual. Col. & J. learn the column together on 77J. Tilt from Veg from Bulbura [Jurveres] in [Sutceny] — Routine as usual.	
	Sept 9th Sat		Strength RR 5148 10D 1St b. D 414 Mules 26 E.b. 18 Routine as usual.	
	Sept 10th Sun			
	Sept 11th Mon		Started all units of Case Emp & MG Bettys — Mess Pret cor stated also the Summary of infantile & injurious with 3313 [Survey] — Jow 170 & Tuesday Aug — Bear Notes received at weekly — Rail loud.	
	Sept 12th Tues		Routine as usual. —	
	Sept 13th Wed		Only ½ ration above normal — New order DD 7507 745/3/11/9/16 — thence rates increase to 1½ oz — Veg Ration increase Eg in lieu.	
	Sept 14th Thur		all ration received "No Ration" 1 PM Biscuit, Tea & Sugar (Bacon No Bacon, Cheese F.M. or Bread — These ration were drawn for the Brigade at Bulbura — Incl. of Sep. 2 Supplies convoy with our ration in camp — Refilling Point stayed at the 366. X 240 15.	
	Sept 15th Fri		Same [Jundes] as Yesterday. All [ten] Bln required Routine as usual. Refilling on yesterday — [tritter] [Survey] [Rgg.]	
	Sept 16th Sat		Refilling Point changed to K 12 a 6.0. (Sheet 36b) in [Nuven] in [Murra] [Survey] Road — [Fresh] Meat Breakening as usual — Jaune [Roll].	

Army Form C. 2118.

WAR DIARY
or
INTELLIGENCE SUMMARY

(Erase heading not required.)

Instructions regarding War Diaries and Intelligence Summaries are contained in F. S. Regs., Part II. and the Staff Manual respectively. Title Pages will be prepared in manuscript.

Place	Date	Hour	Summary of Events and Information	Remarks and references to Appendices
	Sept 17th Sunday		Strength AR 600S Horses MD 213 LD 455 Mules 26 Carts 18. Cement been received (68th) also 1400 lbs potatoes about - Regs. were cement for Railroad siding - Drew 100 yds or cent 1090. Visited all Coy units of Brigade - RO 76th Inf Bde - Refilling point as yesterday.	
	Sept 18th Monday		Routine as usual. Bought a further 720 × Green Veg Khakure under drawn from Railroad - Visited Supplies of Brigade.	
	Sept 19th Tuesday		Routine as usual 100 Veg received from Railway 50 + 20 in Tins of Cheese - Visited all Supplies of Brigade - Cookhouse units received as only 2 1/2 × 3 days per man.	
	Sept 20th Wednesday		Routine as usual.	
	Sept 21st Thursday		Refill no load turn from Railway, no old refilling point - Visited all Supplies - Bad fire last time Pack of Bowworth - 170 Twenty Coys - ale MO & letter of Brown - Letter 7 am repro 7.45 Det Sandetary Section -	
	Sept 22nd Friday		Refilling point Venerness - Bethune Road E.28 central (36B) - Supplies returned by Supp Column 30. Cheese received per PM Lowis.	
	Sept 23rd Sat		Refilling as yesterday Drew suits for 3rd Train 10 am - After refilling came Wandecourt for ALLOUAGNE (a few Kilom S of HA & SRS).	

Kerr. Mgr.

WAR DIARY or INTELLIGENCE SUMMARY

Army Form C. 2118.

Place	Date	Hour	Summary of Events and Information	Remarks and references to Appendices
	Sept 24th Sund		Strength 9 Base Group AR 5262 WO 140 LD 447 Malin 26 Sub 18. Rifle Inspection of Crew Rooms - Allemagne at 8 am - after rifling continued trek to Flechinelle near Estree Blanche whilst the Butterflies Brandin 51 drew in N.S.W. Brigade was being at this Butterflies Brandin 51 drew in N.S.W. from Allemagne - 1st Echelon of Estree Blanche - 767 M Battery 10th Reveil of Liettres - 2 Suppers - Enguin-les-Mines 8 Kinghams - Flechin - 7 Field Ambce Seany also 76 Machine Gun death - KRR B/n ol Engineercatte & Rising Rd - Lingham	
	Sept 25th Mond		Rifling at Flechinelle in road from Estree Blanche - Cohem. Lorries arrive at 750 - Rifling at 9 am - Contact arranged for supply D 43 Vegs daily Div at Bourset - Couper - Lillern Cabbage 10 for work, Cauls 15 for 100 k, Turnips Efos 100 k -	
	Sept 26th Tues		I wait 775 I 447 cannot be guaranteed by Veg merchant on sale so expecting upon rain arising daily. Rifle as yesterday	
	Sept 27th Wed 28th Thurs 29th Fri		Owing Bakery 6 Bttn 1/63 Fletcher the ills daily Routine as usual Rivstead I 69 for her daily I for her daily	
	Sept 30th Sat		Visited Bourre Chapel - Battle of the Btttn maintenance for persons maitri ullintz fooc 100 11 Odctering Ptc	

M Off

SS.O 3rd Division

S.S.O 3rd Div

Vol 10

WAR DIARY
or
INTELLIGENCE SUMMARY
(Erase heading not required.)

Army Form C. 2118

Place	Date	Hour	Summary of Events and Information	Remarks and references to Appendices
BOMY	1-10-16		Refilling as usual. Units milked. No coal at milkers. 30 ton mot received on WARD RECQUES. (10 km to BOMY 10 km to FLÉCHINELLE.	
"	2-10-16		Units at 3 b, 4 b, & 9 b also milkers. No coal owing to asks I Army & others order to tons to tons I Army ordered all Purchases being supply little to be F.P. held 13 to 4 tonnes — at no duty to keep out more f/water 1 ft. Same at same hour.	
"	3-10-16		Units at 4 b at 2 b also milkers. No coal. Attempt arranged from RECQUES to proceed to tank tipflaches at Army mine depot. Operation unless received for move to Fifth Reserve Army.	
"	4-10-16		Units 4b, 5b, 2b, to tipflaches. Another 10 tons coal however from BRAY in to complete total of 30 ton arranged by A.D.S.Q. Also 30 tons at milkers which were handed over to Thirty Fifth Bn CW[?] not now required, no owing to move are refilling at 4 b... All arrangements handed of full bns in to have ready to move tomorrow [?]	

Army Form C. 2118

S.S.O. 35 Nn

WAR DIARY
or
INTELLIGENCE SUMMARY
(Erase heading not required.)

Place	Date	Hour	Summary of Events and Information	Remarks and references to Appendices
MONCHY CAYEUX	5/10/16		All supply wagons moved loaded to the new Establishments to units on principal wagon lines to refilling points as follows:- 76th Bde HEUCHIN, 85th Bde LISBOURG, 9th Bde SAUTRECOURT (WAVRANS), Bde ANVIN. Lorries arrives (with rations to complete 4 g) at 4 a.m. units were refilled & rations for all were ready by 9 a.m. on 7th were released to units (demonstrating) all things & units to trans port & rails were left on Supply park lines ready was taken to trans port B lines ready to send and not by Government. The all RFA were carefully handed over to month were carefully handed over to units were carefully transferred to B lines ready to units and ready to send tomorrow. Units reached & set from troop train.	[signature]
MONCHY CAYEUX	6/10/16		Visited rail heads LILLERS, all supply refills in PREVENT. ETREE VAM in No. 5 (A8 equipped on 8th) unto railhead PREVENT in reference to loading him up there in morning.	[signature] G W Lyall

WAR DIARY
or
INTELLIGENCE SUMMARY

Army Form C. 2118

S.S.O. 325 Div.

Place	Date	Hour	Summary of Events and Information	Remarks and references to Appendices
BERTRANGOURT	7/10/16		Major PREVENT takes S. All dumps etc entrusted to this man. RFA hole got completely away S. Visited BELLE EGLISE trenches loading there tomorrow. Guns amount to 8 heavy Cat. Walter Reserve Army D.B.O.B. 4 of the rest dries on this (also advanced 3 inch Bns. of course Burnage are training from to LOUVENCOURT - LEAL VILLERS) front.	
"	8/10/16		Took command in BERTRANGOURT. Entered Wheeles. Visited R.E.O. training very late. Line to landing 12 noon at BELLE EGLISE, have transport ready, commences landing 2.30 one landing & more nearly Bde. group. Night Bde takes 6 have nearly 1000 pm matters to last once Pack horse Capt nobles's 2.5 B.G. train in close at BERTRANCOURT will be taken after to Cart dumps. Daily resume will be issued in course of...	

Army Form C. 2118

WAR DIARY
or
INTELLIGENCE SUMMARY
(Erase heading not required.)

S.S.O 2nd Div

Place	Date	Hour	Summary of Events and Information	Remarks and references to Appendices
BERTRANCOURT	9-10-16		Visited outposts — also R.E.O. train still carrying back several cart-loads of rifle oil — went to 9th Bde who also divisional stores — rifle oil demanded — (45 galls) to be kept with Bde O's. Arranges with O.C. 1/6 train to detail an officer to take over Horse Patrol this morning on No.16 Suff. Coln, Visited E.O.C No. 16 Suff. Coln. — went to there lines. Refused to take place — nothing to do — this Coln. at war at farm No. Yds. 7.30 a.m. at west nestled Jt. Point near Company steels — lunched at wheelers Companies at 9.15 am Major returned to Company lines afterwards landed 7 pm Carts of in the morning.	CWWard Capt RAVC
	10/10/16		Received letter 9th Visit. Train 12 mules, 1 cart chained sickness to BERTRANCOURT Went... lists all S.O.'s limit interpreted at Wheelers wtr for company loading at mules 5. 7.45 pm Wagon stones to Company lines ready to receive our company.	

1875 Wt. W593/826 1,000,000 4/15 J.B.C. & A. A.D.S.S./Forms/C. 2118.

Army Form C. 2118

WAR DIARY
or
INTELLIGENCE SUMMARY
(Erase heading not required.)

S.S.O. 35. Div.

Place	Date	Hour	Summary of Events and Information	Remarks and references to Appendices
BERTRANCOURT	11-10-16		Visited all S.O's. Wants D.A.D.o.S. to arrange for purchase of fresh vegetables in AMIENS. Reply now unsuccessful in the afternoon. Coke returned (1000 to 1200 lbs daily) required on Q work daily. En Q ordered a lorry daily to purchase vegetables. This was commenced 13". Details re B.E.F. Kit A/C sent to divisions to complete. Vegetables wanted in AMIENS. Capt St Prendt from Remount at DOULLENS for 13 & 14". Visited all S.O's, also smiths, blacksmiths. Staff at workshops at 4 p.m. Refilling Pt. Clothes outside village from Railhead S. Supplies Ordnance from Doullens.	
"	12-10-16		Commenced lorry service at 12.45 from Rlhd retrieves the return. All arrangements all S.O's. Visits all S.O's. Waiter D.D.O.S. in reference to motor returns.	T.W.Wentele

Army Form C. 2118

WAR DIARY
or
INTELLIGENCE SUMMARY
(Erase heading not required.)

Instructions regarding War Diaries and Intelligence Summaries are contained in F.S. Regs., Part II. and the Staff Manual respectively. Title Pages will be prepared in manuscript.

Place	Date	Hour	Summary of Events and Information	Remarks and references to Appendices
BERTRAN COURT	13/10/16		Working commenced at reached 11 a.m. watch at S.O.	
	14/10/16		Looking at villages & inflatables for horses. 11 a.m. Went Amiens re purchase two bed supply for the troops. Stopped contract for other inflatables from Amiens which arrive at reitheon.	
			17th Btn 11 Plns (Pioneers) to be relieved by us from Coy. 16th wind attached 9th Sn. Pigle. went D.O.A.P.T. Name amongst the overlays pour grain of two met Phoenix required for tactical purposes. Trades fine.	
	15/10/16		Reached working at 11 a.m. Received from tomorrow will be at Ae Heut, I am P.S.O. that?; relative supply Col s at S.O. Interviewed L Col to exchange woods retain freedom for orders at 3 F.S. Depot. Hitherto ration (1870) from the fighting troops for 3 days lined in reserve until required. Instructions issued by Q to Col and S.O. aeroplane weatherfine.	Address copy S.O.

Army Form C. 2118

WAR DIARY
or
INTELLIGENCE SUMMARY
(Erase heading not required.)

Instructions regarding War Diaries and Intelligence Summaries are contained in F.S. Regs., Part II. and the Staff Manual respectively. Title Pages will be prepared in manuscript.

Place	Date	Hour	Summary of Events and Information	Remarks and references to Appendices
BERTRAN COURT.	16/7/16		Milked at ACHEUX. Loading commenced about 11.15 am. train several hours late. All 6 train Q. moved this morning to O.S.C.D. wagons after loading notified in new camp area. Lorry decided H.Q. & proceed to arrange divl. motor lorries supply for horses; weather fine.	
	Night		Loading commenced at 11.30 pm. @ Prev. meal 30% more rv 30%. T all transits as arrived today; these supplies are to be dumped in Brigade Co. Camp. There as a reserve. Consignments no repealing or delivery lorries takes place today. 8th Inf Bgde. to LOUVINCOURT, 7th Bgde to LOUVENCOURT, 9th Inf Bgde to COURCELLES today, Divl. HQ'rs to BUS tomorrow. Pilots & coul. Hyd. in BUS today; weather fine, cold.	

[signature] Capt.

1875 Wt. W593/826 1,000,000 4/15 J.B.C. & A. A.D.S.S./Forms/C. 2118.

WAR DIARY or INTELLIGENCE SUMMARY

Army Form C. 2118

Place	Date	Hour	Summary of Events and Information	Remarks and references to Appendices
BUS to ARTOIS	13/10/16		Lushed at CONTEVILLE from today - this place is 25 miles distant from our area. Necessitates Horse 7 Supply Columns again. Based D.S.T. drawn Fuel to Bulk Issue, no distance beyond — Can't if from Coutenville & Bertrancourt. Loading at railhead to any gun — tractor without refilling points — weather fine.	
	14/10/16		Hauled railhead refilling points - arrangements made to ensure day ration held in reserve, but S. Col dumps seem to be spread between two. This was necessary to expedite further petrol at 6.m. transit from the heavy tractors. Obtained 30 him trial from the 1st Canadian Division. Instructions issued by Q. Division to us own artillery. The order was subsequently cancelled. Weather very cold. Brigs to S.Col. Seymour. No spare lorries are available Continue Controls at Amiens for supply of roofs for horses — an endeavour to procure tarpaulins.	Memos Oct. S.S.O

WAR DIARY or INTELLIGENCE SUMMARY

Army Form C. 2118

Place	Date	Hour	Summary of Events and Information	Remarks and references to Appendices
BuS	29/10/16		Went Railhead, no fuel available. Lorries dumped this morning supplies for tomorrows consumption. Supply situation now normal. Today at railhead 12 tons G.S. T.M. butter attached trend slip for rations drawn, wastage, fuel, etc.	
	30/10/16		S.C.C through Corpering withdraws close to coal today. Lorries Lorring Coopers Moved from Ordnance for issue to troops tomorrow. Rly return of butter today. Wagon Line - C.R.E. calculation for R.T.A horses under R.O. Army R.O. 1875-21-19 10/16 withdrew to-. Shortage fuel in Consignees from two sources yesterday arranged meat to obtain 15 tons coke + 10 tons coal from Rosse only. This area receives sufficient.	
	31/10/16		Nothing further from Mr Phennis Nations issues have been returns at Nightly rounds from the day returns during the past 3 + 4 days sufficient but slight to make one return for all Supply troops in view that each new chance can be an extra day on their dumping to become effective. Rations stripterham supply matters weather cold Completed of wada treatyo [?]	Horses coff [?] OO 1138 OO 114/[?]

WAR DIARY or INTELLIGENCE SUMMARY

Army Form C. 2118

Place	Date	Hour	Summary of Events and Information	Remarks and references to Appendices
BUS	23/10/18		Difficulty experienced in getting fuel for the Division. Spoke to S. Col. Instructed the Church ration section to set cooks working for tomorrow. Relieved 146th Inf. Bn. butting for tomorrow. Up to the Supply Farm with OC Train transport convoy in case supplies have to be carried up to line by pack horses. Issued splendid service and Bell Syrie of coal. Also much to be thankful for. Weather cold. Amusement BOO 115 received.	
	3/11/76		Sent repairing parties to potatoes railhead also to BST which is potato turnover at Michael. 20 wheelers Capt Veal to proceed recon. Grounds in Orvillers – obtained ordnance Lorry to fetch them. Repairing points: 10000 rations (men) for issue to fighting troops rations from Active railhead today. (1) Top cups Church delivered. Owing the removal 5308 per men at Michael on the 26th inst. This division write the additional issue 1308 potatoes from the stations. Remains short of all day. Amusement (2) 000 115 received Orbs.	

WAR DIARY
INTELLIGENCE SUMMARY
(Erase heading not required.)

Army Form C. 2118

Place	Date	Hour	Summary of Events and Information	Remarks and references to Appendices
BUS LES ARTOIS	28/9/16		Very Cold with Bull Eglise & S'Olymer refilling points. Withdrew truck of coke removed from S. Cloud's shops. Weather unsettled.	
	29/9/16		Iron Begins repair, also refilling points & Contenille continue. Only 2.5lb 7 inch Newson Bombs from to a truck being unloaded on the line somewhere. Another one recd. Consignment of B.O.115 was —	
	30/9/16		Iron & Bull Eglise at first refilling points & Depot Column. Saw R.S.O. between at Chilaye of 17 pdr supper at Boro ferry. Retiring companies were stable then, but R.S.O. on the way tried up again — altogether 8000 S.I.T 10 feet length by here 7 1st Army. Bren cartridges to 80% from today. Saw R.S.O. Iron Contiens Maricourt. Arage by horse transport at Bull Eglise Thiepval — asked B.O.G.S.T Brieuna came removed from 7 trucks water & G — & Smith's. No transport not equal to demand. Also of 100 rubber — may be furnished for lorries at 10ft — for 100 rubber — Agree in effect life. Weather unsettled. Armament work B.O.A 115 returned. O.P.D 116 returned.	Alexander S. Cloyd's Oven.

Army Form C. 2118

WAR DIARY
or
INTELLIGENCE SUMMARY
(Erase heading not required.)

Instructions regarding War Diaries and Intelligence Summaries are contained in F. S. Regs., Part II. and the Staff Manual respectively. Title Pages will be prepared in manuscript.

Place	Date	Hour	Summary of Events and Information	Remarks and references to Appendices
Brus to Cohan	28/10/16		Loading at Belle Eglise from toting by horse transport – train arrived about 1.30, loading commenced 2pm. all wagons (Supp Ʒ) and 6 refill in camp through the following day, thus keeping the Supp Ʒ situation normal – train left refuelling points nothing water not.	
	29/10/16		Loading at newhouse commenced 1.30pm. trains arrived refuelling Pond water not.	
	30/10/16		3am to 9. went received today. train arrived at 4pm 69my, much rain/have camps. weather very wet.	
	31/10/16		train arrived at 11am but was not in position for loading until 4pm. 3pm matter reported D.R.T.O. in want to my chart only 3 ams he did. 3 ams be previously being received, write troops I.T expect for ridens – Received McKenzie Capt SSO	JSSO Sgt

SO 3RD Div. TROOPS

Army Form C. 2118.

WAR DIARY
or
INTELLIGENCE SUMMARY.
(Erase heading not required.)

SO 3rd D. Troops.

Instructions regarding War Diaries and Intelligence Summaries are contained in F.S. Regs., Part II. and the Staff Manual respectively. Title pages will be prepared in manuscript.

Attached cols.
S.O. 3rd D. Troops.

Place	Date	Hour	Summary of Events and Information	Remarks and references to Appendices
St QUINTON	Oct 1st		Lorries arrive 7.45am. Refilling 8am.	
"	" 2nd		Routine as usual.	
"	" 3rd		Routine as usual. Div are now purchasing 2500 kilos of oat straw daily fr. R.F.A. horses, this is bailed & issued at refilling point.	
"	" 4th		Refilling as usual in morning, in afternoon second refilling at Div. HQrs. waggon return & A.S.C. coys & part of supply coy moved at 7pm. Supply waggon march with Bgd. & deliver rations & write at ANVIN. Lorries arrive ANVIN 4pm. all Cols HQ. & coats units refill 5.30pm. through march & R.F.A. will refill in morning.	
ANVIN	" 6th		Refill R.F.A. 6.30am. Supply waggons march with Bgd. to ETREE-WAMEN & deliver rations. Lorries arrive 12m. & units refill as they return from units, finishing well by of night.	
			Supply waggon march with Bgd. deliver rations at ACHEUX & return & camp	
ETREE-WAMEN	" 7th		RAINCHEVAL. No refilling.	
RAINCHEVAL	" 8th		Lorries arrive 8am. refilling 8.30am. at sheet 57.D.O.51.D.5.3.	
	" 9th		Routine as usual	

Army Form C. 2118.

WAR DIARY
or
~~INTELLIGENCE~~ SUMMARY.
(Erase heading not required.)

Instructions regarding War Diaries and Intelligence Summaries are contained in F.S. Regs., Part II. and the Staff Manual respectively. Title pages will be prepared in manuscript.

S.O. 3rd D. Troops.

Place	Date	Hour	Summary of Events and Information	Remarks and references to Appendices
RAINCHEVAL	Oct. 10		Ration drawn by M.T. from railhead at BELLE-EGLISE. Refilling held in camp at 3pm	
	11		Routine as usual.	
	12th		Routine as usual.	
	13th		Routine as usual.	
	14th		Routine as usual.	
	15th		Routine as usual.	
	16		Refilling held as usual. Cony moved A LOOC EAUCOURT.	
	17		The ration was drawn by M.T. & a reserve being made in camp. No issue.	
LOUVENCOURT	18		Convoy arrives 3pm refilling 3.30pm at Sheet 57 D. 1. 29. a. 2. 3.	
	19		1 Lewis cover. H. Capt. Hawkins. Refill from reserve dumped in camp on 17 inst at 3pm — a little Fresh meat & Bread sent up Specially by Lorry to Bdes — remainder Q.M. Biscuits	
	20		Lewis arrived in VAUCHELLE - AUTHIE road (Sheet 57 D. 1. 27. b. 2. 2.) at 7 p.m. Refill 7.45 a.m. All units as usual. Routine as usual.	
	21st		Refilling as usual. Routine as usual.	
	22nd		Refilling at 2 pm. Reserve of 15 galls. Whale oil kept. Routine as usual	

E. Marshall Ingot
SO 3rd D. Troops

O. A. Luckaw Capt.
SO 3rd D. Troops.

Army Form C. 2118.

SO 3rd D Troops

WAR DIARY
or
INTELLIGENCE SUMMARY.
(Erase heading not required.)

Instructions regarding War Diaries and Intelligence Summaries are contained in F.S. Regs., Part II. and the Staff Manual respectively. Title pages will be prepared in manuscript.

Place	Date	Hour	Summary of Events and Information	Remarks and references to Appendices
LUCHEUXCOURT	23/10/16		Refilling ud for 22nd. Extra forage received in dump to-day (R.A. Ru. 173. 19/10/16) viz:- 5 lbs Hay for H.D. breed & 2 lbs oats for L.D. for artillery units only. Rations as usual. Also ration 14.6 T.M.B.s on dray only.	
"	24/10/16		Rations as usual & refilling ud for 23rd inst	
"	25/10/16		at 11 a.m. from reserve. Rations as usual.	
"	26/10/16		" for 24th " " "	
"	27/10/16		" for 25th " " "	
"	28/10/16		" for 26th " " " . 3 rg. characters received to-day – Vegetable ration reduced to 8 ozs. Dump moved about 400 yds up road nearer AUTHIE (122.c.17.) Rations as usual (all fighting troops (i.e. T.M.B's & KRR's) have now a full grocery ration & 1 ration Biscuit & 1 ration M&V with them in reserve). Horse transport at BEUG EGLISE railhead at 2 p.m. Dump in camp at 4 p.m. & refill. 15 g.s. service loaded in company lines	
"	29/10/16		Supply wagons leave for units at 9 am & return to railhead (Belle Eglise) & load at 1 pm refill in camp at 4 p.m. Authority was given to purchase extra rations from units (i.e. Hay H.D. & L.D. Hay L.D.) even though they are receiving the extra amount from railhead. Units informed.	
"	30/10/16		Supply wagons deliver rations – return to railhead – load & return to camp & park overnight.	
"	31/10/16		Refill at 8 a.m. in camp. Wagons deliver troents – load at railhead & remain loaded all night in camp. Rations as usual.	

G. Marshing-Bright
SO 3rd D. Troops

Army Form C. 2118.

S.O. 8th Inf Bde

WAR DIARY
or
INTELLIGENCE SUMMARY
(Erase heading not required.)

Instructions regarding War Diaries and Intelligence Summaries are contained in F. S. Regs., Part II. and the Staff Manual respectively. Title Pages will be prepared in manuscript.

Place	Date	Hour	Summary of Events and Information	Remarks and references to Appendices
Millufell	1-10-'16		Visited units.	
"	2-10-'16		Visited units	
"	3-10-'16		Routine as usual	
"	4-10-'16		Rifle time – second time at 4 p.m.	
			Supply wagon returned to Company's camp.	
	5-10-'16		Company marched to LISBOURG. Batt. Hd. Qrs. at SQUIRREL.	
			Refilling at LISBOURG at 5 p.m.	
	6-10-'16		Company marched to PETIT BOURET with Brigade transport.	
			Refilling at 5 p.m. on main road at GRAND BOURET	
	7-10-'16		Company marched to Camp at O.1.f.3.3 – Sheet 57 7	
			Nose fitting. Batt. Strength.	

All ranks   H.Q.   L.D.   Cobs.   Small Mules.
4103 –   108 –   391 –   18 –   9

A. E. Robinson Lieut

S.O. 8th Inf Bde

Army Form C. 2118.

WAR DIARY
or
INTELLIGENCE SUMMARY
(Erase heading not required.)

Instructions regarding War Diaries and Intelligence Summaries are contained in F. S. Regs., Part II. and the Staff Manual respectively. Title Pages will be prepared in manuscript.

Place	Date	Hour	Summary of Events and Information	Remarks and references to Appendices
In the field	8.10.'16		Resting at O.11.d. Horses arrived 8 a.m. Runs exercised daily from an onwards. Bde. Hdqrs. 4R.S.F. at BEAUSSART. 2nd R.S. & 7th. M. Gun Co. at AUTHUIE WOOD. 7 K.S.L.I. 8th E.Y. 8th A.&.S. Highrs. Bill. Coy. R.E. at MAILLY. Railhead loading & horse transport at BELLE EGLISE at 7 p.m.	
"	9.10.'16		Resting in camp at 7 a.m. Visited Bde. Hdqrs.	
"	10.10.'16		Visited all units. Rationing Town Major of MAILLY-MAILLET.	
"	11.10.'16		30 all ranks. Routine as usual. Refitting 6 p.m.	
"	12.10.'16		Refitting 3 p.m.	
"	13.10.'16		Visited all units.	
"	14.10.'16		Routine as usual. Bde. strength:-	

All ranks. H.D. L.D. Cbe. Small M.G.
4060 - 97 - 391 - 15 - 9

A.C. Robertson
S.O. 8A. I.I. Bde. Lieut.

Army Form C. 2118.

WAR DIARY
or
INTELLIGENCE SUMMARY
(Erase heading not required.)

Instructions regarding War Diaries and Intelligence Summaries are contained in F. S. Regs., Part II. and the Staff Manual respectively. Title Pages will be prepared in manuscript.

Place	Date	Hour	Summary of Events and Information	Remarks and references to Appendices
In the field	15-10-16		Visited units.	
"	16-10-16		Company moved to O.11.a.8.9. Sheet 57 D. Railhead orders at 11 a.m. at ACHEUX. Refilling in camp. M.H's for infantry R.E. held in reserve.	
"	17-10-16		No head of rail heat of railhead. Days ration dumped in camp held in reserve	
"	18-10-16		Refitting at O.57.b.2.6. Lorries arrived at 1.30 p.m. Refitting b, Sp. Bt. in place.	
"	19-10-16		Brigade moved. Bearer Sub Hd. Qrs. to BUS-LES-ARTOIS. 75 R.E. L.F. 8th E.Y. v.t. R.S.F. 6 BUS. 2nd Royal Scots to MAILLY-MAILLET. Ambce Aid Pt. R.E. to COURCELLES. 8th Fld. Amb. to FORCEVILLE. Refilling at I.27.b.3.3. Sheet 57 D. Small issue.	
"	20-10-16		Lorries arrived at 8 a.m. Co. moved to LOUVENCOURT at I.35.a.7.7. Visited all units. Enemy 1 M.N. TT present ration for every man going on leave.	AGR Robinson Lieut S.O. 8th Div.

2449 Wt. W14957/M90 750,000 1/16 J.B.C. & A. Forms/C.2118/12

WAR DIARY
or
INTELLIGENCE SUMMARY

Army Form C. 2118.

Place	Date	Hour	Summary of Events and Information	Remarks and references to Appendices
Sethepe	20-10-16		Sent down M.M. strength return. Pale strength :—	
			B QM rate. H.Q. L.D. Offs. R&F mules.	
			8=277 98 – 394 – 18 – 9	
"	22-10-16		Sent Higgins Heaters. Visited units.	
"	23-10-16		Routine as usual.	
"	24-10-16		Received instruction that from 27th Cheese ration will be below	
			to 3oz + reg. ration 8 ozs. Fresh meat 40%.	
"	25-10-16		Oxo cubes to be daily issue for men in trenches.	
			Visited units	
"	26-10-16		Routine as usual.	
"	27-10-16		Fresh meat ration reduced to 50%.	

A.C. Robertson Col
S.O. St L.f. Bde.

WAR DIARY
or
INTELLIGENCE SUMMARY

(Erase heading not required.)

Army Form C. 2118.

Place	Date	Hour	Summary of Events and Information	Remarks and references to Appendices
In the field	28.10.16		Visited all units. Refilling in Camp.	
"	29.10.16		Railhead loading at 11 a.m. 8th Inf. Bde. Relieved 76th Inf. Bde.	
"	30.10.16		Handed over to Lieut H.L. Kindt.	
"	31.10.16		Refilling 8 a.m. Routine as usual.	

A.P. Ruxton, Lieut
S.O. 8th Inf. Bde.

H.L. Kindt, Lieut
Co. Mk Sup Bde.

SO 9th INF BRIGADE

Army Form C. 2118.

S.O. 9 Inf. Bde.

WAR DIARY
INTELLIGENCE SUMMARY.
(Erase heading not required.)

Instructions regarding War Diaries and Intelligence Summaries are contained in F. S. Regs., Part II. and the Staff Manual respectively. Title pages will be prepared in manuscript.

Place	Date	Hour	Summary of Events and Information	Remarks and references to Appendices
BONCOURT	30/9/16		Refilled from 16" D.S.C. on CUHEM - BEAUMETZ - les - AIRE road. Lorries arrived 8.10 a.m. Refilling completed 9.30 a.m. All stores as usual including green fodder for all purchases and vegetables purchased by D.P.O. Used the units of the Hdqts Division, Hdqts R.E. Hdqts Train, Div. Hdqts Sig. Bn, 3rd Signal Coy & A.O.C.	
" "	1/10/16		As for 30th inst entirely.	
" "	2/10/16		As for 1st inst entirely. Rum issued at 6.6 p.m to all Brigade units.	
" "	3/10/16		As for 2nd instant entirely except that no Rum was issued.	
" "	4/10/16		Refilled as for 3rd inst entirely at same time (8.30 a.m.) Refilled again in afternoon. Lorries arrived 4 p.m. All stores as usual including green fodder. After refilling wagons returned loaded to company lines & parked overnight.	
" "	5/10/16		Company 10 a.m. to BETHONVAL. Supply wagons march loaded with company & trek off en route to different "billets" units. Refilled again at a on main St. POL - ANVIN road at crossroads Fleury - Bethonval at SAVTRICOURT horw arrived 4.15 p.m. Refilling as usual less 3" Div. Hdqts, Hdqts R.E., Hdqts Train, 3rd Signal Coy; A.O.C. & Hdqts Company. After loading wagons proceeded a few & units. The lorries took off all return required by these for men proceeding	

Capt. Bastonal 4.5
p L C

Army Form C. 2118.

WAR DIARY
or
INTELLIGENCE SUMMARY.
(Erase heading not required.)

Instructions regarding War Diaries and Intelligence Summaries are contained in F.S. Regs., Part II. and the Staff Manual respectively. Title pages will be prepared in manuscript.

S.O. 9th Inf. Bde.

Place	Date	Hour	Summary of Events and Information	Remarks and references to Appendices
			by train to new area on 7" inst. (for concentration 7") I left one wagon at old area for transport going by road. (Rums were issued to all units). All wagons then loaded were returned to camp & marched to Bethonval 6th.	
BETHONVAL	6/10/16		Company leave 9 a.m. to CANETTEMONT. Supply wagons with supplies for transport actual units dumped supplies with 1st line transport which had all marched with us & were parked in same field & afterwards proceeded to refilling point at Frevent - Eliré - Wamin main road at road junction CANETTEMONT - REBREUVIETTE. All done as usual (No green flags) No horse arrived 4 p.m. Refilling finished 5.30 p.m. Wagons returned to company lines	
CANETTEMONT	7/10/16		Company leave at 6 a.m. to ARQUEVES with all other Brigade Transport. The latter took off a week & proceeded to meet Brigade area Supply wagons followed on & dumped supplies returning to our camp on cross-roads 600 yds N.W. of Arqueves on VAUCHELLES-AUTHIE - RAINCHEVAL road. No refilling to-day.	
Arqueves	8/10/16		Refilling took place at 8 a.m. on LEALVILLERS - LOUVENCOURT road. All division units as usual. After refilling wagon proceeded to units off-loaded & returned to camp. Loaded in bulk by horse transport at BELLE-EGLISE railhead at 9 p.m. Wagons	B Hawshurst Capt AEC

T/134. Wt. W708-776. 500000. 4/15. Sir J. C. & S.

Army Form C. 2118.

WAR DIARY
or
INTELLIGENCE SUMMARY.
(Erase heading not required.)

S.O. 9th Inf. Bde.

Place	Date	Hour	Summary of Events and Information	Remarks and references to Appendices
ARQUEVES	9/10/16		returned to company lines & parked. Heated overnight. Brigade goes in trenches. Supply wagons proceeded loaded to dump on road leading from camp to ARQUEVES 2000 yds North of road junction with road "ARQUEVES - RAINCHEVAL. Wagons dump at 7 a.m. Refilling completed at 8.30 a.m. All issues as usual including Rum which was issued as yesterday's (8/10/16) strength. Whale oil (15 galls N.14 units) was sent out to all units of Brigade at 7 p.m. Wagons load at Belle Eglise railhead at 9 p.m. Two issues of Rum were made overnight by Convoy - then will be issued tomorrow (10th inst.)	
"	10/10/16		Dumped a.m. 4 units & units as before. Double issue of Rum to catch up load again at 9 p.m. as per 9th inst.	
"	11/10/16		Refill as 10th inst. – rum issued to all units, load again at railhead at 4 p.m. Refill 5.15 p.m – completed 6 p.m. All issues as usual including Rum. Refill in company camp. Supply Reinforcements at 7 a.m. Return direct to railhead & load at 1 p.m. Refill in own	
"	12/10/16		own camp at 9.15 a.m. at 11 inst. at 2 p.m. Completed 2.45 p.m. All issues as usual including Rum. Supply wagons leave loaded for units at 3 p.m. Refill in afternoon at 3 p.m. All issues as usual including Rum. Some fresh	
"	13/10/16		vegetables obtained from D.P.O.	

G.H. Maitrieu Capt.

T/131. Wt. W708-776. 50,000. 4/15. Sir J.C. & S.

WAR DIARY
or
INTELLIGENCE SUMMARY.
(Erase heading not required.)

Army Form C. 2118.

S.O.9* Inf: Bde.

Place	Date	Hour	Summary of Events and Information	Remarks and references to Appendices
ARQUEVES	14/10/16		Supply wagon leave at 6.45 a.m. for units. Return to railhead at 11 a.m. and return to camp. Refill in camp at 3 p.m. completed 4 p.m. All done as usual including Rum & some fresh vegetables obtained from D.P.O.	
"	15/10/16		Supply wagon leave at 6.45 a.m. for units. Return to railhead at 11 a.m. All went on usual. Divisional Canteen opens to units.	
LOUVEN COURT	16/10/16		Supplies delivered to units. Wagons returned to new camp. Refill took place near Camp. Brigade transport parks for the night. All arms as usual.	Arrived at BELLE EGLISE to this Company.
"	17/10/16		Captain de Vergie took over to be liaison. Ration numbers rechecked.	Arrived at ACHEUX — miles S. Wagons to be left from Amp reserve.
"	18/10/16		Lorries arrives 2.30 p.m. at nextfilling point. All drawn as usual. Refills from Divis reserve. Other duties as usual	
"	19/10/16			
"	20/10/16		Refills — VAUCHELLES - AUTHIE — 4 to 5 . Lorries arrived 4.50. all drawn as usual.	

E.W. Neal
Capt.

Army Form C. 2118.

WAR DIARY
or
INTELLIGENCE SUMMARY.
(Erase heading not required.)

S.O. 9th Infantry Bde

Place	Date	Hour	Summary of Events and Information	Remarks and references to Appendices
LOUVENCOURT	23/10/16		Reveille sounds 7.30 am. Seven days in training as usual	
"	24/10/16		Reveille sounds 7.15 am. Seven days in training as usual	
"	25/10/16		Reveille sounds 7.0 am. Rifles S.O.S. all ranks training as usual	
"	26/10/16		Routine as usual	
"	27/10/16		Reveille sounds 8.45 am. Army told men to be sent up to training camp. Other routine as usual	
"	28/10/16		Reveille sounds 8.0 am. Leave granted including fresh vegetables. Others lay head purchase.	
"	29/10/16		Routine as above	

W. Neil
Capt

Army Form C. 2118.

S.O. 9th Inf Bde

WAR DIARY
or
INTELLIGENCE SUMMARY.
(Erase heading not required.)

Instructions regarding War Diaries and Intelligence Summaries are contained in F.S. Regs., Part II. and the Staff Manual respectively. Title pages will be prepared in manuscript.

Place	Date	Hour	Summary of Events and Information	Remarks and references to Appendices
LOUVENCOURT	28/10/16		Annie arrives. E.O. Officiated by 8.45 am on VAUCHELLES – AUTHIE Road. Supplies Rations & Returns to camp. Lorried on trek at BELLE EGLISE midday & men gone returned to Company lines.	
"	29-10-16		Refilled new camp at LOUVENCOURT. M.T. transport to meet & deliver supplies. Loaded on yesterday at midnight. Refilled again near new Coy. lines in Coy lorries.	
"	30-10-16		Supplies delivered to units. Loaded at BELLE EGLISE midday. All guns returned to Company lines. Weather very wet.	
"	31-10-16		Refilled. Supplies delivered to units. Loaded in trek at midday as usual.	

C.W. [signature] Capt

S.O. 76th INF BRIGADE
S.O. 76 Inf Bde

Army Form C. 2118.

WAR DIARY
or
INTELLIGENCE SUMMARY
(Erase heading not required.)

Instructions regarding War Diaries and Intelligence Summaries are contained in F.S. Regs., Part II and the Staff Manual respectively. Title Pages will be prepared in manuscript.

Place	Date	Hour	Summary of Events and Information	Remarks and references to Appendices
FLESHINELLE	Sunday 1/10	—	Feeling strong the 9th Brigade AT 5394 Shirt 142 L.D. 452 Cts 18 Sheets 26. Known Hope but Refilling point Main road FRESNELLE – ESTRÉE BLANCHE on 17.4r – Refilling at 9/15. – Ration as usual – Rations as D.R.O. continued to regiment arriving infant train – by/infantry ostensibly coming to regulation. Coy/10th Wood 2/Lt + 1 NCO out 1 limited 7 Units – gunnery Ord Crummuce Cpl 16 Blamed /Lt lt. – also Sent 1 Show follows 4th Gunner Reg War – in wood of trunk – Club watched but Regt 1 Gunner for war – in wood of trunks – Club watched but Regt 1 Gunner at 1am – tonight Serverie with 9 under live Regt 7th. Bas Caure Brigade – Succeeds by Lt. Col. Pryor –	
	Monday 2/10	—	Routin as usual – Purchase of Regt continued – End supp on Phaleville exhausted –	
	Tuesday 3/10	—	Purchase of Regt continued – Orders rec'd that Bn moves on Thursday Routin as usual	
	Wednes 4/10	—	Stin orders from Brigadier Col Mee leaves Bn up for approximate 5th. – Routin as usual. Lt Parker arrives late 20. Chili leaving in stores or special leave Reptt since 17/7am + 4.30pm H.M.	
	Thurs 5/10	—	Left Flechinelle 11am Black via Helshi L'Meuchin ready of travel Billets no three were in their neighbourds as weeks ago Reptt 7pm. – Routin of kinds appears as before	

H. Wilkins Major

WAR DIARY
or
INTELLIGENCE SUMMARY

Army Form C. 2118.

Place	Date	Hour	Summary of Events and Information	Remarks and references to Appendices
MEAULTE				
	Friday 6/10		Transport & all kits left via ST Pol thro' back YPRES REUVE (L Patten as Q dropping off & bring stretchers) - Rifles to man Rd 600 yds 8|B|9 Rihoum - Louvre of Rum	
	Satby. 7/10		Continue trek with Barled waggons flown Rd 1000 yds NE - N of RAINNEVAL (S.E.S. (DOULLENS) Infantry arrived in new area by trains, buses, women or a lake of Rum.	
	Sunday 8/10		Rifling at 12 midday (manoeuvres) at BELLE EGLISE - Rain turning cold wet arms wet lubr'n again & supplies lowered - however Rain cheated wind 400 yds S of Rifling front Vaumelles - Rain etc spoilt care - of Croisards - Louvre of Rum	
	Monday 9/10		Rifling at 7am - Rain in turnout - Late arr from L Barker - Rifling as yesterday - Went to Doullens - ration supplies disagreeable & June (Limit Qm Return) - Me	
	Tuesd 10/10		Rifling as yesterday - Went to Doullens ration returns exp'd arrivals disagreeable & June (Limit Qm Return) - Me	
	Wed. 11/10		Ratio as usual - Louvre at Railhead cnlr refilled during afternoon Complaint forwarded STO re shortage of bacon, these began - I	
	Thurs 12/10		Arranged for purchase of ways at Amiens - after doing so I am informed that one will be required after hull as 10g will arrive at Railhead - Rifles during afternoon as yesterday J	

Army Form C. 2118.

WAR DIARY
or
INTELLIGENCE SUMMARY.
(Erase heading not required.)

Instructions regarding War Diaries and Intelligence Summaries are contained in F.S. Regs., Part II. and the Staff Manual respectively. Title pages will be prepared in manuscript.

Place	Date	Hour	Summary of Events and Information	Remarks and references to Appendices
Acheux	13/10/16		Purchase of Vegetables at Acheux & Amiens — the former the fullest stop the latter however — Routine as usual	
Acheux	14/10/16		Routine as usual — Went to Amiens to settle up purchase Jugs made ordered Lunch brought in exchange for bread — commencing to-th is supplying 17th —	
Sunday 15/10			Routine as usual — landed over to Henson —	Witnessed H/O/SC 20.7Co? Supps.
Monday 16/10/16	15/10/16		20th over duties of S.O. 76th A/5 Btn from Lt Phidr. Tasked with No 2 by trews camp in vicinity of Louvencourt on the Louvencourt-Bertuillers road	
Tuesday 17/10/16			Routine as usual	
Wednesday 18/10/16			Refilling from Supply Column on Louvencourt Acheum road Dump changed to vicinity of Louvelles on Louvelles-Authie road	
Thursday 19/10/16 20/10/16			Reserve Ration of 1 P.M. & Biscuit issued — Supply column dumps at refilling point on both days sufficient fresh meat & make up ration	[signature] S.O. 76th A/5 Bn

2353 Wt. W2544/1454 700,000 5/15 D. D. & L. A.D.S.S./Forms/C. 2118.

Army Form C. 2118.

WAR DIARY
or
INTELLIGENCE SUMMARY.
(Erase heading not required.)

Instructions regarding War Diaries and Intelligence Summaries are contained in F.S. Regs., Part II. and the Staff Manual respectively. Title pages will be prepared in manuscript.

Place	Date	Hour	Summary of Events and Information	Remarks and references to Appendices
	Saturday 21/10/16		Extra reserve ration of MRN issued to units.	
	Sunday 22/10/16		Issue of Canteen stores to units.	
	Monday 23/10/16		Did not attend refilling - left for Amiens at 7 a.m. on duty for Divn HQrs - Afternoon went on duty to Doullens.	
	Tuesday 24/10/16		Routine as usual.	
	Wednesday 25/10/16		Extra Reserve Grocery ration issued to fighting troops - Sugar short - deficiency to be made up later.	
	Thursday 26/10/16		Routine - No vegetables in dumps - 175 extra corders issued troops known to be deficient on first issue. Cheese ration increased by 1½ oz bring it up to normal 3 oz. Extra 2 oz vegetable ration issued.	
	Friday 27/10/16		Proportion of Bread heat decreased to 40% - Order of Army for tactical reasons. - Units advised of this. Refilled in morning from supply column at Louchelles (Léhence) to units - Second Lorry in afternoon from BELLE-ÉGLISE to Rhead. Refilled in camp for Sunday at Frévillers next morning.	

E. Kennard Capt. F. B/M.
20 V.S. B/Co.

Army Form C. 2118.

WAR DIARY
or
INTELLIGENCE SUMMARY.
(Erase heading not required.)

Instructions regarding War Diaries and Intelligence Summaries are contained in F. S. Regs., Part II. and the Staff Manual respectively. Title pages will be prepared in manuscript.

Place	Date	Hour	Summary of Events and Information	Remarks and references to Appendices
	Sunday 29/10/16		Routine as usual. Feet much short.	
	Monday 30/10/16		Routine as usual. " " "	
	Tuesday 31/10/16		Routine as usual. " " "	

John T. Lemon
Lt. Col.
C.O. 76th 2/Bn.

WAR DIARY or INTELLIGENCE SUMMARY

(Erase heading not required.)

Army Form C. 2118.

S.S.O. 3rd Division
SSO 3rd Div
Vol XI

Place	Date	Hour	Summary of Events and Information	Remarks and references to Appendices
BUS to ARTOIS	1/1/16		Pack Train arrived at 11 AM but was not put in position for H[orse] T[ransport] loading until 7.30pm — heater reported to DDST Fifth Army. Undue increase delay at Bull Ejust [?] Midlands in getting our Train into position after their arrival, as all other increased locating the supplies in darkness led to quantities transferred from train transport. Coms made arrangements with the Q.M. & me Corps scale. No sup[plies] within the establishment as consumed for working parties coming down from the line. Weather fine.	
	2/1/16		174 & 50bn (Pioneers) were drawn this am. Supplies from Reduced ration from today — Train arrived 3pm — in position 5pm.	
	3		Conduit at Wilhaine fumes 11am. Supp[lies] Officer notified again in writing of keeping Supers &c. Kum Pkt issues today reduced, OCoH feedings 3oz up as mentioned above	— Capt

WAR DIARY or INTELLIGENCE SUMMARY

Army Form C. 2118.

Place	Date	Hour	Summary of Events and Information	Remarks and references to Appendices
BUSBO ADDIS	4/11/16		Train not in position until 8pm. Loading finished 11.30 am. Had M.O. who started down to 25/70 on first train. Showery during night.	
	5/11/16		Train arrived 7pm. Loading finished 1pm. Empties left at 2.5pm for man kitted - Received no reply. Lt Curren (S.O.) left on special boat. Capt Paskin (L.O.) does during his absence. Gang for Amino duty 6pm supply O. Noto for troops.	
	6/11/16		Hay's rations drawn B.T.S. today. Saw cake allowance 7½ kg to B.T.S. Forces Diospitol – Orders from D.O.S.T. stating all troops would have be furnished lunch under army arrangements returning to Corps. Supply Officers would be moved to arrange any local purchase refunded from Amino to supplement noto up to 5,000 kilos daily for troops – CO 164 + 165 leaving for business briskly.	Copy

Army Form C. 2118.

WAR DIARY
or
INTELLIGENCE SUMMARY.
(Erase heading not required.)

Instructions regarding War Diaries and Intelligence Summaries are contained in F. S. Regs., Part II. and the Staff Manual respectively. Title pages will be prepared in manuscript.

Place	Date	Hour	Summary of Events and Information	Remarks and references to Appendices
BN. S-bn MORTARS	7/11/16		Orders from 87th Corps to clear 3157 yds key in Conjunction with 51st Divn — Coys to comprise 3 trench mortar bty. Could only obtain 1350 Pdrs. Seny Cy Flicuit [?] Stornston to Nroto. [?] trench ground ammun. to first line today — Borrowed 8 round Coke returned from Reinforcement B.Rice. — under any ditty ammunition all day. train closed 7pm. to meet these demands later.	
		5/11/16	1875 K. Bay 400 pyf rounds + 750 Kirkoredcosted distributed to this divn, by ordo. Instructed Capt. Newton to arrange clearance up to the front. Sent Cl Hude to review all units — As the troop mine from Corps is totally inadequate to meet the demands of the Division, I recommend brought into the difference (in [?] rounds) by the purches of limbers. Two limbers unobtainable in division, 5 this force is much in arrear of the front line. Instructions were issued — set forth from reinforce by line transport. Must transports this is all taken to divide as OSB + 9 hun Government — weather wet during morning — Capt. Veal (U.D.) left for England on Special leave — Capt Ostley acting O in his absence. Roll been commend 11 am. in position 3.20 pm	

WAR DIARY or INTELLIGENCE SUMMARY

Army Form C. 2118.

Place	Date	Hour	Summary of Events and Information	Remarks and references to Appendices
Bus les Artois	19/1/16		Glorious sunshiny morning, wrote forward for [?] journey to obtain work from Bois Jhuré. No[?] instructions from him to Reconnoissance of infantrymen for cutting fuel. There are in addition 670 supplies of fuel in reserve. 200 at fuel dump from 57th Divn. at Beauvoisins 155 tons. Ord 30 two tons — Started my visit to Capt. & then started for Beauvisaux & Bus [?] Divn — Divns interviewed at 1.35 p.m. by Second Capt Harrison Hops w/ Lieut Swik w/ [?] On return to hay supply — Wrote minor [?] Ivan in position at Bisson — knew on [?] Bois Jhuré may 3 & 9 tons — [?] The first lot dumps are completed at [?] [?] the nights [?] there to Canaris[?] on the [?] Such conditions on all guards of [?] cannot [?] be obtained. He sent my servants about 3000 tons Bailey (in [?] the [?] [?] [?] from St. Leger Div. British Army now our [?])	

Army Form C. 2118.

WAR DIARY
or
INTELLIGENCE SUMMARY.
(Erase heading not required.)

Instructions regarding War Diaries and Intelligence Summaries are contained in F.S. Regs., Part II. and the Staff Manual respectively. Title pages will be prepared in manuscript.

Place	Date	Hour	Summary of Events and Information	Remarks and references to Appendices
Bus le Artois	continued 10/1/16		Owing to Regiments arrival Bypoorch during a report has been sent to H.Qrs. 3rd Army pointing this out and suggesting that Supply officers to know Divisions of they supply as S.N.L.O. Even small details become no.	
	11/1/16		11 noon. 11:00 am Conference worked for arms to troops now stationed - Port return showed 65,000 duds to horses O.C. 2nd Divest Battalion to furnish in forward of will take place for issue Early - meanwhile this Depots required to topfilate issue stretches for supply. Eventually returned bombedlo from SSO me own. 12 noon ADO DAO "6 called discussed trend in new Theood - As the Supply Depot at present crowded from Army is insufficient troops demands Sent report there through the Divisions furnished this out. Also furnished a report respecting the very local amount of hay received from SSOcept. Telephoned the Director Jolls m this hay return required Arrangements for Supply of wire trains Resumondation deal up to mel Derwent Methodist. Service is of 11 am Winchester sulphur SSD	

WAR DIARY
or
INTELLIGENCE SUMMARY.
(Erase heading not required.)

Army Form C. 2118.

Place	Date	Hour	Summary of Events and Information	Remarks and references to Appendices
Bns HQ RKINS	13/11/16		From in position at 11 am. Wired BDE/808? Head wished any orders. 10 then went to bn's lines and huts in regiments. Capt A Friend & ammn bearers if posble, unable carry — he replied none available — Rum was available after taking. None, with further orders. 0-0630 minutes — Relieve for Bsons 9.130 units the survivor from Dochan to BDE. 1 Coil to Pack Arill Gunp the Bestructured — trenches and mining. Lieutenant attacked this morning though from SSW fl. How. battly west from Trumn & to billets in Sector. Causalities estimated at about 2900 — Subsequently found as about 1500 all weather windy.	
	14/11/16		Train to position 11p.m. Relieves not commenced during battle detailed from 35st? Evening slaugh troops despatched weather windy.	[signature] O.C.

2353 Wt W2544/1454 700,000 5/15 D. D. & L. A.D.S.S./Forms/C. 2118.

WAR DIARY
or
INTELLIGENCE SUMMARY.
(Erase heading not required.)

Army Form C. 2118.

Place	Date	Hour	Summary of Events and Information	Remarks and references to Appendices
Bus Les Artois	11/11/16		Train in position 8.15 pm. Arrived posn. 635 pm now from 7 aerts so then sent Advan.Guard by order of 11th Corps. R- fielding strongly. 14 bg 3 (wounds all ditto reprodn. were commenced during position.) Weather cold & fine.	
	12/11/16		Train in position 8 pm. Now a old refugee horses from Thiepval - Junction retained from BOISE[?] of fifth army & they up transport for 110 litres for wound case. Weather keep area fine	
	13/11/16		No news of train up brunchnight. Return Strength 16/6 & 6 OR. Weather fine rather	
	14/11/16		Yesterdays train arrived at 6 am - it was detained at Candas for some extra union. Since 11.30 am this fremen day. Officers placed & lorries to Bois Henri travelers for word. Full trust ration today - no news of looking train up brunchnight. Raining all day.	

J. Munro Capt
SSO

Army Form C. 2118.

WAR DIARY
or
INTELLIGENCE SUMMARY.
(Erase heading not required.)

Instructions regarding War Diaries and Intelligence Summaries are contained in F. S. Regs., Part II. and the Staff Manual respectively. Title pages will be prepared in manuscript.

Place	Date	Hour	Summary of Events and Information	Remarks and references to Appendices
Rus le ARRAS	27/11/16		Halluys Train arrived here this morning. Went up to wire Station in Blair wood. Received from Bois Grenier Trolley 1.3.30 am wood. Carried railway. Holenp Train in position at 2.30pm. Weather cloudy, no rain. Ration Strength 167 >> OR	
	28/11/16		Holenp Train in position at 10.30pm. — Relieved [by] 1200 train Breakfast detail, was refused without Corps authority. Informed "Q", Bns Officers to continue to furnish gutts. Weather fine. Ration Strength 169 >> OR	
	29/11/16		Down Tet in up to midnight. Relieved by Brig ? divn. SK legn undl 2a troops them At Cunco Attacked two lines working pice. Holenp Train in position from this morning. Sydney train in position 5pm. Back on train down to 6 to pickets between head up from Vacant puck. Turn to Bois then became arrangement for wood cutting by a pty of 35 men uneler G Hatchin from this Division — received unpimal made. Sent 6 to 13th Corps Knife for See true Schsyfield alphal— Weather fine. Reco	G.M.

2353 Wt. W2544/1454 700,000 5/15 D. D. & L. A.D.S.S./Forms/C. 2118.

Place	Date	Hour	Summary of Events and Information	Remarks and references to Appendices
Bus to Libru	28/11/16		Train in position at 2 p.m. — A great [?] when from fuel trips & rations — apparne a [?] great one than trucks in future. have entirely broken under O/Meller left today for Paris. Hun accompanied home with Corps to the new H/Q training area, to and home from there fuel dump at the [?] Convercourt — start on 30th inst. Say return to train up to 8 o'clock from today. Headquarters train in position at midnight. Orders received that we will be BEUSSART.	
	29/11/16		Neither Train nor [?] weather dull.	
	29/11/16		Moving to Beauvent received from today, train in position at new [?]. To be available today to leave fuel — arrived O/c for take lorries instructions [?] the afternoon and return to Pub Rosoan [?] was — 16 minutes by train this out duty. Arranged with O/C Supp/[?] Cal. b Cwc & Officer [Duff?] details rations lorries to Bus, as [?] Suff Col. is to go for rations weather was no [?] barrow from Moma Heavy [?].	EO Sprs?

Army Form C. 2118.

WAR DIARY or INTELLIGENCE SUMMARY

Army Form C. 2118.

Place	Date	Hour	Summary of Events and Information	Remarks and references to Appendices
Bois de Antico	26/11/16		Train arrived in position at 3pm - No wood known from Bois Piers Estang. Weather dull. Mojo chief kermit battery.	
	27/11/16		Train in position 7.30pm Off 4/6 motor ? War Camp. Re arranged batteries. No interior shares from R.O. Bulb. S/here in future - detail from I.G. cancelled. Three officers to No Ontario Headquarters in the morning. Lost bayoneted at railhead other rations received by coal dump - batteries being battered into weather sull. Train not in position up to midnight - destroys shelves at noon today 11 Am sullen.	
	28/11/16		Yesterdays train in position at 1.30 am - Today's train stopped at 8.30am - took fired 10 hour on Third. which arrived at railhead on the stretcher was not cleared by the Division. Afterwards cleared by overside chainway - R.O. informed. Arrived but 2 full ration - 6 tonnes [illegible] ration, troops word dust from Bois Picus. Rations could ?	
			dust.	

WAR DIARY or INTELLIGENCE SUMMARY

Army Form C. 2118.

Place	Date	Hour	Summary of Events and Information	Remarks and references to Appendices
Dues les Aves	30/11/16		Train in position 9.30 am — 150 rd. free DR.C. attached 9.9th Bgde. For return from tomorrow. Applied 13th Corps Troops for Ecottier Directrice a total (with R.S.) wants 4 train without Copper endorsing. Applied to Corps through D.D. — He went between railhead and Bus is as step had condition. During the last week wheat received from army purchase Board through 13.th Corps, 6,500 Kilos hay, 1500 K between oats, 1500 t. wheat straw — Capt Heurskin B. Binitzio has been detailed to look after the receipt distribution of all props received from A. P. Board. Length 73,914 yds meters by wire	Holburn Capt D.D.O Stevenson

S.O. 3rd Div: Troops

Army Form C. 2118.

WAR DIARY
or
INTELLIGENCE SUMMARY.
(Erase heading not required.)

S.O. 3rd Div: Troops.

Instructions regarding War Diaries and Intelligence Summaries are contained in F.S. Regs., Part II. and the Staff Manual respectively. Title pages will be prepared in manuscript.

Place	Date	Hour	Summary of Events and Information	Remarks and references to Appendices
LOUVENCOURT	1/11/16		Supply wagons which had loaded overnight in bulk, dump supplies and refill at 8. a.m. in camp on LOUVENCOURT–LEALVILLERS road (Sheet 57d O.11.a.8.5.) Routine as usual. Wagons load again at railhead (BELLE-ÉGLISE) at 5 p.m. & returned to company lines & park loaded.	1
"	2/11/16		Routine as for 1/11/16.	
"	3/11/16		Routine as for 2/11/16.	
"	4/11/16		Routine as for 3/11/16.	
"	5/11/16		Routine as for 4/11/16 Roots issued & purchased locally.	
"	6/11/16		Routine as for 5/11/16. Roots issued. Hay ration reduced to 8 lbs per horse (including H.D.) Same railhead. Rations also is being bought by A.P. Board & handed over chits to C.R.A.	
"	7/11/16		Routine as for 6/11/16 Roots issued as before.	
"	8/11/16		Routine as for 7/11/16 Roots issued also 1875 Kilos Rye Hay & 400 Kilos Rye Straw obtained from Army Purchase Board AUTHIE (Rillet 51) & chits issued to C.R.A. for distribution.	
"	9/11/16		Refill at 6. a.m. wagon load at railhead at 11.30.a.m. Refill again at 3.30. p.m. Wagon park loaded overnight. Roots issued.	
"	10/11/16		Supply wagons issue to units & return to railhead to load at 5.30 p.m. Wagon park loaded overnight. No refilling	

HArthur Capel

2/

Army Form C. 2118.

WAR DIARY
or
INTELLIGENCE SUMMARY.
(Erase heading not required.)

S.O. 3rd Div. Troops.

Place	Date	Hour	Summary of Events and Information	Remarks and references to Appendices
LOUVENCOURT	11/11/16		Refill 6 a.m. Routine as usual & nothing issued. Supply wagons loaded at railhead at 2 p.m. Refill at 3.30 p.m camp. Routine as usual & nothing issued.	
"	12/11/16		Supply wagons deliver to units – load at railhead 2 p.m. No refilling.	
"	13/11/16		Refill 6 a.m. Routine as usual except rum wine stopped. Rum issued. Load railhead at 2 p.m. Refill 3.30 p.m. Routine as usual. Rum issued.	
"	14/11/16		Supply wagons deliver to units – load at railhead at 10 p.m. No refilling.	
"	15/11/16		Refill 6 a.m. Bread arrived very late (9.30 a.m) on refilling point till done. Routine as usual. Ration 504 D. How Batty. for 1st time with two days rations – consumption 15" & 16". Load railhead at 10 p.m. – no refilling.	
"	16/11/16		Refill 8 a.m. All issues as usual including roots. Load railhead tomorrow (17/11/16) as train did not arrive until Friday morning (17/11/16).	
"	17/11/16		Load railhead 6.30 a.m. Refill 10.45 a.m. All issues as usual – routine as usual load railhead at 10 p.m.	
"	18/11/16		Refill 8.30 a.m. All issues as usual. load at railhead at 7 a.m. next morning 19/11/16	
"	19/11/16		Load railhead at 7 a.m. Refill 10 a.m. All issues as usual including roots load railhead again 4 p.m.	

C.H.Austin Capt.

Army Form C. 2118.

3

WAR DIARY
or
INTELLIGENCE SUMMARY.
(Erase heading not required.)

S.O. 3rd Div. Troops

Instructions regarding War Diaries and Intelligence Summaries are contained in F. S. Regs., Part II. and the Staff Manual respectively. Title pages will be prepared in manuscript.

Place	Date	Hour	Summary of Events and Information	Remarks and references to Appendices
LAVIENCOURT.	20/4/16		Refill 8.30 a.m. All issues as usual including 100 G. Only 12 lbs oats per L.D. horse from this day inclusive instead of 14 lbs. Load railhead 10 p.m.	
"	21/4/16		Refill 8.30 a.m. All issues as usual. 63rd T.M.B. returned by us for last time - leave to-day.	
"	22/4/16		Load railhead at 6.30 a.m. Refill 9.30 a.m. - all issues as usual including 100 G. Load again at railhead at 4.30 p.m. Park loaded overnight.	
"	23/4/16		Refill 8.30 a.m. All issues as usual including 100 G. Load again at 3.30 p.m. - wagons park overnight.	
"	24/4/16		Refill 8.30 a.m. All issues as usual including 100 G. Hay ration increased to 10 lbs per horse from to-day onwards. 49th D.A.C. do not draw issues which of 3316 in future. Load again at 12, mid night.	
"	25/4/16		Refill at 8.30 a.m. All issues as usual including 100 G. Rhats obtained from F.P.O. at AVTHIE for 2200 kilo oats at Sarton. 2 guns to R.A. for distribution amongst RE artillery. Load at REAUSSART railhead at 4 p.m.	
"	26/4/16		Refill at 9 a.m. All issues as usual including 100 G. Load at Reaussart railhead at 4 p.m. Rhats obtained from F.P.O. AVTHIE for 1000 kilo Hay in farmer at MARIEUX.	
"	27/4/16		Refill at 9 a.m. All issues as usual including 100 G. Load railhead 6.30 p.m.	

G. Hawkins, Capt.

Army Form C. 2118.

WAR DIARY
or
INTELLIGENCE SUMMARY.   S.O. 3rd Div: Troops,
(Erase heading not required.)

Place	Date	Hour	Summary of Events and Information	Remarks and references to Appendices
ROUVENCOURT	28/11/16	9 a.m.	Refile 9 a.m. All wires as usual including route. horse railhead 12 midnight. Chit obtained from F.P.O. BERNAVILLE for 1500 Rats wheat straw in gunny at the Vicogne. But obtained from F.P.O. BEAUVAL for 3700 Rats Hay in gunny at BEAUQUESNE.	
"	29/11/16	11 a.m.	Refile 11 a.m. All wires as usual including route, horse railhead 12 midnight.	
"	30/11/16	10.30 a.m.	Refile 10.30 a.m. All wires as usual including route. Obtain chit from F.P.O. Kerisant for 1500 Rats of Hay from Rubempre, horse railhead at midnight. Wagons park loaded overnight.	

Ottoussine &cpt
S.O. 3rd Div: Troops

Army Form C. 2118.

S.O. 8th Inf. Bde.

WAR DIARY
or
INTELLIGENCE SUMMARY.
(Erase heading not required.)

Place	Date	Hour	Summary of Events and Information	Remarks and references to Appendices
In the field	1/11/16		Rifling 6 & 9 am. Routine as usual – £	
	2/11/16		Rifling 9am – Went to Dranoutre funeral at 10.30. 2 boys & Co men in Bn.t Corp. Kitchen – Later rode up to the type 146th Rest up. Julius 10th Upper 1st Lord Colls. Bupper Stale – Under Sig Sugs moved from Rickard £	
	3/11/16		Rifling 9am – Brown letter tools teeth terms Picket Sings – Purchase of funf (Park) at Annice for divisione hotest Sunday – Routine as usual £	
	4/11/16		Brigade having been relieved by 9th No. came back to screnes – visited 1st Rifle Brown & the Bregoon £	
December	5/11/16		Origini things AA 4326 AD 111 AD 369 CB 18 Imader 9. Routine as usual – Replies at 9am £	
	6/11/16		Routine as usual –	
	7/11/16		Arr. present made for the troops to be practiced at Southern – £	
	8/11/16		turned at Browns settled Replies at 9am & also at 9am – going to the front that ar necessary for all Rigades the back to trenches tomorrow at 11am – £	
	9/11/16		Routine as usual £	

H. Weaver Lieut Col
So 8th Inf Bde

Army Form C. 2118.

WAR DIARY
or
INTELLIGENCE SUMMARY.
(Erase heading not required.)

Instructions regarding War Diaries and Intelligence Summaries are contained in F. S. Regs., Part II. and the Staff Manual respectively. Title pages will be prepared in manuscript.

Place	Date	Hour	Summary of Events and Information	Remarks and references to Appendices
In the field	10/11/16		Train did not arrive till this evening – Supplies parked in bulk on S Waggons for night. [illegible]	
	11/11/16		Refilling 7 am to enable waggons to return for refilling at Railhead 11am –	
			Routine as usual – Loading Railhead during afternoon & refilled immediately on return of waggons – Solidified Alcohol drawn from 9th Bde issued to all units in Bay Bde. Orders received for daily issue of rum to all troops – Bde to trenches –	
Sunday	12/11/16		Strength of Brigade Group AR 4285 HD. 110 LD 392 Cobs 18 S Mules 9.	
			Routine as usual – Bde still in trenches – No extra forage from DDO	
	13/11/16.		No more daily issues of Rum or Pea Soup to be made – Bde still in trenches – Double Forage recd from Doullens. –	
	14/11/16		Routine as usual – Big reduction in strengths of all Units of Bde – Train arrived late at railhead –	
	15/11/16 –		Routine as usual – Train again late at railhead –	
	16/11/16.		Routine as usual –	
	17/11/16		" " "	
	18/11/16		"	
Sunday	19/11/16.		Brigade Group Strength AR 3417 HD 114 LD. 391 Ch. 18 S Mules 9. Visited 87 [illegible] Ambce. –	
	20/11/16		Visited all Infantry Units of Brigade group –	
			H.H. [illegible] Lieut ASC.	

2353 Wt. W2544/1454 700,000 5/15 D. D. & L. A.D.S.S./Forms/C. 2118.

Army Form C. 2118.

WAR DIARY
or
INTELLIGENCE SUMMARY.
(Erase heading not required.)

Place	Date	Hour	Summary of Events and Information	Remarks and references to Appendices
In the field	21/11/16		9 Section Bread returns to A & B and being surplus are required for rich remade. Routine as usual.	
	22/11/16		Men did not arrive till late nightly conveying as not take place until 11 am.	
	23/11/16		Worked S.A.M. Battery. Employed in Col Index List in relation to J, and SOO. Routine as usual.	
	24/11/16		Rubber of [?] in Bois Eglise & Beaussart.	
Sunday 26/11/16			Rubber changed from Bois Eglise & Beaussart. Stanger of Brit Sgr. AR. 3609 wts. 106 & 397 En. 18 Serve. 9. Visited Supply trucks father and Staff Capt- purchased 200 Eggs returned via Puchy Contre at Humbletton noon - Got Rail Station - Report by them. trapped june & Lieut Wgn. Replying 9 am. Routine as usual.	
	27/11/16		Rain set in & rain till 11.30 pm although due at ginsday.	
	28/11/16			
	29/11/16		Letter to P.O. 4c. at troubles. Routine as usual.	
	30/11/16		La Transing	

30/11/16

H. H. Ninds Lieut. M.T.
S. O. 8th Supply Col.

S.O. 9th Inf. Bde.

WAR DIARY
or
INTELLIGENCE SUMMARY.
(Erase heading not required.)

Army Form C. 2118.

S.O. 9th Inf. Bde.

Place	Date	Hour	Summary of Events and Information	Remarks and references to Appendices
LOUVENCOURT	1-11-16		Rations were brought here by our supplies delivered to units. Loaded on truck by horse transport at BELLE EGLISE without 10 guns & lorries to Company lines	SMW Capt
"	2-11-16		All services routine as usual	SMW Capt
"	3-11-16		Routine as usual	SMW Capt
"	4-11-16		Routine as usual	SMW Capt
"	5-11-16		Routine as usual 9th Bde relieves 76th Bde in line	SMW Capt
"	6-11-16		Supplies delivered at railhead as usual.	SMW Capt
"	7-11-16		Routine as usual.	W.D.
"	8-11-16		Rations & supplies at railhead. Refilled again at 6 p.m.	W.D.

Army Form C. 2118.

WAR DIARY
or
INTELLIGENCE SUMMARY.
(Erase heading not required.)

I.O. 9th Inf Bde

Instructions regarding War Diaries and Intelligence Summaries are contained in F. S. Regs., Part II. and the Staff Manual respectively. Title pages will be prepared in manuscript.

Place	Date	Hour	Summary of Events and Information	Remarks and references to Appendices
Liverpool	9.11.15		Landed at railhead 11.30 am. Replied 3 p.m.	MSO
	10.11.15		All went on usual. Loaded at railhead 5. p.m. Replied at 7 p.m. usual	MSO
	11.11.15		Loaded at railhead 2 p.m. Replied 4 p.m. usual	MSO
	12.11.15		Loaded at railhead 1 p.m. Replied at 3 p.m. usual. Run issued out of stores.	MSO
	13.11.15		Loaded at railhead 2pm. Replied 4 pm. Run drawn & put into reserve.	MSO
	14.11.15		Loaded at railhead 7 p.m. NO Bread drawn	MSO
	15.11.15		Rifles ? am Bread drawn at 12 noon. Special Major out round usual. Att at	MSO
	16.11.15		Loaded at railhead 9 p.m.	MSO

WAR DIARY
or
INTELLIGENCE SUMMARY.
(Erase heading not required.)

Army Form C. 2118.

S.O. 9th Suffolk Rifle

Instructions regarding War Diaries and Intelligence Summaries are contained in F. S. Regs., Part II. and the Staff Manual respectively. Title pages will be prepared in manuscript.

Place	Date	Hour	Summary of Events and Information	Remarks and references to Appendices
LOUVENCOURT	16/11/16		Rations 8.0 am. Limbers as usual, loaded at mulchers at 11 pm.	SMV
"	17/11/16		Rations 10.0 am. Routine as usual	SMV
"	18/11/16		Rations 9.0 am. Routine as usual	SMV
"	19/11/16		Rations 8.0 am. Loaded in back at BELLE EGLISE at 3 pm.	SMV
"	20/11/16		Rations 8.0 am. Loaded at mulchers 12 midnight. Routine as usual	SMV
"	21/11/16		Rations 9.0 am. Routine as usual, loaded at mulchers at 11 pm.	SMV
"	22/11/16		Rations 8.0 am. Supplies deliveries, loaded at mulchers at	SMV Capt acc

Army Form C. 2118.

WAR DIARY
or
INTELLIGENCE SUMMARY.
(Erase heading not required.)

S.O. 9th Dn. Bde.

Place	Date	Hour	Summary of Events and Information	Remarks and references to Appendices
LOUVENCOURT	23/11/16		Refilled 9.30 a.m. on Company lines. Supplies delivered to units. Loaded in bulk at BELLE EGLISE wollers at 3 p.m. Wagons returns to company lines.	SMW
"	24/11/16		Refills 8 a.m. Loaded at wollers in bulk at 11.30 p.m. Other work as usual	SMW
"	25/11/16		Refills 9 a.m. Loaded in bulk at BEAUQUART wollers at 1 p.m.	SMW
"	26/11/16		Refills 10 a.m. Loaded in bulk at BEAUQUART wollers at 6 p.m. Other work as usual	SMW
"	27/11/16		Routine as usual	SMW
"	28/11/16		Routine as usual	SMW

Army Form C. 2118.

S.O. 9th L. Bde

WAR DIARY
or
INTELLIGENCE SUMMARY.
(Erase heading not required.)

Place	Date	Hour	Summary of Events and Information	Remarks and references to Appendices
LOUVENCOURT				
	29/11/16	10 am	Reported to new Co-forming hives, Louvencourt at BEAUSSART - billets at midnight. Other units on move.	9MN
" "	20/11/16	10 am	Arrived 10 am. Louvencourt - billets at 4p. Other units on move.	9MN

JW Neal Captain
S.O. 9th L. Bde

S.O. 76th Inf. Bde.

Army Form C. 2118.

WAR DIARY
or
INTELLIGENCE SUMMARY.
(Erase heading not required.)

Instructions regarding War Diaries and Intelligence Summaries are contained in F. S. Regs., Part II. and the Staff Manual respectively. Title pages will be prepared in manuscript.

76 m/y/y Bde.

Place	Date	Hour	Summary of Events and Information	Remarks and references to Appendices
LOUVENCOURT.				
	Wednesday 1/11/16 to 4/11/16		Routine as usual	
	Sunday 5/11/16		From this date, vegetables known daily from Amiens per D.P.O. Supplement extra hay ration handed over also. Capt H.S. Parkin Att. during temporary absence.	
	Monday 6/11/16		Issues as usual. Splendid electric lines to camp	
	Tuesday 7/11/16		Issues as usual. Pack train coming up at uncertain times necessitates repeating being held 3 hour later.	
	Wednesday 8/11/16 to 12/11/16		Issues as usual.	
	Sunday 19/11/16		Visited all units of the Brigade including Bde. Headquarters. Units were quite satisfied with everything.	
	Monday 20/11/16 to 20/11/16		Routine as usual. Issues as usual.	
	Tuesday 21/11/16		Usual routine.	
	Wednesday 22/11/16		Lieut. E. Kinnago took over duties of Supply Officer 76 Inf. Bde.	

A. Pickin Capt
For S.O. 76 Inf. Bde.

Army Form C. 2118.

WAR DIARY
or
INTELLIGENCE SUMMARY.
(Erase heading not required.)

Instructions regarding War Diaries and Intelligence Summaries are contained in F.S. Regs., Part II. and the Staff Manual respectively. Title pages will be prepared in manuscript.

Place	Date	Hour	Summary of Events and Information	Remarks and references to Appendices
LOUWENCOURT.				
	Wednesday 22/11/16		Resumed duties of S.O. 78th Inf/Bde. Took over from Captain H.E. Parkin attd.	
	Thursday 23/11/16		Usual Routine. Previous arrangements as to distribution of Soldiers elected cancelled – Weekly allowance of 600 tins expected. Issues to be made only to Brigades actually in trenches at time of receipts. To come to R.F.A. Arrangements made for issue of 1 tin of coal per week to 7th Field Ambulance – to be drawn from S.O. 5th Corps. Know the wants from 6th Corps Coal yard as no transport available to bring fuel to Armencourt.	
	Friday 24/11/16		Usual Routine. Amount of hay at Railhead increased, trucks were to be increased from 25 to 26 per horse.	
	Saturday 25/11/16		Routine as usual	
	Sunday 26/11/16		Routine as usual	
	Monday 27/11/16		Rations for 50 men and 1 horse sent to Tincheller by Supply wagon for 3rd Bris'de Grenade School.	
	Tuesday 28/11/16		Usual Routine. Refilling held late owing to late arrival of pack team.	

John T Newman
Lieut A/S/O 78 Bde

Army Form C. 2118.

WAR DIARY
or
INTELLIGENCE SUMMARY.
(Erase heading not required.)

Place	Date	Hour	Summary of Events and Information	Remarks and references to Appendices
LOUVENCOURT	Wednesday 29/9/16 Thursday 30/9/16		Routine as usual	Short Stevenson Event Att to 2/4 Bn 20-76

Army Form C. 2118.

Vol 7
S.S.O. 3rd Divn.

WAR DIARY
or
INTELLIGENCE SUMMARY.
(Erase heading not required.)

Instructions regarding War Diaries and Intelligence Summaries are contained in F. S. Regs., Part II. and the Staff Manual respectively. Title pages will be prepared in manuscript.

Place	Date	Hour	Summary of Events and Information	Remarks and references to Appendices
Bus lès Artois	1/3/16		Train in position at 6 p.m. weather very cold.	
	2/3/16	7 pm	Bombardment. Buses moved closer for repairs. Train in position at 10.30 pm to 10 am. N/E. Trouble car in workshop also leave one of the train for mild duties.	
	3/3/16		Two train Sections moved from 3 F.S.D. machine of 11 cames worth reported. Train in position 4.15 am. Sent particulars to D.D. Officer at the auction of vehicle required taken from parked a number of Dodge ferrays spent. (Distributed)	
	4/3/16	11 am	weather very cold. Train in position uneventful. Pull off are number of ville 2 ton coal truck no 40.187 which a 2 ton and 1 truck 7637 not used at Beaumont weekly update WDRS T type.	
			Army. weather cold.	

Army Form C. 2118.

WAR DIARY
or
INTELLIGENCE SUMMARY.
(Erase heading not required.)

Place	Date	Hour	Summary of Events and Information	Remarks and references to Appendices
Aux. le Rio.	5/8/16		Regt. in position R# Ferme Belgique about 1 Louvser creek. No reports from patrols from OKO Camp below trench driven from forward dumps today. 036 6 comm. and G.9 covered for attack at Betrapon Woods (ridge) relieved hay — Palemo Betrupper. No 2,3 Pt Co. more town Camp on Rue Auctie and today refilling period entrée camps. Weather was healthan annum. Have during morning.	
		1·30pm	Down in position 1·30pm. No 2, 3 rd Co. more today from Louvemesrt two Camps at Bois WARNUNONT on Rue Auctie Rd — Refilling Parade. > 6. I st D.S.T. 3 . 6. J. 19. C > 8. 4. 6. I st A.G. > 7. to enter home charging Just from Richard Weather was. Round first N day.	

Army Form C. 2118.

WAR DIARY
or
INTELLIGENCE SUMMARY.
(Erase heading not required.)

Place	Date	Hour	Summary of Events and Information	Remarks and references to Appendices
Bushy Artie	8/9/16		Train ordered by R.T.O. in King in position at 11 am but actually not in until 2.30pm. 8th Car; Purser Co. arrive they the retained from 9h. was - attached Pct. 13 M. for returning Dct 277, 7, 6, 62 spinta RHP in 3rd him for stabling our staff from southest - accommodate gunners this is kept then from am Tenters at Beverlook, etc. I think it took I police control much reported O.R.T.D. wasthe sad - hull.	
	9/9/16		Train in position 9 am ; an engine came at my time which racked before 11 am when they came straight from santo direa of the warking during Teturna for Hammor Consumption 151 Kits Overland 2 c.o. astrelin 176th Indefm. for returns from Interior headed hull.	[signature] Corbey

Army Form C. 2118.

WAR DIARY
or
INTELLIGENCE SUMMARY.
(Erase heading not required.)

Place	Date	Hour	Summary of Events and Information	Remarks and references to Appendices
Bustle Camp Arras	9/9/16		Train in at 9 a.m. — Detrained Started march via [Mouvry] at 3.75 depot.	
	10/9/16		Train in at 9 a.m. arrange for RTR on ORVILLE & out in to [supply] form. Owns they over return the marches that [supply] wagon [proceed direct]. & [airlines] in turn to the [critical bodies]. [Supplies] [furnished] that we could feed [troops] & [Cavalry] if [Parks] [fails]. The weather was [is] [improve] of. The [Beaucourt] Roads which as now in a very bad condition. Weather very [rainy].	
	11/9/16		Train in at 7 a.m. attacked carried out difficult methods. Also sent to draw ashore. AT B troop gun, [Skype] gun, [Steam] (with own platoon) — C+D troop [Steel] troops & [Skype] from [Sudan Green] [Sector] 2 ([between from] [Brown]) — AT+B troop — [Sudan] troops & [Skype] gun [Serbury] Also drew from behind with CEO [Seaton] — This was to form [Troops] of [Wiscombi] on [Road] in [Beaucourt] area — Troops into operation on [Materials] much less [heavy] [during] [training]	

Army Form C. 2118.

WAR DIARY
or
INTELLIGENCE SUMMARY.
(Erase heading not required.)

Place	Date	Hour	Summary of Events and Information	Remarks and references to Appendices
Bus. Co. Arras	17/1/916		15" and 76 R.E. have for 37th Divn, returned for some retained. "Q" suggested to Corps that fuel for this Divn should in future be drawn from Bellegline retailed to it in order to take transport off Noreuil & Beaumont - nowhere Beaumont & Batrancourt in very bad condition - we tried Evren. Evening storm night.	
	18/1/916		Went 0.3/3rd T. Division packtrain 1y 400 men into horse lines etc.	
	19/1/916		Lines loading at railhead starts. Today - Some complication owing to the T of no train being on train was by R.O.D. Traffic control at Beaucourt railhead is bad, made him is always confused with traffic marched is full. Lorries T. interior Evening R.E. material consignment the Corps is working all promises getting into railhead rest somehow thes 3 to 4 hours behind. Weather unsettled & snow. Report here in re departments of Anstruck Batt. for this Divn - Regimentals fraternally mil. Weather colder	J Dunnington SSO 3rd Divn

WAR DIARY
INTELLIGENCE SUMMARY.

Army Form C. 2118.

Place	Date	Hour	Summary of Events and Information	Remarks and references to Appendices
Busle Anfio	16/9/16		Train in position again. Weather still good. Telegrams & Intelligence received from today. Strings of lorries moving West from forward positions refilling points at P11C. Fast food lorries transport lorries from the forward dump very heavily. Using Bertrancourt road.	
	17/9/16		The M.T.O. on foot basis, 1st & 3rd Depots — refilled works to D.S.&.T. supplied a reserve. Should be kept at railhead. Forward Brigades instructed to draw from forward dumps by first line Transport from 19th inst. Difficulty as Belle Église. Motor lorries fuel and 3rd Divn claim all the fuel on their pack train. D.S.&T. advised. 100 men attached from 51st Divn Pentayne. 9100 men. (b) 665 tpts from Watsons.	
	18/9/16		No petrol at railhead today. 3rd Divn Drawing Depot to draw 2 new trenches tomorrow at Beauxencourt. Arrangements made for listening train.	

WAR DIARY
or
INTELLIGENCE SUMMARY

Army Form C. 2118.

Place	Date	Hour	Summary of Events and Information	Remarks and references to Appendices
Busla Lutaia	19/1/16		1st Cav Pioneer Regt relieve 8th Pioneers on arrival. Train in at 9am — Composition at nairkina still continues. The question of allotting fresh trains at nairkina does not turn itself with hopes intended as menus have many dump troops arriving (as Buissons approvals), relieve under 7 weapons remain in the mar. 3 attached here (100 each) from 7th & 31st Btns left Febry. 153 men from 3rd Bison beginning attached Bn.s + 0.C.3. accompanied. Cooks returning returning by final line slacks today from forward dumps by 7th Regr Bgde. Weather fine. Train 9.30am no wounded received from railhead since returned. Ambulance trains 1000 & 1 car from A.P.B.a review. Returns freely from today 8PO to Recommend 90 2nm major. Nation happen sufficient by DAC.	Wimmler 8603rd

2353. Wt. W2544/1454. 700,000 5/15 D.D.&L. A.D.S.S./Forms/C. 2118.

Army Form C. 2118.

WAR DIARY
or
INTELLIGENCE SUMMARY.
(Erase heading not required.)

Place	Date	Hour	Summary of Events and Information	Remarks and references to Appendices
Boulogne Astra	2/1/16		Train in at 9 am. Party to difficulty friends line transport arranged with B.E. of Brigade that in future Notes found and not Capt's report would deliver us mostly weary Amiens dumping & return for battles in the line at Querrieu.	
	22/9/16 23/9/16		Train in at 9 am. Into abri Train in at 9 am. Cannaveiheil Carpentin Phosphates at railhead Querrieu null.	
	24/9/16		Train in at 8a.5 am. Reports rats about in train engagements Muse at train in from Road. Trucks null.	
	25/9/16 26/9/16		Train in at 9 am. Trucks steel shot. Aux fuel tank trimming gear. Train in at 9 am. only a portion given full regime in Russia from 3rd Division. Trucks reported to army. 333 Kilo Petroifies alcohol issued by M Aspen. Tracks null recce.	[signature]

2353 Wt. W2514/1454 700,000 5/15 D. D. & L. A.D.S.S./Forms/C. 2118.

WAR DIARY or INTELLIGENCE SUMMARY

Army Form C. 2118.

Place	Date	Hour	Summary of Events and Information	Remarks and references to Appendices
Bus les Artois	27/10/16		Train in at 9 am. 1000 turkeys shot, thinned from Pool. Very little fuel still continues to come up, trench for two Divisions — Horses supply from Bois Jean had much replaced orders received. Return from 13th Corps from recent of deep Latrine replacing trenches to drainage ventilation for trenches. Thanks for change workers where are unwell have for extra Pay at present among other transport as now available. Canteens being in workshops. Capt. Hawkins left in tent. Capt. Pattern acting for him. Received shell fire.	
	28/10/16		while empty trains sent on from Fery - Sent to load for him. I attended 1000 copies purchased arranged off. So him coal deep for these days from SO 7119 Corps Troops. Train but in up tonight. No inspection received from R.T.O. Arrangement reference Areas of the 78 &. Division Tropper arrived. Read Boulogne — no emergency? but necessary to put up pontoon meeting near that Hiumps m Bois - avoided rd.	J. M. [signature] SSO 5 Corps

2353 Wt W254/1454 700,000 5/15 D/D. & L. A.D.S.S./Forms/C. 2118.

Army Form C. 2118.

WAR DIARY
or
INTELLIGENCE SUMMARY.
(Erase heading not required.)

Place	Date	Hour	Summary of Events and Information	Remarks and references to Appendices
Busto Arsizio	3/1/916		Yesterday train in at 1.30am and dug out - sent O'Neal to a refilling point during the morning but only 7 tons received. It is hoped that in morning lorries from the APC's going to Busseto in full. Numbers from reserve [Dumps?] etc. Won't [Dinner?] sent OBy S.T. 2 lorries [Murray?] received from CRS. two lorries Col. Russell 67/1 K Bye. 7353 train to-night 9pm. Train in at 8.30am. 1 truck oats cut. Dumbbell to [march?] up. have been in great shortage of [?] Baris Truck train on wagon letting pay 10 ton trucks. an additional 10 men 2 t.D. wagons, working 3 t in out of 7 D. wagons. Army will give us 1 ton [wagon?] for every 2 ton [?] [?] [?] travel trans, weather cooler,	[signature]

2353 Wt. W2544/1454 700,000 5/15 D. D. & L. A.D.S.S./Forms/C. 2118.

Army Form C. 2118.

WAR DIARY
or
INTELLIGENCE SUMMARY.
(Erase heading not required.)

Place	Date	Hour	Summary of Events and Information	Remarks and references to Appendices
Bus les Artois	31/12/16		Down in 9 am. Just putting rather short round to hom except I find at latitude; however ran to Capt West in Spencer in town tomorrow.	[signature] LtO 2nd Durh.

S.O Div Troops
Dec. 1916
S.O. 3rd Div Troops.

WAR DIARY
INTELLIGENCE SUMMARY.
(Erase heading not required.)

Army Form C. 2118.

Place	Date	Hour	Summary of Events and Information	Remarks and references to Appendices
LOUVENCOURT	1/12/16		Refill at 10 a.m. from supply column which had loaded at railhead overnight (30/11/16). In company camp (Louvencourt - Beauvillers road. Sheet 57d. O.11.a.8.5.) All issues as usual including rum. Load again at BEAUSSART railhead at 7.p.m.	
"	2/12/16		Refill 10.6.a.m in camp. All issues as usual including rum. Load at 2.p.m.	
"	3/12/16		Refill 7.30 a.m. All issues as usual including rum. Obtd trains from F.P.O Neuvillat for 3200 klos hay from Septenville. Load at railhead at 5.p.m.	
"	4/12/16		Refill at 8 a.m. All issues as usual including roots. Obtd ottrucks from F.P.O Beauval for 150 klos hay from Boisnoyenne. Load again at railhead at 3.p.m.	
"	5/12/16		Refill at 8.a.m. All issues as usual including roots. Obt. ottrucks from F.P.O. Beauval for 12500 klos hay from Prouville. Load at railhead at 4.p.m.	
"	6/12/16		Refill at 8.30 a.m. All issues as usual including roots. Load at railhead at 3.p.m.	
"	7/12/16		Refill at 8.30 a.m. GS issues as usual including roots. Load at railhead at 3.p.m.	
"	8/12/16		Refill at 8.30.a.m. All issues as usual including roots. Move with company to BUS-AUTHIE road (Sheet 57d J.19.C.8.7.) Load at railhead at 2.p.m.	
BUS.	9/12/16		Refill 8 a.m near refilling point. All issues as usual including roots. Obtain from F.P.O Neuvillat fr 1500 klos hay/p. R.F.A. Load at railhead at 1.30.p.m.	

C.Hawkins A/Capt.

WAR DIARY
or
INTELLIGENCE SUMMARY.
(Erase heading not required.)

Army Form C. 2118.

S.O. 3rd Div. Troops.

Place	Date	Hour	Summary of Events and Information	Remarks and references to Appendices
BUS.	10/12/16		Refill at 8 a.m. All stores as usual including roots. Load at railhead at 1 p.m. Refill again at 8.15 p.m. (S.S.O's order received 3 p.m.) All stores as usual including roots. Attached with where Transport does not park with us. Refill tomorrow morning program.	
"	11/12/16		Load at railhead at 12.30 p.m. Refill at 5.30 p.m. All stores as usual including roots.	
"	12/12/16		Load at railhead at 11.30 a.m. Refill 4.30 p.m. All stores as usual including roots. 20th K.R.R's leave us today to go to S.O. 8th Bgd. Order obtained from F.P.O. A. littie gr 1500 kilos Hay at Marieux	
"	13/12/16		Load at railhead at 12 noon. Refill at 4 p.m. All stores as usual including roots.	
"	14/12/16		Load at railhead at 12 noon. Refill 3.30 p.m. All stores as usual including roots. Order obtained from F.P.O. Acusset for 800 kilos Hay at Grolle, 500 kilos Wheat straw at Grolle & 200 kilos wheat straw at Vaucelles.	
"	15/12/16		Load at railhead at 12 noon. Refill at 3.15 p.m. All stores as usual including roots.	
"	16/12/16		Load at railhead at 12 noon. Refill at 3.30 p.m. All stores as usual including roots.	
"	17/12/16		Load at railhead at 12 noon. Refill at 3.30 p.m. All stores as usual including roots.	
"	18/12/16		Load at railhead at 12 noon. Refill at 3.30 p.m. All stores as usual including roots.	
"	19/12/16		Load at railhead at 12 noon. Refill at 3.15 p.m. All stores as usual including roots. But was	

Capt Hawkins Baft

Army Form C. 2118.

WAR DIARY

INTELLIGENCE SUMMARY.

(Erase heading not required.)

S.O. 3rd Div. Troops

Instructions regarding War Diaries and Intelligence Summaries are contained in F.S. Regs., Part II. and the Staff Manual respectively. Title pages will be prepared in manuscript.

Place	Date	Hour	Summary of Events and Information	Remarks and references to Appendices
BUS.	20/12/16		Attached from A.P.B. RAINCHEVAL 8,000 kilos Hay (260 bundles) from dump at CANDAS — only 3000 kilos (240 bundles) was drawn today. (Hut No. 11)	
"	21/12/16		Load at railhead at 12 noon. Refill at 3.15 p.m. All issues as usual including oats.	
			Hay obtained from Candas dump further to chit No. 11 for 15,000 kilos.	
"	22/12/16		Load at railhead at 12 noon. Refill at 3.15 p.m. All issues as usual including oats.	
"	23/12/16		Routine exactly as 22nd.	
"	24/12/16		To be noted Plum pudding issued today to All Ranks.	
"	25/12/16		Load at railhead at 11.45 a.m. Refill 3 p.m. All issues as usual including oats.	
"	26/12/16		Load at railhead at 11 a.m. Refill 2.30 p.m. All issues as usual including oats.	
"	27/12/16		Arrived at railhead at 6 p.m. The weights a/h wagons landed at railhead at 10.30 p.m.	2mm
"	28/12/16		Rations 7.30 a.m. Coffee 3.0 p.m	2mm
"			Refilled at 7.30 a.m. Usual issues.	
"	29/12/16		Refilled at 10.30 a.m. proving the Pack Train arriving very late.	
"	30/12/16		Pack Train in at 9 a.m. Refilled at 3.20 p.m.	
"	31/12/16		Refilled at 3.20 p.m. 43 bales of hay short.	

W. Watkin Capt.
for S.O. 3rd Div. Troops

S.O. & T. Staff
Sept 1916

Army Form C. 2118.

WAR DIARY
or
INTELLIGENCE SUMMARY.
(Erase heading not required.)

Place	Date	Hour	Summary of Events and Information	Remarks and references to Appendices
Fovant				
Thurs:	30/11/16		Ryfleng 10.30 am Routine as usual —	
Friday	1/12/16		Authority given by D.V.S. for the Col. 1/c the expt week to visit Brigade when horses were moved I transfers. Notified this most urgently possible when it is not of use. — Also Staff Capt. for Gun Park Stores nearly to be drawn by Regiment at Lavington — Ryfleng 10 am —	
	2/12/16		300 Can Id detail drawn for Base — Relieved Stn. for distribution stock in lieu only. — Ryfleng 10 am.	
Sunday	3/12/16		Ryfleng Down Mealed Brigade group — Strength no 3588 H.S. 102 <D377 C.Dr. 18 S Mules 3	
	4/12/16		Ryfleng as usual — Gun arrived only 2 rations somewhat late Raining afternoon — Orders received tomove 1 Bro du WARNIMONT on Ron L Aukie Rne —	
	5/12/16		New Camp at about 57D. I 23 6 (inverse) Ryfleng Route Larne about T.19. 0 3.6.	
	6/12/16		Routine as usual —	
	7/12/16		Ryfleng 8 am — A great deal is being done with Sand bags from men by — also use astles ten broken up today — Return the drawn for Cavalry Division Artilly joining up from ryfleng between Capt Mackay forward. Hay cart on loan —	

M. Matthews
U.N.S.

Army Form C. 2118.

WAR DIARY
or
INTELLIGENCE SUMMARY.
(Erase heading not required.)

Instructions regarding War Diaries and Intelligence Summaries are contained in F. S. Regs. Part II. and the Staff Manual respectively. Title pages will be prepared in manuscript.

Place	Date	Hour	Summary of Events and Information	Remarks and references to Appendices
Aista	9/7/16		Reporting 8.30 am – Stem took stay from Brimville – at JRO Reported for their rations. Delayed Alcohol received to be told no answer – Hardly Known Regt started answer	
	11/7/16		Fighting 5 am – Routine as usual – Plenty Regt armed for the rations this morning – Reporting at 5 am – again at 3 pm as as known any am coming in to	
End 13/7/16			Rations – morning – P.R. 4149 J+K 110 LD 407 Cb 13 Decoder 8.	
	14/7/16		Examination received Carrs Amm Ammo before afternoon rifling points. Reporting at 3 pm – Steward rations for 20th KRR Op who went from on for ammunition with.–	
			Tea for consumption 14th. – 20 KRR Op from 5.Yps. Reporting about your with exception of George which did not answer – could speak – he was left. He looks lazy or annoying.	
	15/7/16		Replacements from CO r coffee received thirsts when and chewer on 3316 – Sponded at that Unite do not belong any yet supposed not to	
			Long into traunch, however I was instructed not belong any Act of hand ship to in tune light – 7KR D anno shorty afterwards asking for this dut to charged – what Inspence revealed then that I am satisfied template for RR	
			[signature]	

2353 Wt W2544/1454 700,000 5/15 D. D. & L. A.D.S.S./Forms/C. 2118.

WAR DIARY
or
INTELLIGENCE SUMMARY.

(Erase heading not required.)

Army Form C. 2118.

Place	Date	Hour	Summary of Events and Information	Remarks and references to Appendices
A.D.S.	14/7/16 15/7/16		Routine as usual — Visited Supply Dump of 8th Bde — O.M. been moving today to new camp in fact J.Big wood —	
	16/7/16		Visited Beattie at Carnelles — Routine as usual — Continue to	
			pull down afternoon — Routine as usual —	
	17/7/16 Sunday 18/7/16		The anzacs came in from the front at 9 & 1 9 — am for some opening fire on our side opposite the line — As the Bigness is always ready in want it is necessary for my Supply details to man 1 lt. and camp — 100 yds past Church on road leading past Church near by at BEAUSART — today they have moved up there there supplies in a Camp in back of line opposite in a spitting position there — And it is where the 1st line transport staff drew supplies. This is our flying town — Indent wagons am horsed in new camp house — transferring to camp — These supplies are offloaded early & taken by 1st line transport at 8.30 am (Contd)	

WAR DIARY
or
INTELLIGENCE SUMMARY.

Army Form C. 2118.

(Erase heading not required.)

Instructions regarding War Diaries and Intelligence Summaries are contained in F. S. Regs., Part II. and the Staff Manual respectively. Title pages will be prepared in manuscript.

Place	Date	Hour	Summary of Events and Information	Remarks and references to Appendices
Anka	18/11/16 (contd)		Further to Klein Tempst are to do their detail came over.	
	19/11/16		All too has been uneventful, 58 Coy R.E. (ordered wiring to pushers of Carnels from Cpr Res) Rep 87 Anks.; Rusbey Rouen Rgt. moved out. Slypen time — Only two days truts known man has returned from line up to KR — 1 RSR unknown — Shells on the undercar. In the hispane of Ba Kpillens, restart running of trucks.	
	20/11/16		Routine as usual — Only 20 KR's to their detail wagons camp reported fired to target.	
	21/11/16		Plankers as usual — Sheefom Rly shoot at wadleam.	
	22/11/16			
	23/11/16		Zeppelin Shot down transport attempts stopped — In order that Belgrave can be watched after delivering supplies is necessary to keep telliers some afternoon as received instructions.	
	24/11/16 Sunday		Train late at Railhead in haste for refilling at midday — Supplies delivered as usual during morning — Capt Cupegnon Coy — In as on	
			Coy Klein —	
	25/11/16 Xmas Day.		Train arrived Klein — Routine as usual.	
	26/11/16		Train did not arrive ready for Ofloading till 6pm trught — Liverpool refilled at 10pm — Lad wagon reached camp at 3.10 a.m. — 27th	

Army Form C. 2118.

WAR DIARY
or
INTELLIGENCE SUMMARY.
(Erase heading not required.)

Instructions regarding War Diaries and Intelligence
Summaries are contained in F. S. Regs., Part II.
and the Staff Manual respectively. Title Pages
will be prepared in manuscript.

Place	Date	Hour	Summary of Events and Information	Remarks and references to Appendices
Auchie	27/12/16		Train inspection at Midday — Checked LL/Cpl Thirks complaint from 86 R.S.F. re shortage 9 ozs — Fruit Consigned to train — only 880 lbs Potatoes have been received at railhead for 17th Div since 20th inst.	‡
	28/12/16		[struck through]	‡
	29/12/16		Train did not arrive at all day. All supply details returning from dumps to old dumps — On Q.my station as provide rearward march — Train from Gratevilles arrived 7.20 am — No cat on train, have new delivered first troops Groups by Army. 4 days train arrived at 5.30 pm. No day received — She is to be delivered tomorrow by Army — Rest stores reversed from forward dumps.	‡
	30/12/16		Refilling 6.30 am — No train arriving early today 3 wagons which were open & empty & some time — No candles received	‡
	31/12/16		See Jany. '17.	

A. H. Hewett Lt.
O.C. 8th Supply Coln.

2353 Wt. W2544/1454 700,000 5/15 D.D. & L. A.D.S.S./Forms/C. 2118.

S.O.9. Sept. Bn.
December 16 S.O. 9th S. L. Rde

WAR DIARY
or
INTELLIGENCE SUMMARY.
(Erase heading not required.)

Army Form C. 2118.

Instructions regarding War Diaries and Intelligence Summaries are contained in F. S. Regs., Part II. and the Staff Manual respectively. Title pages will be prepared in manuscript.

Place	Date	Hour	Summary of Events and Information	Remarks and references to Appendices
LOUVENCOURT	1/12/16		Refilled. 10 a.m. new Company lines. Supply wagon proceeded direct to BEAUSSART - rations & cooker. Truck at 7 pm. Supply wagon returns 8 p.m. to lines.	EMW
"	2/12/16		Refilled 10 a.m. Loaded at midday 3 pm. Alternative as usual.	EMW
"	3/12/16		Refilled 8 a.m. Loaded at midday 5 pm.	EMW
"	4/12/16		Refilled 8 a.m. Loaded at midday 3.0 pm. Returns	EMW
AUTHIE	5/12/16		Refilled 8 am. Cookers & P to unit & wagon proceeded direct to BEAUGHART - rations & loaded supplies in her. Company moves to new Camp. Supply wagon proceeds to Company lines no rations from lorries	EMW EMW

Army Form C. 2118.

WAR DIARY
or
INTELLIGENCE SUMMARY.
(Erase heading not required.)

S.O. 9th [illegible]

Place	Date	Hour	Summary of Events and Information	Remarks and references to Appendices
RUTHIE	6/12/16	8.0 am	Rations &c. as usual. Routes as usual	SMV
"	7/12/16		Routes as usual	SMV
"	8/12/16		Routes as above	SMV
"	9/12/16		Routes as usual	SMV
"	10/12/16	8.0 am	Rations &c. Supplies delivered to units. Wagons proceeded direct to units. Landed in sub groups. Failures to unloading point. Rebels open at 4 pm. Wagons. Parks were empty by [illegible]	SMV
"	11/12/16		Supplies delivered to units. Wagons proceeded to unload at 11.30 am. Refilled 2.30 pm. Wagon Parks as usual Co lines.	SMV

E M Maud
Capt ASC

T2134. Wt. W708-776. 500000. 4/15. Sir J.C. & S.

Army Form C. 2118

WAR DIARY
or
INTELLIGENCE SUMMARY.
(Erase heading not required.)

S.O. 9th Inf Bde

Place	Date	Hour	Summary of Events and Information	Remarks and references to Appendices
AUTHIE	12/12/16		Supplies delivered to units. Wagons provided to BEAUSART trenches & loaded supplies to huts. Rations 2.30 pm Wagons parks on road outside company lines.	SMV
"	13/12/16		Routine as above	SMV
"	14/12/16		Routine as above	SMV
"	15/12/16		Routine as usual	SMV
"	16/12/16		Routine as usual	SMV
"	17/12/16		Routine as above	SMV
"	18/12/16		Routine as above	SMV
"	19/12/16		Routine as above	SMV

EM Vaugh
Capt RE

Army Form C. 2118.

WAR DIARY
or
INTELLIGENCE SUMMARY.
(Erase heading not required.)

S.O. 9th Inf Bde

Place	Date	Hour	Summary of Events and Information	Remarks and references to Appendices
AUTHIE	20/10/16		Supplies A/M to units & then in buck carts to camp. Refilling took place & lines lorries were for parks until evening.	EMW
"	21/10/16		Capth Watt visits Supple details & lorries to BEAUSART ready for shifting tomorrow. Capth Megson landed stores (& supplies left over from own refilling point) down there to AUTHIE	EMW
"	22/10/16		Supplies drawn from BEAUSART entirely by the lorries. Transport. Routine as yesterday	EMW
"	23/10/16		Supplies arrive from BEAUSART by 1st line transport. Capth Megson arranges — drew from Ditches & refilled after. Supplies A/M to COURCELLES. Horses drawn etc from Div	EMW

E M West
Capt ASC

T2134. Wt. W708-776. 500000. 4/15. Sir J.C. & S.

Army Form C. 2118.

WAR DIARY
or
INTELLIGENCE SUMMARY.
(Erase heading not required.)

S.O. 9th Inf Bde.

Instructions regarding War Diaries and Intelligence Summaries are contained in F. S. Regs., Part II. and the Staff Manual respectively. Title pages will be prepared in manuscript.

Place	Date	Hour	Summary of Events and Information	Remarks and references to Appendices
AUTHIE	24/7/16		Capt. Mayne proceeded to mislad BEAUCOURT & Rosieres immediately at the supplies. Duck Rosieres immediately regularly. Quick BEAUCOURT transports A/H to start	E.M.V.
"	25/7/16		Routine as yesterday	E.M.V.
"	26/7/16		Routine as usual. Trains very late. Rogilles at 9 pm	E.M.V.
"	27/7/16		Routine as usual	E.M.V.
"	28/7/16		Supply details returns 5 to 6½. Train did not arrive at Rogilles.	E.M.V.
"	29/7/16		Reported at midnight for convoy (30 t.) at 2 am. Mayne returns to field at Rogilles. Supplied immediately to the points of eggs. proceeded to militia & hohunsed with back. Returns to follow. Proceeded to lunkes 5 limited	E.M.V.

E.M. Veal
Capt a/c

T2131. Wt. W708—776. 500000. 4/15. Sir J. C. & S.

Army Form C. 2118

S.O. 9th L[?] Bde

WAR DIARY
or
INTELLIGENCE SUMMARY.
(Erase heading not required.)

Place	Date	Hour	Summary of Events and Information	Remarks and references to Appendices
AUTHIE	30/12/16		Refills 8.20a.m. Supplies d/d to units Lewgons framework direct to wallers blankets in sack.	EMV etc
"	30/12/16		Took over duties of Supply Off. 9th Inf Bde.	
"	31/12/16		Wagons moved off to units 6.30 a.m. (refilled 30.12.16) returned from R.Hd. 12.30. refilling completed 3.15pm Dump near Camp repaired. 9am →	R.O.C.

R.T. Cooper Capt. RASC
So. 9th Inf Bde

Army Form C.2118.

S.O. 76th Bde

WAR DIARY
or
INTELLIGENCE SUMMARY.
(Erase heading not required.)

Place	Date	Hour	Summary of Events and Information	Remarks and references to Appendices
LOUVENCOURT.				
Friday	1/12/16		Routine as usual.	
Saturday	2/12/16		Sahie allowance of 5 cwt coal and 5 cwt coke to No.7 Field Ambulance is discontinued as they are drawing 1 ton per week from Acheux (Corps Supply Dumps). 800 Zinc petroleum alcohol arrive at dumps — 400 forwards to 76th Bde HQ in one lorry for use in trenches (15,15 Man). 200 forwarded to 0.8th Bde (F.C.O 1/12/16). Return from E.L.O. Frevre Eu365 of cwt weekly to last type 78 not Gps 76 Gps, M:	
			Saw 1st Wine Bruxelles — no wine made.	
Sunday	3/12/16		Usual Routine — Wheatstraw Profiteh (x150x400). Have enter'd up daily (x 300) Returning from L.O. 3rd Div hospo.	
Monday	4/12/16		Brought Potato factory. So 7th Bde asked to return oil of lastcoke. to qum (not Now).	
Tuesday	5/12/16		Hay (x160 pone) for 1st div transport my reception from L.O. 3 Div Xropo Hy (x160 900) received from L.O. X Troops	
Wednesday	6/12/16		2 Company moves camps to Bois de Warnemont — B.Sn — Authue Road Routine as usual.	
Thursday	7/12/16		Heck starts 7/12/16 — Hy of Corp kitchen supplies	
Friday	8/12/16		Usual Routine	

Thos. T. Tenken
Lieut. A.S.C.
S.O. 76th Inf. Bde

Army Form C. 2118

WAR DIARY
or
INTELLIGENCE SUMMARY.
(Erase heading not required.)

Instructions regarding War Diaries and Intelligence Summaries are contained in F.S. Regs., Part II. and the Staff Manual respectively. Title pages will be prepared in manuscript.

Place	Date	Hour	Summary of Events and Information	Remarks and references to Appendices
BOIS DE WARNIMCOURT				
Saturday	9/12/16		Routine as usual. Note from S.O. Paraffin stored at Railhead — Centralised diversion 5.	
Sunday	10/12/16		Routine as usual.	
Monday	11/12/16		No. 18 Coy. Rdt. Batteries attacked for Rations — Authority to issue of 1 lb. meat, 1 lb. bread weekly for troops electing to Brigade (to Rest).	
Tuesday	12/12/16		Manual Routine.	
Wednesday	13/12/16		500 tins Solids elected from S.O. 8th Bde. issued to 76th Bde. H.Q.	
Thursday	14/12/16		Starting from 14/12/16 76th Brigade draws supplies at Rlhd. Beaussart from 7th Div'l Pack Train; (See 9).	
Friday	15/12/16		Routine as usual.	
Saturday	16/12/16		Routine as usual.	
Sunday	17/12/16			
Monday	18/12/16		Supply details and trains now tres forward a pulling-point at Beaussart. Supplies drawn from Rly. Pt. Beaussart by 1st line Transport. Regimental distribution made in dumps — No. 7 F.A. Ambulance and No. 18 Rdt. Baker Company transferred to 9th Bde. for Rations. Worthy part (7th Div) attached 78th Inf'y Bde III Div) Strength 105. No ration were not drawn for 4 days were debited to us.	

John Henning Capt.
Temp. S.O. 76th Inf. Bde.

Army Form C. 2118.

WAR DIARY
or
INTELLIGENCE SUMMARY.
(Erase heading not required.)

Instructions regarding War Diaries and Intelligence Summaries are contained in F.S. Regs., Part II. and the Staff Manual respectively. Title pages will be prepared in manuscript.

Place	Date	Hour	Summary of Events and Information	Remarks and references to Appendices
BOIS DE WARNINCOURT	Wednesday 20/12/16		Routine as usual	
	Thursday 21/12/16		Routine. Wrist-watch drawn for new things.	
	Friday 22/12/16		78th Bde relieved by 9th Bde. Refilling at old dumps. Bois le Warnincourt. 7th, 8th and 142nd Fd Ambulances and 8th Cav Pioneers attached to 74th Bde for Rations. Sect Ridey R.E. attached to 9th Brigade for same purpose.	
	Saturday 23/12/16		Routine.	
	Sunday 24/12/16		Routine. Men pretty sour - word shot of from Ypres.	
	Monday 25/12/16		Christmas Day.	
	Tuesday 26/12/16		Routine - Boxing Day.	
	Wednesday 27/12/16		Severe coal shortage. Fuel for drying purposes cancelled.	
	28/12/16		Routine - Forward Refilling abolished.	
	29/12/16		Routine - 76th Bde relieves 9th Bde.	
	30-31/12/16		Routine as usual.	

John L Leman
Lieut. A.D.S.
A.D.S. 78th W/3 Bde

www.ingramcontent.com/pod-product-compliance
Lightning Source LLC
Chambersburg PA
CBHW080840010526
44114CB00017B/2339